DAY HIKING

Bend and
Central Oregon

Monkey Face is Smith Rock State Park's most notable landmark.

A green-banded mariposa lily near Hand Lake Shelter

Previous page: Views of the Three Sisters from Tumalo Mountain

Snow-capped views of the Cascades from Sparks Lake

A grove of bright yellow aspen can be seen through the fire-thinned forest.

A hiker heads back to Camp Lake after summiting Middle Sister.

Abundant manzanita is gorgeous when flowering.

Looking down into Smith Rock State Park from Summit Ridge

Hikers walk toward Teardrop Pool on their descent from South Sister.

A scenic footbridge crossing over Fall River

Bright red Indian paintbrush runs rampant around Todd Lake.

North Sister pokes out above a lava flow.

DAY HIKING

Bend and Central Oregon

mount jefferson • three sisters • cascade lakes

Brittany Manwill

MOUNTAINEERS BOOKS

For my parents, who taught me to crave adventure

MOUNTAINEERS BOOKS

Mountaineers Books is the publishing division of The Mountaineers, an organization founded in 1906 and dedicated to the exploration, preservation, and enjoyment of outdoor and wilderness areas.

1001 SW Klickitat Way, Suite 201, Seattle, WA 98134
800.553.4453, www.mountaineersbooks.org

Copyright © 2016 by Brittany Manwill

Printed in the United States of America
First edition: 2016

Copy Editor: Julie Van Pelt
Cover and Book Design: Mountaineers Books
Layout: Jennifer Shontz, www.redshoedesign.com
Cartographer: Lohnes + Wright
All photographs by Brittany Manwill unless otherwise noted.
Cover photograph: *Broken Top Mountain and Fall Creek*, by Corbis Photography
Frontispiece: *Benham Falls on the Deschutes River*

Maps shown in this book were produced using National Geographic's *TOPO!* software.

Library of Congress Cataloging-in-Publication Data
Names: Manwill, Brittany.
Title: Day hiking Bend & Central Oregon : Mount Jefferson/Three Sisters/Cascade Lakes / Brittany Manwill.
Description: First edition. | Seattle, WA : Mountaineers Books, [2016] | Includes index.
Identifiers: LCCN 2015037071 | ISBN 9781594859342 (paperback) | ISBN 9781594859359 (ebook)
Subjects: LCSH: Hiking—Oregon, Central—Guidebooks. | Hiking—Oregon—Bend Metropolitan Area—Guidebooks. | Oregon, Central—Guidebooks. | Bend Metropolitan Area (Or.)—Guidebooks.
Classification: LCC GV199.42.O74 M36 2016 | DDC 796.5109795/8—dc23 LC record available at http://lccn.loc.gov/2015037071

 Printed on recycled paper

ISBN (paperback): 978-1-59485-934-2
ISBN (ebook): 978-1-59485-935-9

Table of Contents

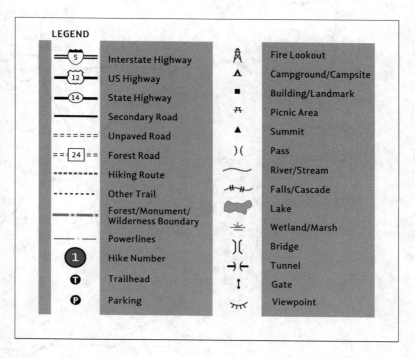

LEGEND

═══5═══	Interstate Highway
═══12═══	US Highway
──14──	State Highway
────	Secondary Road
=======	Unpaved Road
== 24 ==	Forest Road
-----------	Hiking Route
---------	Other Trail
─ ·─ ·─	Forest/Monument/Wilderness Boundary
─── · ───	Powerlines
1	Hike Number
T	Trailhead
P	Parking
🀲	Fire Lookout
△	Campground/Campsite
■	Building/Landmark
🎋	Picnic Area
▲	Summit
)(	Pass
~	River/Stream
╫╫	Falls/Cascade
▬	Lake
☰	Wetland/Marsh
)(	Bridge
→←	Tunnel
↕	Gate
⋎	Viewpoint

Central Oregon Hike Locations

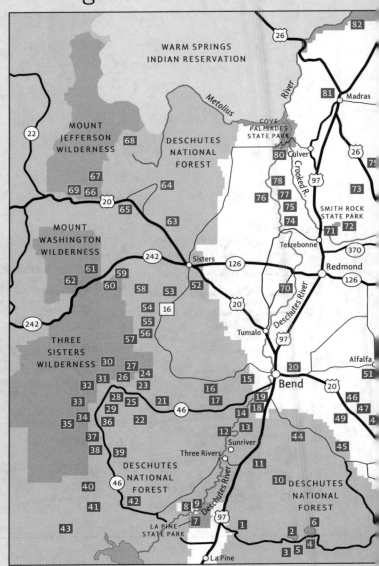

WARM SPRINGS INDIAN RESERVATION

MOUNT JEFFERSON WILDERNESS

DESCHUTES NATIONAL FOREST

Metolius

COVE PALISADES STATE PARK

Madras

Culver

Crooked R.

SMITH ROCK STATE PARK

MOUNT WASHINGTON WILDERNESS

Sisters

Terrebonne

Redmond

THREE SISTERS WILDERNESS

Deschutes River

Tumalo

Bend

Alfalfa

Sunriver

Three Rivers

DESCHUTES NATIONAL FOREST

Deschutes River

LA PINE STATE PARK

La Pine

DESCHUTES NATIONAL FOREST

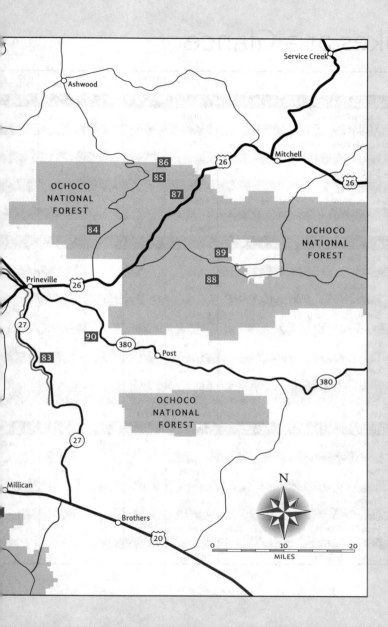

Hikes at a Glance

HIKE	DISTANCE	RATING	DIFFI-CULTY	KID-FRIENDLY	DOG-FRIENDLY
NEWBERRY CALDERA AND LA PINE					
1. Paulina Creek	5 miles	***	3		•
2. Paulina Lake	4.3 miles	****	3		
3. Paulina Peak	6 miles	****	4		
4. Lost Lake	6.2 miles	****	4		
5. Big Obsidian Flow	0.8 mile	****	2	•	
6. Cinder Hill	6.75 miles	****	3		
7. Cougar Woods and the Big Pine	4 miles	***	2	•	
8. Fall River Springs and Old Guard Station	1.6 miles	***	1	•	•
9. Fall River and Falls	5 miles	***	3	•	•
BEND					
10. Lava Cast Forest	0.9 mile	**	1	•	
11. Lava River Cave	2 miles	***	3	•	
12. Sun-Lava Path to Benham Falls	5 miles	***	2	•	
13. Lava Butte's Trail of Molten Land	1.3 miles	**	1	•	
14. Dillon and Benham Falls	8 miles	****	3		
15. Shevlin Park	4.7 miles	***	3		•
16. Upper Tumalo Falls	4 miles	****	3		•
17. South Fork Tumalo and Bridge Creeks	3.7 miles	***	3		
18. SW Canal Trails	3.3 miles	***	2		•
19. Deschutes River Trail to South Canyon Bridge	3.6 miles	***	3	•	•
20. Pilot Butte	2 miles	****	3		
UPPER CASCADE LAKES HIGHWAY					
21. Tumalo Mountain	3.5 miles	****	4		
22. Mount Bachelor Summit	6.2 miles	***	5		
23. Todd Lake	1.7 miles	***	2	•	
24. Broken Top Saddle and "Hidden" Lake	7 miles	*****	4		
25. Sparks Lake	2.6 miles	****	3		
26. Green Lakes	9 miles	*****	4		•
27. Soda Creek and Lower Crater Creek Falls	4.5 miles	***	3	•	•
28. Devils Lake	1.4 miles	***	2	•	
29. Quinn Meadow	7.8 miles	**	3		

BARRIER-FREE	WILD-FLOWERS	WILDLIFE	BIRD-WATCHING	VIEWS	HISTORICAL	ENDANGERED TRAIL	SAVED TRAIL
				•			
				•			
		•					
				•			
		•		•			
•							
					•		
•							
•							
•				•	•		
					•		
							•
					•		
					•		
				•	•		
	•			•	•		
				•	•		
	•						
	•			•			
•				•	•		
	•			•			
	•						
	•						
	•						

HIKE	DISTANCE	RATING	DIFFI-CULTY	KID-FRIENDLY	DOG-FRIENDLY
30. South Sister Summit	11 miles	*****	5		
31. Moraine Lake	7.5 miles	*****	4		
32. Le Conte Crater	6.5 miles	***	4		
LOWER CASCADE LAKES HIGHWAY					
33. Sisters Mirror Lake	6.7 miles	***	3		•
34. Horse Lake	8.6 miles	***	3		
35. Horse Mountain Lakes	9.5 miles	***	4		•
36. Elk Lake	1.5 miles	**	3	•	
37. Blow and Doris Lakes	4.75 miles	***	3		•
38. Lucky Lake	2.7 miles	****	2		•
39. Blue Lagoon	1.3 miles	***	2	•	•
40. Teddy Lakes	7.8 miles	***	3		•
41. Merle Lake	8.75 miles	***	4		•
42. Osprey Point and Billy Quinn Gravesite	0.9 mile	**	1	•	
43. Lily and Charlton Lakes	5.25 miles	***	3		•
THE BADLANDS AND HORSE RIDGE					
44. Bessie and Kelsey Buttes	10.5 miles	***	4		
45. Pictograph Cave	5 miles	**	4		
46. Flatiron Rock	6 miles	***	2		
47. Badlands Rock	6 miles	***	2		
48. Dry River Canyon	4.8 miles	****	3		
49. Horse Ridge via Sand Canyon	7 miles	***	4		
50. Pine Mountain	4 miles	***	4		
51. Tumulus Loop	4.5 miles	**	2		
SISTERS AND MCKENZIE PASS					
52. Peterson Ridge Trail	4.7 miles	**	2		•
53. Logjam Falls	3.5 miles	***	3		
54. Whychus Creek Falls	6 miles	****	3		•
55. Park Meadow	10 miles	***	4		
56. Little Three Creek Lake	1.3 miles	***	2	•	•
57. Tam McArthur Rim	5.2 miles	*****	4		
58. Camp Lake	13.5 miles	*****	5		
59. Black Crater	7.5 miles	****	4		
60. Matthieu Lakes	6 miles	****	3		•
61. Little Belknap Crater	5.3 miles	***	4		
62. Hand Lake Shelter	1 mile	***	1	•	

BARRIER-FREE	WILD-FLOWERS	WILDLIFE	BIRD-WATCHING	VIEWS	HISTORICAL	ENDANGERED TRAIL	SAVED TRAIL
	•			•			
	•			•			
	•			•		•	
	•						
	•						
		•	•		•		
				•			
					•	•	
	•	•					•
	•	•	•				•
		•	•	•	•		
							•
				•	•		
	•	•					•
							•
						•	•
							•
	•			•		•	
				•			
				•			
	•			•			
	•			•	•		
				•	•		
				•			
	•			•	•		

HIKE	DISTANCE	RATING	DIFFI-CULTY	KID-FRIENDLY	DOG-FRIENDLY
MOUNT JEFFERSON AND SANTIAM PASS					
63. Black Butte	4 miles	****	4		
64. Metolius River and Wizard Falls Fish Hatchery	6.5 miles	**	3	•	•
65. Suttle Lake	3.7 miles	***	3	•	•
66. Square Lake	4 miles	***	3		•
67. Canyon Creek Meadows	5 miles	****	3		
68. Cabot and Carl Lakes	9.6 miles	****	4		
69. Three Fingered Jack	10.5 miles	****	4		
CROOKED RIVER AND SMITH ROCK					
70. Maston Area Trails	5 miles	***	3		
71. Smith Rock: Misery Ridge and Monkey Face	3.9 miles	*****	4		
72. Smith Rock: Perimeter	7.2 miles	****	4		
73. Gray Butte	3.8 miles	***	3		
74. Steelhead Falls	1 mile	***	1		
75. Sand Ridge	2 miles	***	3		
76. Alder Springs Trail	6 miles	****	3		
77. Lone Pine Trail	1.8 miles	***	3		
78. Scout Camp Trail	2.3 miles	****	3		
79. Rimrock Springs	1 mile	**	1	•	
80. Tam-a-lau Trail	6.5 miles	*****	3		
81. Willow Creek Canyon	6 miles	***	3		
82. Old Oregon Trunk Railroad and Trout Creek Bluffs	2.5 miles	****	3		
PRINEVILLE AND OCHOCO MOUNTAINS					
83. Chimney Rock	2.75 miles	****	3		
84. Steins Pillar	4.1 miles	***	3		
85. Twin Pillars	6 miles	***	4		
86. Cougar Creek	7 miles	***	4		
87. McGinnis Creek	5.2 miles	**	3	•	
88. Lookout Mountain	6 miles	***	4		
89. Walton Lake	2 miles	***	2	•	
90. Eagle Rock Agate Beds	3.6 miles	**	3	•	

BARRIER-FREE	WILD-FLOWERS	WILDLIFE	BIRD-WATCHING	VIEWS	HISTORICAL	ENDANGERED TRAIL	SAVED TRAIL
	•			•	•		
			•				
							•
	•						
	•						
	•					•	
	•			•			
		•					•
				•			
		•	•	•			
	•			•	•		
		•					•
	•			•			
	•	•		•			
		•		•			•
				•			•
•		•	•				
	•			•	•		•
				•	•		
		•		•	•		
			•	•			
	•			•			
		•		•			
					•		•
	•	•					
		•		•	•		
			•				•

Acknowledgments

I'm lucky to have such an amazing support group in my life. I am forever grateful to the following people who were instrumental in completing this book.

First and foremost, a big thank-you to the team at Mountaineers Books. Thank you for giving me so much freedom and allowing me to be myself on paper. Kate Rogers, thanks for reaching out and giving me the opportunity to be a part of such an amazing series. Thank you to Kirsten Colton for giving me such valuable feedback on my draft materials, and to Laura Shauger for being so patient with me and answering a myriad of questions. Thank you to Christine Hosler, Julie Van Pelt, Margaret Sullivan, whomever had to decipher my map scrap, and the rest of the behind-the-scenes crew.

To other writers in the outdoor industry, I'm deeply thankful for your knowledge, inspiration, and guidance. Thanks to those who forged this terrain before me, namely William Sullivan, whose trusty guidebooks showed the way and made Central Oregon's wilderness more accessible for many. A special thanks to Eli Boschetto at *Washington Trails Magazine*: your experience and leadership have been instrumental in getting my writing career off the ground.

A million thank-yous to my wonderful family, starting with my parents. Dad, thanks for passing on your addiction to staying active. Mom, thanks for accompanying and helping me on so many hikes. I'm so grateful to both of you for instilling such a deep love of the outdoors in me. Skylar, thank you for always being up for adventure. It's contagious.

I'm also deeply thankful for my two trusty hiking buddies. Tonka, you're a super pup. Rowan, thanks for being the most adaptable newborn in the world and letting me drag you on a hundred hikes during your first year.

Last but not least, thank you to my wonderful husband, Derek. Thank you for encouraging me, hiking with me, and helping when my spatial reasoning failed. Whether I disappeared all weekend for hiking or served you leftovers for three nights in a row, you've been extremely understanding during this entire process. I love doing life together; I'm lucky to have you.

Preface

Our son was born right at the beginning of the hiking season when I researched this book. Since Derek works during the day, that meant that the little man was going to be joining me on all my hikes. I carried him—up mountains, across deserts, and through canyons—fastened to my chest by means of a simple infant carrier.

As I slowly but surely completed all the hikes for this book, we had all sorts of mishaps. Hiking with an infant is hardly a walk in the park. Almost daily, people would ask if I was crazy, adding, "Is it even *okay* to have a baby this young out here?" Sometimes I would ask myself the same questions. More often, however, the experience made me reflect on my own childhood and how I got to where I am today.

My experience in the outdoors started at an early age. Looking back, I fondly remember every single chaos-filled camping, skiing, rafting, hiking, and biking trip with my family, although I'm sure there were a few trips where I was less than thrilled about wild animals and sleeping on the ground. What started as nothing more than a requirement for being part of my family developed into a love of the outdoors that has grown stronger and stronger over time. The fresh air, solitude, and challenge of testing my mental and physical strength fulfill a deep craving.

I can't stress strongly enough how much these early experiences in the outdoors affected my life. Being active and being outside taught me how to be prepared, work hard, and respond to emergencies, as well as the basics of survival. In some ways more importantly, it also taught me how to live a healthy lifestyle, relax, have fun, and find balance in the chaos of everyday life.

I completed my last hike for this book just as my son took his first steps. When I think of his first year, I finally understand how fast time goes by. I'm sure my parents think the same thing when they look at my brother and me. I'm lucky to have grown up in a family that was so focused on adventure and making memories—a lifestyle I hope to pass down to my own kids. Life is short, but it's absolutely amazing.

I've truly enjoyed working on this book. I hope that reading it helps you create as many new memories and reach as many new heights as I did writing it.

Newberry Caldera's Paulina Lake

Introduction

There's a strange dichotomy going on in our country right now. For as much as we all talk about living in the now, focusing on what really matters, and seeing the world, our actions reflect the opposite. Walk down any street in almost any city and you'll see people looking down, staring at a little screen. It used to be just the "youths," but now it's everyone. Even Grandma probably has a smartphone. Technology is awesome, but our obsession with it does more than just make people-watching exceptionally boring: it makes the world a sad place, a tiresome place. Look up and smell the fresh air! Life goes by fast. It's easy to get so caught up in capturing and recording every moment that actually *living* in the moment gets pushed to the side.

Obviously, the world would fall apart if we all just quit our jobs and threw our phones in the trash. But that doesn't mean you can't take back a small portion of your life. Even a quick stint outside can boost endorphins for your entire day. Instead of looking at the world through the filter of your camera, get out and see it with your own two eyes.

Hiking is all about getting outside, connecting with nature, pushing yourself, and creating memories. It's the kind of "real living" that shines life into your day instead of sucking it out. This Day Hiking series was created to make it as easy as possible to incorporate this kind of awesomeness into your day. Backpacking requires extensive planning and packing, but almost anyone can do a day hike without much notice. Adventure is more accessible than

people think. This book showcases ninety of the best day hiking routes throughout Central Oregon.

Once dependent on timber for its livelihood, Central Oregon is now a mecca for outdoor enthusiasts and adventurers. From the grasslands around the steep Crooked River Gorge, to pristine alpine lakes and jagged peaks, this is a uniquely diverse area. Even the snow brings a welcome change, allowing hikers to rediscover areas with snowshoes or backcountry skis.

Central Oregon is generally defined as the land in the middle of the state but east of the Cascades—the rest of its boundaries have always been a little more fluid. The "official" Central Oregon territory includes Deschutes, Jefferson, and Crook counties. The unofficial guidelines allow these borders to be a little blurry, including basically any hike on the east side of the Cascades that's somewhat high-desert-like.

As a compromise, the hikes in this book fall somewhere in between these confines. Almost all the hikes are located within the three aforementioned counties. Those that aren't are both near the boundary and so filled with the characteristics that make up the Central Oregon landscape that it seemed only natural to include them.

To make navigation easier, the hikes in this book are organized by regions within Central Oregon: Newberry Caldera and La Pine, Bend, both Upper (northern) and Lower (southern) Cascade Lakes Highway, the Badlands and Horse Ridge, Sisters and McKenzie Pass, Mount Jefferson and Santiam Pass, Crooked River and Smith

Rock, and Prineville and Ochoco Mountains. These regions split the hikes up by general geographic area and by access point.

This book covers a lot of ground and a unique set of landscapes. You'll find everything from casual urban strolls to arduous climbs up some of the Cascades' highest peaks. You'll find hikes for kids, hikes for dogs, and hikes for those needing barrier-free (paved or ADA-accessible) trails. Several hikes incorporate various historical sites, including old fire lookouts, wagon roads, Native American pictographs, and other landmarks with intriguing histories.

In terms of natural features, Central Oregon has everything on the "perfect hike" list. You'll find exceptional views in every region, including panoramic vistas of the Cascades, gorgeous alpine lakes, stunning

lava fields and rock formations, and deep canyons with vibrant rivers. Central Oregon also features stunning wildflower displays from late spring through early fall and excellent wildlife viewing. Animal species differ, but you may see Rocky Mountain elk, bear, cougar, bobcat, deer, rabbit, marmots, and other little critters. Look up and you'll likely see peregrine falcons and golden eagles soaring high above the canyon walls, while great blue herons perch in the middle of the river below. This part of the state is also home to one of the largest osprey nesting sites in the country.

This list merely scratches the surface. From the high alpine lakes to the flat ancient-juniper deserts, I truly believe that Central Oregon is one of the most beautiful places in the world. It's a special place. No

A lizard suns itself on a log near Rimrock Springs.

matter what kind of adventure you're looking for here, you can find it in this book. They say that those who visit Central Oregon *move* to Central Oregon. You've been warned.

USING THIS BOOK

These Day Hiking guidebooks strike a fine balance. They were developed to be as easy to use as possible while still providing enough detail to help you explore a region. Fellow guidebook authors and series partners Craig Romano and Dan Nelson set the path with their Washington volumes by creating easy-to-follow guidelines for using this book.

This summary uses their expertise and advice while expanding on topics of particular pertinence to the types of things you may encounter in Central Oregon. As a result, *Day Hiking Bend and Central Oregon* includes all the information you need to find and enjoy the hikes, but it leaves enough room for you to make your own discoveries as you venture into areas new to you.

What the Ratings Mean

Every hike described in this book features a detailed "trail facts" section. Not all of the details here are facts, however.

Each hike starts with two subjective ratings: the first rating of 1 to 5 stars is for the hike's overall appeal; the second rating, difficulty, is based on a scale of 1 to 5. This is subjective, based on my impressions of each route, but the ratings do follow a formula of sorts. The overall **rating** is based on scenic beauty, natural wonder, and other unique qualities, such as potential for solitude and wildlife viewing.

The **difficulty** rating is based on trail length, steepness, and how difficult it is to hike and navigate. Generally, trails that are rated more difficult (4 or 5) are longer and

steeper than average. But it's not a simple equation. A short but steep scree ascent may be rated 5, while a long, smooth trail with little elevation gain may be rated 2. Additionally, bad weather can quickly turn an easy hike into something much more challenging.

To help explain those difficulty ratings, you'll also find the **roundtrip mileage** (unless one-way is noted), total **elevation gain**, and **high point** for each hike. The distances are not always exact mileages. Your own mileage may differ slightly, as trails are occasionally rerouted due to snow, blowdown, fire, or restoration efforts. The elevation gains report the cumulative difference between the high and low points on the roundtrip. It's worth noting that not all high points are at the end of the trail—a route may run over a high ridge before dropping into a lake basin, for instance.

The recommended **season** is another subjective tool meant as a guide and not an absolute rule. Some years, a heavy winter snowpack may not melt in the high country until early September. In other years, the highest trails may be snow-free by June. Several regions can be explored year-round, while others are definitely snowed-in during the winter. Keep in mind that even if a trail is snow-free, that doesn't necessarily mean it's hikable. Ice and thick mud can be just as, if not more, encumbering than snow. Use the suggested season as a tool to help you plan your trips. But because no guidebook can provide all the details of a trail, or stay current with constantly changing conditions of trails, stream crossings, and access roads, make sure to check with the land or road manager before you head out. Phone numbers and websites are listed in Appendix II to make it easy to get the latest information on conditions.

A hiker and two dogs head across a plateau toward Moraine Lake.

To help with trip planning, each hike lists which **maps** you'll want to have on your hike, as well as whom to **contact** to get current trail conditions. Hikes in this guidebook primarily use Green Trails and US Forest Service (USFS) recreation maps. Certain regions have specialty maps, many of which are downloadable for free on the appropriate land manager's website. US Geological Survey (USGS) maps are listed for areas not covered by these other maps. Some hikes also reference the Bend Adventure Map. While primarily a biking and skiing map, it is useful for a few hikes for which it shows more detail than other maps.

Green Trails maps use the standard 7.5-minute USGS topographical maps as their starting point. But where USGS maps may not have been updated since sometime in the 1950s, Green Trails has researchers in the field every year, checking trail conditions and changes. Many hikers still use USGS maps, which remain useful for looking at mountains, lakes, contours, and the like because natural features don't change rapidly. But human-made features do change, and Green Trails does a good job staying abreast of those changes. These maps are available at most outdoor retailers in the state, as well as at many US Forest Service and national park visitors centers. Geo-Graphics also makes quality maps for the various wilderness areas in Central Oregon, although they are harder to find nowadays. **Notes** include any additional details or tips that may be helpful for visiting a particular area.

Finally, given that we now live in a digital world, **GPS coordinates** for each trailhead are provided—use this both to get to the trailhead and to help you get back to your car if you get caught out in a storm or wander off-trail.

Hike Descriptions

Icons at the beginning of each hike description provide a few quick-glance details that may be important as you plan your hike.

 Kid-friendly

 Dog-friendly

 Barrier-free (paved or ADA-accessible)

 Exceptional wildflowers in season

 Good chance of viewing wildlife

 Good bird-watching

 Exceptional scenic views

 Historical relevance

 Endangered trail (threatened with loss or closure)

 Saved trail (rescued from permanent loss)

Kid-friendly hikes are generally easier, pose few if any obstacles, and often consist of natural features that should intrigue and engage youngsters. A **dog-friendly** icon means not only that dogs are allowed but also that the hikes are friendly on your pooch's paws, contain adequate shade and water sources, and in many cases follow lightly traveled trails. Dog leash laws vary depending on the area and time of year, so check at the trailhead to make sure you're obeying the trail rules. A **barrier-free** hike is either fully or partially paved or otherwise ADA-accessible. The **wildflower** icon means you'll find seasonally occurring blooms throughout the hike, ranging from large, colorful meadows to more understated but equally beautiful desert flowers. A **wildlife viewing** icon means you have a greater chance of spotting wild animals on the hike; the **bird-watching** icon tips you to abundant birdlife. Hikes marked for **exceptional views** identify trips with more than just average pretty scenery. These hikes typically have sweeping panoramas of surrounding mountains or otherwise extraordinary vistas. **Historical** hikes have some type of significant human interest in addition to natural highlights. Examples include fire lookouts, shelters, gravesites, or other interesting landmarks. The **endangered trail** icon spotlights trails that are threatened due to lack of maintenance, motorized encroachment, abandonment, or other acts detrimental to their continuance. A **saved trail** icon denotes a formerly threatened or abandoned trail that has been revived and restored.

Take these designations with a grain of salt. They're meant to be helpful—not restrictive. You know your kids, your dog, and yourself better than I do, so use your best judgment. Wildflowers are more likely in late spring and summer than in the dead of winter. And excellent views are often squashed by weather and/or wildfire.

The route descriptions themselves provide directions to get you to the trailhead, an overview of what you'll find on your hike, and in many cases additional highlights beyond the actual trails you'll be exploring. Always bring a map, as there's no way to guarantee that signs will be where they should be or that trails will be as clear as they were when they were originally hiked.

Of course, you'll need some information

Yellow arrowleaf balsamroot

long before you ever leave home. As you plan your trips, the following several issues need to be considered.

PERMITS, REGULATIONS, AND FEES

It's important that you know, understand, and abide by the regulations that apply to the trails in Central Oregon. As our public lands have become increasingly popular, and as both federal and state funding has declined, regulations and permits have become necessary components in managing our natural heritage. To help keep our wilderness areas wild and our trails safe and well maintained, land managers—especially the National Park Service and US Forest Service—have implemented a sometimes-complex set of rules and regulations governing the use of these lands.

Generally, any developed trailhead in Oregon's national forests falls under the Region 6 forest pass program. For many of these designated national forest trailheads in Central Oregon, you must display a Northwest Forest Pass in your windshield in order to park legally. These sell for $5 per day or $30 for an annual pass good throughout Washington and Oregon (which constitute Region 6). It's safe to assume that a pass is required, although the Ochoco Mountains are generally fee-free. In recent years, fees have been eliminated at several (but not all) sites in the Deschutes National Forest as well.

If you visit national parks, in Oregon or elsewhere, the America the Beautiful National Parks and Federal Recreational Lands Pass may be a good choice. The $80 annual fee grants you and three other adults in your vehicle (children under sixteen are admitted free) access to all federal recreation sites that charge a fee. These include national parks, national forests, national monuments, national wildlife refuges, and Bureau of Land Management areas, not only here in Oregon, but throughout the country. All park and forest pass monies go directly to the agencies managing our land. You can purchase passes at national park and forest visitors centers as well as many area outdoor retailers. The passes are valid for one year from day of purchase.

Some state parks charge a $5 parking fee not covered by the Northwest Forest Pass or America the Beautiful Pass. Annual parking passes for Oregon State Parks are available for $30. In Central Oregon, both Cove Palisades and Smith Rock state parks charge for parking, while La Pine and Pilot Butte don't. As a general rule, assume that trailhead fee stations will only accept cash.

In addition to parking fees, many hikes that enter wilderness areas require visitors to carry a wilderness permit. These permits are free and can be obtained at self-service kiosks at any trailhead that requires them. They're required for both day and overnight

A tranquil tributary of Soda Creek

visits between Memorial Day weekend and October 31. Please fill out the permit. Not only do they track usage trends, which helps to allocate funds appropriately, but they also aid in search-and-rescue operations. Plus, you can be fined if you aren't carrying one when you should be.

WEATHER

Central Oregon is famous for its sunny days and bright blue skies. This part of the state reports over three hundred days of sunshine per year. But even though land east of the Cascades has a dry-side ecosystem, high-alpine areas can still be susceptible to less-than-ideal hiking weather.

Central Oregon is home to both high-desert and canyon terrain, both of which can get excruciatingly hot in the summer. Flat desert hikes, especially on the east side of Bend, are dry, with very little shade and few water sources. Canyon hikes are similarly exposed, but they also bring the additional danger of trapped heat. Temperatures are often 15 degrees Fahrenheit higher at the canyon floor. When combined with a low-humidity climate and increased moisture loss from exercise, these conditions can cause heath problems. To limit dangers:

- **Hike in the morning** or on cooler days.
- **Hydrate** before, after, and during your hike.
- **Wear light, breathable, sun-protective clothing** and sunscreen.
- **Watch for signs of heatstroke**, including increased body temperature, confusion, rapid heart rate, and decreased fluid output. If you or a hiking buddy exhibits any of these signs, get help immediately.

Thunderstorms can roll in with very little notice. To reduce the risk of getting struck by lightning, take the following precautions:

- **Keep track of weather** forecasts and changes by using an NOAA weather radio.
- **Avoid travel on mountaintops and ridge crests.**
- **Stay well away from bodies of water.**
- **If your hair stands on end, or you feel static shocks, move immediately**—the static electricity you feel could very well be a precursor to a lightning strike.
- **If there's a shelter or building nearby, get into it.** Don't take shelter under trees, however, especially in open areas.
- If there's no shelter available, and lightning is flashing, **remove your pack** (any metal in the pack construction will conduct electricity) **and crouch down**, balancing on the balls of your feet until the lightning clears the area.

Even though Central Oregon has plenty of sunny weather, the Cascades also get a lot of precipitation. Rain isn't as serious over here as it is on the west side, but check the weather and be prepared anyway. A small rainstorm in town can be a windy snowstorm on top of high peaks. Leftover snowpack can last well into summer, which can make establishing stable footing and routefinding tricky. Hiking poles and crampons are both handy for crossing snowfields and glaciers.

ROAD AND TRAIL CONDITIONS

In general, trails change very little from year to year. Most are fairly durable, but when change occurs, it can happen quickly. One brutal storm can change a river's course, washing out sections of trail in just moments. Wind can drop trees across trails by the hundreds, making the paths unhikable. Snow can obliterate trails well into the summer.

Access roads face similar threats and are in fact more susceptible to closures than the trails themselves. With this in mind, each hike in this book lists the land manager so you can contact the appropriate agency prior to your trip and ensure that your chosen road and trail are open and safe to travel.

Snow

While Central Oregon is much drier than the western side of the mountains, the Cascades in Central Oregon receive a lot of snow each year. This is great for skiing but not quite as great for hikers. Trails in the higher alpine areas, such as near the Three Sisters, are often snowed-in until midsummer.

Many hikers think, "No worries! I'll just snowshoe!" That's certainly a possibility with several hikes, but you need to check into road closures first. Most alpine recreation roads close for the winter due to heavy snowpack and the reality that keeping them plowed would be far too expensive and cumbersome to make it justifiable. The Oregon Department of Transportation (ODOT) closes and reopens these roads at different times each year depending on snowpack, temperatures, and weather forecasts. Check on road conditions before you go out.

Additionally, heavy snow puts a lot of pressure on trees. Limbs and branches fall under their weight, and rough winter storms can blow whole trees right over. Even when trails are finally snow-free, there's a good chance that the trail will have significant blowdown blocking parts of the path. Volunteers work hard each spring and summer to clear areas, but if you get there before they do, expect to hop over some downed trees.

Fire

B&B, Pole Creek, and Two Bulls. These names might not mean much to you, but say them to a Central Oregon resident and that person will immediately recall three of the area's most destructive wildfires in recent history. Because of a dry climate and plenty of trees, fire is just a part of life in Central Oregon. It seems like there's a big wildfire almost every summer, either due to lightning or careless behavior by campers and hikers.

When it comes to fire, prevention is key. Pay attention to weather conditions, and heed all warnings put out by the Forest Service. Don't build a fire somewhere you shouldn't, and make sure it is 100 percent extinguished before you leave it. Roads and trails may be closed due to fire, and they may be rerouted for several years following a blaze. Restrictions are put in place to protect you, so adhere to them.

Should you find yourself caught in a wildfire, you need to act quickly. If you're out on a hike and you think you see or smell smoke, see ash falling, or see flames or a reddish-orange glow on the horizon, there's a good chance that a wildfire is nearby. Wildfires are fast and unpredictable, and you can't outrun one. Call authorities if you have cell service, even if you believe the fire has already been reported. Stay calm and dictate your location as clearly as possible. In the unfortunate and dangerous event that you come face to face with a wildfire, follow these guidelines:

- **Hike downhill and upwind.** Fires produce updrafts that force the blazes uphill more quickly than downhill.
- **Cover your nose and mouth with a damp cloth** to limit smoke exposure.
- **If you're in a canyon, get out.** Canyon walls act as a natural chimney.
- **Seek water.** If the body of water is large enough, stay there. If it's just a tiny creek, drench your clothes and backpack with water and keep moving.
- If you know the wildfire will be imminently overtaking you, **you may need to wait it out**. Look for a space relatively free of brush, logs, or other fire fuel. Dig a quick trench or find a hole in the ground. Lie facedown with your feet pointing toward the fire, and cover yourself with wet clothing or dirt to shield yourself from the blaze.
- **Remove synthetic clothing.** Synthetic fibers melt in high temperatures and will burn your skin.
- **Stay calm.**

While fires can be destructive, they can also be very beneficial for our forests. In fact, prescribed fires are actually very good at helping to prevent extreme wildfires! Fires are nature's way of cleaning up a forest. If too many years go by without a burn, an ecosystem can suffer from overcrowded trees, excessive brush and debris, and the spread of destructive insects and diseases that further harm our forests. The forest crews in Central Oregon perform prescribed burns annually to keep our forests healthy. Officials do their best to limit smoke and trail disruption. Even though these fires are controlled, fire is still fire. Obey all guidelines and posted road and trail closures that are in effect during controlled burning.

Rain

Rain isn't that big of an issue in Central Oregon, or at least not very often. But occasional heavy downpours, or snow that quickly melts, can create extremely muddy trails. When the trails are muddy, it's best to stay off them. Using soft and muddy trails can cause long-term tread damage and negatively affect the conditions for all users.

HIKING WITH DOGS

Charles de Gaulle once said, "The better I get to know men, the more I find myself loving dogs." In hikes, just as in life, dogs bring good attitudes and enthusiasm that many people can't. Dogs are man's best friend, and in many cases, their best hiking companions.

Hiking with dogs offers a unique perspective on the natural world. A dog can alert you to dangers along rough trails and show you things you might otherwise miss. For instance, a well-mannered, obedient dog can help you see more wildlife, as dogs are often aware of animals long before you notice them.

The real benefit to hiking with dogs, though, is the sheer pleasure they bring. The absolute joy a dog experiences when

Dog begging to be let off-leash to swim

hiking with its favorite humans is contagious. Just seeing a dog trotting happily up a trail, tongue lolling out and eyes shining with excitement, will elevate most people's moods, forcing them to share and revel in the dog's unabashed excitement and happiness as he frolics.

Central Oregon loves its dogs, and it has even been voted one of the top areas for dogs in the entire country. Many restaurants allow dogs on their patios, and city drinking fountains even have a special spigot and dish for pups. Overall, Central Oregon is a happy place for dogs and their owners.

Of course, not every person is a "dog person," nor are all dogs people pleasers. Simply put, dogs can't be allowed to do as they please all the time. As a hiker with a dog, you're responsible for your own and your dog's actions. To minimize conflicts between people and pups, here are a few guidelines:

- **Follow the rules.** The majority of national forests in the area provide extensive off-leash opportunities for dogs. However, certain high-use areas have seasonal leash laws requiring physical restraint with a leash of no longer than 6 feet. State parks require dogs to be leashed at all times. Some trails prohibit dogs entirely, including those that pass through certain watersheds. No matter where you are, obey the rules for that trail. If you visit an area that doesn't have standing laws regarding dogs, common courtesy and your own best judgment should rule.
- **Keep your dog under control.** When hiking with your dog, you should have your dog on a leash or under strict voice command at all times: on the trail, near campsites, in parking lots, and anywhere else where you may encounter other

people and animals. Strict voice command means your dog will immediately come back to heel when told, will stay at heel, and will refrain from barking. Even if a leash is not required, you should always have it with you.

- **Right-of-way.** Upon meeting any other trail user, you and your dog must yield the right-of-way, stepping well clear of the trail to allow the other users to pass without worrying about "getting sniffed."
- **Horses.** If you meet horses on the trail, it is your first responsibility as a dog owner to yield the trail, but you must also make sure your dog stays calm, does not bark, and does not make any move toward the horse. Horses can be easily spooked by dogs, and it's the dog owner's responsibility to keep her animal quiet and under firm control. Move well off the trail (go downhill off the trail when possible) and stay off the trail, with your dog held close to your side, until the horses pass well beyond you.
- **Good manners.** In practicing good canine trail etiquette, simply being friendly and courteous to other people on the trail goes a long way. If they have questions about your dog and/or her pack, try to be informative and helpful. Additionally, just because your dog *can* be off-leash doesn't mean he *should* be. If your dog is trampling through fragile alpine meadows, chasing deer, or doing his business near a body of water, you should put him on a leash. Also, dog waste needs to be packed out.

Those of us who love to hike with our dogs must be the epitome of respectful and responsible trail users. When other hikers encounter dog hikers behaving responsibly, they come away with a positive impression of dogs. In this way, we also help ourselves by preventing actions that could lead to additional trail closures or restrictions for dog hikers.

OTHER TRAIL ETIQUETTE

Many trails in this guidebook are open to different uses, including horses, mountain bikes, and occasionally motorized use, so when exploring these areas, you might be sharing the trail. When you encounter other trail users—whether they're hikers, climbers, runners, bicyclists, or horse riders—the only hard-and-fast rule is to follow common sense and exercise simple courtesy. It's hard to overstate just how vital these two things—common sense and courtesy—are to maintaining an enjoyable, safe, and friendly situation when different types of trail users meet.

With this Golden Rule of Trail Etiquette firmly in mind, here are other things you can do during trail encounters to make everyone's trip more enjoyable.

- **Right-of-way.** When meeting other hikers, the party going uphill has the right-of-way. There are two general reasons for this. First, on steep ascents hikers may be watching the trail and not notice the approach of descending hikers until they are face-to-face. More importantly, it's easier for descending hikers to break their stride and step off the trail than it is for those who have gotten into a good, climbing rhythm. But by all means, if you're the uphill trekker and you want to grant passage to oncoming hikers, go right ahead with this act of trail kindness.
- **Bicyclists.** Hikers and mountain bikers share many trails in Central Oregon. In general, rules on trails throughout Central

Oregon ask cyclists to yield to hikers. Hikers are more mobile and flexible, however, which makes it much easier for them to step off the trail. In many cases, it's easier to just forgo your right-of-way and volunteer to let the bike pass.

- **Horses.** Both hikers and bicyclists yield to horses. When meeting horseback riders, the hiker should step off to the downhill side of the trail unless the terrain makes this difficult or dangerous. In that case, move to the uphill side of the trail, but crouch down a bit to stay below the horses' eye level and avoid spooking them. Speak in a normal voice to the riders, as this helps to calm the horses. And as noted earlier, if you're hiking with a dog, keep your furry friend under control.
- **Stay on trails.** Practice minimum impact to limit erosion and trail damage. Don't cut switchbacks, make new trails, or create your own shortcut. When conditions or your destination necessitate traveling off-trail, leave the trail in as direct a manner as possible, avoiding fragile plant life and sticking to rocks and snow when possible.
- **Obey the rules.** The rules vary depending on the region and time of year. Some trails are closed to certain uses, so check before you head out.
- **Avoid disturbing wildlife.** Don't approach wildlife. Observe from a distance, and resist the urge to move closer to get a photo. This not only keeps you safer but prevents the animal from having to exert itself unnecessarily to flee from you. Several trails have seasonal closures to protect calving elk, wintering deer, nesting birds of prey, and other special species. Stay off the trails during these closures to protect wildlife.

- **Leave things natural.** Leave all natural elements as you found them. Don't move rocks or logs in rivers, as this could disrupt the natural flow of water. Never roll rocks off trails or cliffs, as you could easily injure someone below you.
- **Do your business in the right way.** If there's an outhouse, use it. If not, pick a location at least 200 feet away from water, campsites, and the trail. Dig a cat hole, do your thing, and then cover the waste with nearby dirt or rocks.
- **Pack it in, pack it out.** This includes toilet paper that isn't placed in a privy, as well as wrappers and apple cores.

These are just a few of the things you can do to maintain a safe and harmonious trail environment. While not every situation is addressed by these rules, you can avoid problems by practicing the Golden Rule of Trail Etiquette: use common sense and courtesy toward others.

WILDERNESS ETHICS

As wonderful as volunteer trail maintenance programs are, they aren't the only way to help save our trails. Such on-the-ground efforts provide high-quality trails today, but to ensure the long-term survival of our trails—and the wildlands they cross—we all must embrace and practice sound wilderness ethics.

Strong, positive wilderness ethics include making sure you leave the wilderness as pure or purer than it was when you found it. As the adage says, "Take only pictures, leave only footprints." But sound wilderness ethics go deeper than that, beyond simply picking up after ourselves when we go for a hike. Wilderness ethics must carry over into our daily lives. We need to ensure that our elected officials

While tempting, it's illegal to remove obsidian from Newberry National Volcanic Monument.

and public-land managers recognize and respond to our wilderness needs and desires. We must make sure that the next generation of Americans has a deep appreciation and respect for the natural world—not an easy task in our urban and materialistic society. If we hike the trails on the weekends, but let the wilderness go neglected on the weekdays—or worse, allow it to be abused—we'll soon find our weekend haunts diminished or destroyed. Protecting trails and wild areas is a full-time job—and one with many rewards, as any hiker can tell you.

Keep in mind that your job is not only to do your part but to help others understand the important role they play as well. Central Oregon has a lot of tourism. In the summer, Bend's population grows by almost twenty thousand visitors. That's a lot of new people hitting the trails and exploring our wild areas. Many are new to hiking and simply don't know what's appropriate. While that's not an excuse for poor behavior and bad wilderness manners, it is a reason for patience. Do your best to be a good steward for the wilder-

ness by teaching those who don't know otherwise. If we continue to pass along good habits, it will pay huge dividends later on.

It's vital that we thank the countless volunteers who donate tens of thousands of hours to wilderness trail maintenance each year. Volunteer efforts step in where limited funding, inappropriate trail use, and conflicting land-management policies and practices fail us. As hikers in Central Oregon, we should make sure to thank the other users who maintain our trails as well. Mountain bikers in this area are especially diligent and hardworking at keeping our trails in good shape.

FOOD AND WATER

While it's smart to pack in your own water and food, living off the land is an enjoyable part of spending time outdoors. As a general rule, you should treat all backcountry water sources. You might not catch a nasty parasite, but it's better to be safe than sick and sorry. Boil the water, chemically purify it with iodine tablets, or pump it through a water filter or purifier.

If you plan on foraging for edibles, including mushrooms or berries, limit what you collect to what you can consume during your visit. Also, some seemingly harmless foods can be dangerous, so know what you're getting into before ingesting anything. If in doubt, it's safer to not eat it.

WILDLIFE

Wildlife is sought by some and avoided by others. Ultimately, whether or not you encounter wildlife is often up to the animals themselves, as they're probably well aware of your presence before you spot them.

There's a hard-and-fast rule that applies to all animals you encounter on your hikes: do not approach wildlife. Remember that you're a visitor. You're in their habitat, territory, and home. Most animals don't seek conflict, but even the gentlest can be provoked into violence if they're threatened. Following are guidelines regarding the more conflict-prone animals native to Central Oregon.

Rattlesnakes

Rattlers are common in hot and dry climates like Central Oregon. Snakes are most active during the late spring and summer, often retreating to their dens in the late fall to hunker down for the winter. These desert serpents are beautiful, but encountering them can be stressful for hikers.

Like most wild creatures, rattlesnakes would much rather do their own thing and avoid humans. It's a misconception that they strike right away. When the fight-or-flight instinct hits, they're more likely to skirt away if they can. It's often said that the third hiker is the one who gets bit: the first wakes the snake up, the second provokes him into rattling, and then he's ready to bite when the third walks by. Depending on how surprised or threatened

the snake feels, he may bite you before you have any time to react to his presence.

To avoid getting bit by a snake, stick to well-defined trails with heavy foot traffic. These sections are usually clear of brush and rocks where snakes can hide. If you have to go off-trail, avoid brushy and rocky areas if you can. Hike with trekking poles and watch your footing. Wearing long pants and high-top boots can provide a layer of protection between the snake's venomous teeth and your body. Dogs are just as susceptible to bites, if not more so due to their curious wandering and desire to stick their noses into holes. Consider keeping your dog on-leash, even if you don't have to.

Should you see a rattlesnake while hiking, follow these Washington Trail Association guidelines: freeze, listen, and then slowly retreat. A threatened rattlesnake will coil into a defensive posture and warn you with its identifying rattle noise before striking. If you can't see the snake but you can hear it, attempt to locate the sound before moving away. You don't want to escalate the situation by stepping on the snake or making it feel more endangered. As you move away, hold your hiking pole between the snake and your leg to create a buffer in case the rattler strikes.

Should you or your pet suffer a snakebite, act quickly:

- **Stay calm and still.** In general snake venom moves slowly, but increased movement and an elevated heart rate will increase blood flow, making the venom spread more quickly.
- **Clean the affected area** with soap and water or an antiseptic wipe.
- **Call 911** from the trail if possible. If not, send another hiker to the trailhead or other cell-service area to seek medical help. **As**

a last resort, walk slowly to seek help. If your dog is the one bitten, carry her, keeping the bite below her heart.

- **Don't attempt a tourniquet or restrict swelling** in any way. Untie shoes or remove socks, watches, or anything else near the bite.
- **Keep the bite below heart level.** Don't elevate it.
- **Don't attempt to cut the wound or draw venom out.**
- You can **cover the bite with a loose moist dressing**, but don't use ice or apply pressure to the area.
- **Don't take painkillers.**

Bears

Bears are definitely among us in the Cascades, although they tend to keep to themselves. Bears prefer solitude to human company, generally fleeing long before you have a chance to get too close. There are times, however, when a bear doesn't hear or smell your approach (bears have a ridiculously powerful sense of smell); or maybe a bear is more interested in defending its food source or young than in avoiding a confrontation. These instances are rare, and there are several things you can do to minimize the odds of an encounter with an aggressive bear.

Hike with a group, keep dogs under control, and make sure a bear can hear you coming. Surprising a bear often makes it feel threatened. Know how to identify bear signs. Tracks and scat are the most common signs of a bear's recent presence, although there are others. Overturned rocks and torn-up deadwood logs often are the result of a bear searching for grubs. Bushes stripped of their berries, with leaves, branches, and berries littering the ground underneath, show where

a bear has fed. Bears use trees as scratching posts and will often leave claw marks; fur in the rough bark of the trees is a sign that says "A bear was here!"

On the rare occasion that a bear seems particularly interested in getting near you, here are a few tips:

- **Give the bear ample personal space**, making a wide detour around it as you leave the area.
- **Remain calm and don't run.** You can't beat a bear in a footrace, so keep calm to avoid triggering its predator-prey response.
- **Speak in a low and calm voice** to identify yourself as a human.
- **Try to appear large** by holding out your arms or raising a jacket over your head.
- **Don't make direct eye contact** with a bear, as this can be interpreted as a threat.

Berry-covered scat indicates wildlife is near.

- **Move upwind** of the bear if you can. It may be able to smell your humanness without coming any closer.
- **Read the bear's body language.** A nervous bear often rumbles in its chest, clacks its teeth, and "pops" its jaw. It may paw the ground and swing its head violently side to side. Watch it closely without staring directly at it, and continue to use low, calm tones.
- **A bear may bluff-charge** to intimidate you. If it turns out to be a legitimate charge, lie down and play dead. If it continues to perceive you as a threat, fight aggressively.
- **Carry bear spray,** and know how to use it.

Cougars

Very few hikers ever see cougars in the wild. Not only are these mountain lions some of the most solitary, shy animals in the woods, but there just aren't that many of them in Oregon. Still, there have been several sightings on both urban and rural trails on the eastern side of Central Oregon. Cougars are most active during dusk and dawn. During late spring and early summer, young cougars often become independent of their mothers and begin a search for unoccupied territory. This is often when conflict can occur.

To avoid negative confrontations, hike in groups and keep children and small dogs close at all times. Avoid dead animals, and be alert to your surroundings. Should you encounter a cougar, you've seen something in the wild that most people never will. Take a mental picture of this majestic beast, but don't be foolish enough to reach for your real camera. To make sure the experience ends up as your best memory and not the opening line of your obituary, you need to understand how cougars think. Cougars are

shy, but very curious. They'll track hikers simply to see what kind of beasts we are, but they rarely (as in, almost never) attack adult humans.

If you do encounter a cougar in the wild, remember that they rely on prey that can't, or won't, fight back. So, as soon as you spot the cat:

- **Don't run!** Running may trigger a cougar's attack instinct.
- **Stand up and face the animal.** Don't hide. Virtually every recorded cougar attack on a human has been a predator-prey attack. If you appear as another aggressive predator, rather than prey, the cougar will back down.
- **Try to appear large;** wave your arms or a jacket over your head. The idea is to make the cougar think you're the bigger, meaner beast. If you *already* have a stick in your hand, wave or throw it.
- **Be loud.** Again, anything that makes you seem scary will motivate the cougar to back down.
- **Pick up children and small dogs,** but otherwise don't bend over, as this may make you seem smaller.
- **Maintain eye contact** with the animal. The cougar will interpret this as a show of dominance on your part.
- **Don't approach the animal;** back away slowly if you can safely do so.
- Should a cougar attack, you must **fight back aggressively.**

GEAR

No hiker should venture far up a trail without being properly equipped. "Feet first" is a good rule. If your feet are happy, you'll be happy. Reliable and comfortable footwear can make all the difference in the world. In many cases, a sturdy pair of boots is essential for traction, support, and keeping your feet dry. I've found that high-quality trail running shoes, however, can do a great job as well. Trail-running shoes or low-cut "hikers" are lighter and have a shorter break-in period than boots. While they're a great option for some hikes, more-strenuous or technical excursions may necessitate the extra cushion and stability that come from higher-height hiking boots. Boots will also protect your feet a bit more from the elements than other less-technical options.

Socks are just as important as shoes, if not more so. Wear whatever is comfortable, unless it's cotton. Never wear cotton. It absorbs moisture and holds onto it, leaving you cold, wet, and susceptible to gnarly blisters. It also lacks any insulation value, so it sucks away body heat when wet. When it comes to your feet, the best advice is to use whatever has worked for you in the past. Buying a brand-new pair of boots for your big trip is a rookie mistake. Test new equipment on short trails close to home instead.

With your feet taken care of, synthetics are generally better than cotton for the rest of your clothing as well. Performance clothing has come a long way. Use whatever will keep you warm, dry, and comfortable. Within those guidelines, what you carry on the rest of your body will vary from hiker to hiker. To stay safe, however, you should always be prepared to spend the night, with emergency food and shelter. Weather can change quickly, especially at high elevations, and you don't want to be entirely caught by surprise.

THE TEN ESSENTIALS

Every member of your hiking party should carry the items in the Ten Essentials list, developed by The Mountaineers.

1. **Navigation (map and compass):** Bring a map for whatever region you're hiking in, as well as a compass. These are definitely important if you end up off-trail, whether on purpose or not.
2. **Sun protection (sunglasses and sunscreen):** At higher elevations, your exposure to UV rays is much more intense than at sea level. You can easily burn on snow, near water, and in the desert where shade is limited. Protect yourself.
3. **Insulation (extra clothing):** Weather changes quickly in the high country, so be prepared at all times of year. The high desert also cools down quickly in the evening, so carry extra layers.
4. **Illumination (flashlight/headlamp):** Getting lost or injured may force you to spend the night in the wilderness. A good flashlight or headlamp is indispensable.
5. **First-aid supplies:** At a minimum, your kit should include bandages, gauze, scissors, tape, tweezers, pain relievers, antiseptics, and perhaps a small first-aid manual. It's recommended that you receive first-aid training through a program such as MOFA (Mountaineering Oriented First Aid).
6. **Fire (firestarter and matches or lighter):** Keep your matches dry or you might as well not bring them. Sealable plastic bags or other waterproof methods work well.
7. **Repair kit and tools (including a knife):** The handy Swiss Army knife and/or a multitool is a must. A basic repair kit includes such things as a 20-foot length of nylon cord, a small roll of duct tape, some 1-inch webbing and extra webbing buckles (to fix broken pack straps), and a small tube of superglue.

8. **Nutrition (extra food):** Always pack more food than you think you'll need, in case you end up spending the night. Also, hiking burns a lot of calories, so you'll be glad you brought extra snacks even if it's not a life or death situation. Calorically dense energy bars are a good option.

9. **Hydration (extra water):** Water is even more important than food. Again, bring more than you need. If you'll be depending on on-trail water sources, make sure that you have a working filter or iodine tablets to treat it first.

10. **Emergency shelter:** No one wants to haul a tent on a day hike. Instead, bring a few garbage bags, a space blanket, or a poncho. Combine this with a bit of rope or cord, and you'll be able to set up a makeshift tent in no time.

ENJOY THE TRAILS

Above all else, I hope that this book allows you to safely enjoy the outdoors in this little pocket of wilderness in our beautiful world. These trails exist for our enjoyment and for the enjoyment of future generations. We can use them and protect them at the same time if we're careful with our actions.

Both on the trail and off, spend some time pondering all the things you love about the great outdoors. Think about how you can share that love with your friends, pass it on to your children, and teach those around you how to appreciate the wonderful natural world that we live in. The more people who get a taste of the wilderness now, the more who will advocate for its safety and maintenance in the next generation. Have fun out there!

Opposite: A gnarled whitebark pine survives along Paulina Lake's shoreline.

newberry caldera and la pine

The Newberry Volcano is responsible for a good chunk of Central Oregon's geological landmarks. It stretches for 500 square miles underground, but the majority of the Newberry National Volcanic Monument is located just outside La Pine, near East and Paulina lakes. These two stunning lakes sit in the middle of dense forest within the large caldera, amid a wide variety of terrain.

This area has several short hikes for families with kids, as well as plenty of longer options. When the higher-elevation hikes are snowed in, explore the nearby peaceful Fall River Trail and La Pine State Park. Both are at lower elevations and feature nice flat trails through ponderosa forests.

① Paulina Creek

RATING/ DIFFICULTY	ROUNDTRIP	ELEV GAIN/ HIGH POINT	SEASON
***/3	5 miles	480 feet/ 4795 feet	Year-round

Map: USFS Deschutes National Forest; **Contact:** Deschutes National Forest, Crescent Ranger District; **GPS:** N 43 43.74, W 121 25.17

Most people drive right by the Peter Skene Ogden trailhead on their way up the long winding road to the Newberry Caldera. Maybe it's a shame, but selfishly, it means more solitude for us. Here you'll find a creekside trail through fragrant ponderosa forests, gradually leading up to Paulina Creek's waterfall at McKay Crossing. The falls are lovely, but the real beauty here is simply the peaceful journey to them.

GETTING THERE
From Bend, take US Highway 97 south for 20 miles toward La Pine. Turn left at Newberry Caldera/Paulina and East Lakes near milepost 161 onto Paulina/East Lake Road 21. Go 2.8 miles and turn left at the Ogden Group Camp, following the gravel road a short distance to the parking area at the Peter Skene Ogden trailhead.

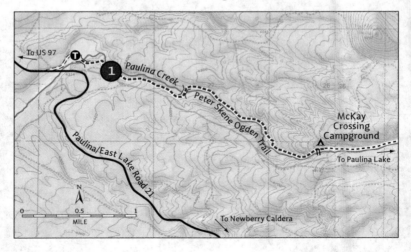

One of Paulina Creek's many trailside splashing spots for pups and their humans

ON THE TRAIL

Find the path near the parking lot and follow it immediately across Paulina Creek on a small footbridge. This is the first of many excellent spots for letting your pup frolic in the water. On hot summer days, you'll find kids splashing around as well. Once on the other side of the creek, turn left to head into the forest.

The trail is soft and starts out alongside the swift and narrow creek and its meadow bank. This hike doesn't require any big-time navigation skills—just follow the creek! With the peaceful stream always nearby, there are plenty of opportunities for dogs and kids to rinse off after trampling along the path. It can be a bit dusty in the summer, but under the shade of the forested canopy above you, it's a very comfortable hike.

The path steadily rises, gaining just under 500 feet over the course of the hike. Near the 1-mile mark, cross the river on a footbridge. You'll then walk for a bit along an old

logging railroad grade. Aren't you thankful there isn't a train busting through here? In such a peaceful environment, the thought of something so loud clamoring along just about makes me cringe!

The trail meanders away from the water every now and then, but it always finds its way back. Such is definitely the case after climbing away from the river for awhile. As you stroll among the trees, you'll lose sight of the water, but you'll more or less stay parallel to it.

At 2.5 miles, you'll realize that you're just as close to the river's edge as you've been the whole time—you're just about 150 feet above it. This aerial viewpoint of a 15-foot waterfall crashing into the rocky gulch below you is a good spot to stop. Scrambling straight down would be dangerously slippery, so don't try it. There's really no need to venture down there anyway. From up here on the trail, you have your own private view.

EXTENDING YOUR TRIP

Continue on this trail for another 6 miles to Paulina Lake, if you'd like. It's all uphill, gaining another 1500 feet as the trail follows the creek into the caldera. Shuttle a car for a one-way trip unless you're up for a 17-mile day.

2 Paulina Lake

RATING/ DIFFICULTY	ROUNDTRIP	ELEV GAIN/ HIGH POINT	SEASON
****/3	4.3 miles	190 feet/ 6560 feet	Late June–Oct

Maps: USFS Deschutes National Forest, Newberry National Volcanic Monument; **Contact:** Deschutes National Forest, Crescent Ranger District; **Notes:** NW Forest Pass or $5 day-use fee. Access road closed in winter. Dogs permitted on-leash. Privy at campground; **GPS:** N 43 42.51, W 121 14.71

Newberry is a 500-square-mile ancient volcano, but its highlight is the actual caldera and the two alpine lakes, Paulina Lake and East Lake, that reside within it—true beauty from the ashes. After a quick climb to a spectacular viewpoint, head back down to the shoreline of Paulina Lake and walk around its rim. Pack a swimsuit if you're planning to take a soak in the Warm Springs, a natural hot spring along the lakeshore.

GETTING THERE

From Bend, take US Highway 97 south for 20 miles toward La Pine. Turn left for

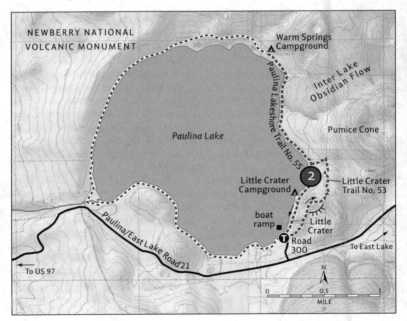

Stairs leading up to the Little Crater viewpoint

Newberry Caldera/Paulina and East Lakes near milepost 161, onto Paulina/East Lake Road 21. Drive 15 miles and turn left on Road 300 into the Little Crater Campground. Park in the day-use area near the boat launch, and find the Little Crater trailhead.

ON THE TRAIL

Instead of starting on Paulina Lakeshore Trail No. 55 right away, head 20 feet or so back up the road and find Little Crater Trail No. 53 on your left. This slight detour takes you up one side of Little Crater and down the other, giving you an awe-inspiring viewpoint in just 0.3 mile of climbing. Head to the right for the viewpoint, where you can look down into massive Newberry Caldera. From here, you can see both Paulina and East lakes, as well as Paulina Peak in the distance. The gaping caldera makes Little Crater seem way smaller than just *little*. Continue around its rim to the other side before turning right to descend 0.6 mile, where you'll pop out at the far end of Little Crater Campground and connect with the Paulina Lakeshore Trail.

You're now on the bumpy and narrow lakeshore path that you'll follow for the remainder of the way. The trail feels like it's been here for a long time, though it seems to have made only as much impact on the terrain as the wandering deer trails just off the beaten path. This probably has more to do with the trail's sturdy and rugged lava rock than the careful treading of visitors.

The lake takes on a different form up close. It's amazing how some of the foliage grows and survives directly in the rock, making the way lusher than you'd expect for such a volcanic environment. In fact, the whole scene feels more tropical than alpine. On a hot day, close your eyes and let the sun hit your face. Take a deep breath, and listen for the small waves lapping the shoreline while the breeze sweeps by. You could just about convince yourself that you're standing on the Hawaiian shores of the Pacific Ocean instead of a chilly lake inside a Central Oregon volcano.

Continue around the lake, passing along the Inter Lake Obsidian Flow at about 2 miles. From here, you'll stomp through a boggy marsh area along a sandy beach. All the extra moisture here breeds mosquitoes. They're very persistent, so it's best to move

swiftly. This is the Warm Springs area, aptly named for a natural hot spring along the sandy beach. About midway through the summer, the lake's water level drops enough to expose the spring. You'll see a small rock-framed pool on the beach just 50 feet or so from the trail. If you've timed it right and the bugs aren't riled up, it's worth a dip.

Turn around on the Paulina Lakeshore Trail when it reaches Warm Springs at just over 2 miles. Instead of turning back up the Little Crater Trail at the junction, continue straight as the trail takes you to the campground road and then leads back to the parking lot.

EXTENDING YOUR TRIP
Continue around the lake past Warm Springs to complete the entire 7.5-mile Paulina Lakeshore Trail.

3 | Paulina Peak

RATING/ DIFFICULTY	ROUNDTRIP	ELEV GAIN/ HIGH POINT	SEASON
****/4	6 miles	1650 feet/ 7984 feet	July–Oct

Maps: USFS Deschutes National Forest, Newberry National Volcanic Monument; **Contact:** Deschutes National Forest, Crescent Ranger District; **Notes:** NW Forest Pass or $5 day-use fee. Access road closed in winter. Dogs permitted on-leash. Water and restrooms at visitors center; **GPS:** N 43 39.96, W 121 16.56

Paulina Peak is the highest spot on the Newberry Caldera rim. With Paulina Lake sitting far below and the entire basin spread out before you, this is simply the best spot to really gain an appreciation for this

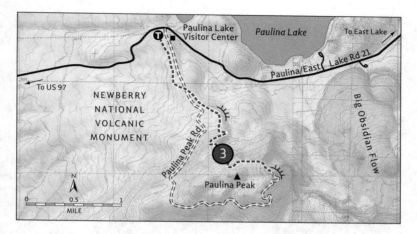

magical area. You'll have to work for it, though. You'll gain over 1600 feet on the hike up, meaning your quads will be quaking on the way down. This one's a toughie, but the final view is worth every step. Short on time? Drive up bumpy and swervy Paulina Peak Road to catch the views sans hike.

GETTING THERE

From Bend, take US Highway 97 south for 20 miles toward La Pine. Turn left for Newberry Caldera/Paulina and East Lakes near milepost 161, onto Paulina/East Lake Road 21. Drive about 13 miles and park in the day-use area on the left, across from the Paulina Lake Visitor Center.

ON THE TRAIL

From the parking area, cross the main road to the Paulina Lake Visitor Center. Then find the signed Paulina Peak Trail on the right, just 0.1 mile or so from the wooden information kiosk outside the visitors center. Shortly after leaving the trailhead, you'll pass through a dead and dying forest. You'll

find similar damaged forests around Central Oregon, and most people assume that the dead trees are from long-ago wildfires. Not so. This destruction can actually be attributed to western pine beetles. Wildfires seem like the scarier foe at first glance, but they're almost easier to recover from than a pest infestation.

Leave the devastation behind and take the dusty trail through lodgepole pine and hemlock forests before reaching the unpaved Paulina Peak Road at 1 mile. Don't take this road, or all the cars heading to the summit will, quite literally, leave you in the dust. Instead, cross the road and find the trail on the other side. You may see a few cars parked here, most likely those of hikers who opted out of the hike's first mile. That's certainly an option, but the parking is limited up here. To me, it's worth it to park at the bottom and commit to hiking from the trail's start, rather than risk driving extra distance just to turn around because there's no parking and hike the first mile anyway. Plus, you *are* here to hike, right?

Paulina Lake as seen from the top of Paulina Peak

After crossing the road and laughing quietly to yourself while cars turn back down the road, continue on the trail. Though you've been climbing since the trailhead, until this point it's been at a fairly comfortable incline. Now things start to get a bit more difficult. Continue on, and get ready to feel those legs burn! You're about to gain another 1450 feet on your way to the top.

Fortunately, opportunities for viewpoints and quick breaks abound as you climb. In just 0.5 mile, you'll snag your first glimpse of Paulina Peak's pointy pinnacles (try saying that five times fast). Over the final 1.5 miles, peekaboo views give you hints at what's to come. But the best views come when you reach the top at 3 miles.

A few struggling whitebark pines grace the summit, but otherwise, your view is nearly unobstructed in every direction. Both Paulina and East lakes fill the basin below, adorned by the Big Obsidian Flow and scattered cinder cones. The Three Sisters, Broken Top, and Mount Bachelor sit to the northwest, with Mount Jefferson and Mount Hood poking out beyond them. If you look to the south, you can see Diamond Peak, Mount Thielsen, and perhaps even all the way to Mount Shasta if the sky is clear.

Obviously, watch your step up here. The north face of Paulina Peak is just about completely vertical and nearly 1500 feet high. It's not the place to slip. Instead of wandering about, pick a comfy spot to settle in for a bit. There's even a picnic table. Direct your gaze toward your favorite Cascade view, or admire the up-close views of Newberry Caldera that you can't see from town. Ultimately, it doesn't matter what direction you're pointing when you plop down. You'll find views that abound all around. Head back the way you came when you're ready.

4 Lost Lake

RATING/ DIFFICULTY	ROUNDTRIP	ELEV GAIN/ HIGH POINT	SEASON
****/4	6.2 miles	1335 feet/ 7220 feet	Late June–Oct

Maps: USFS Deschutes National Forest, Newberry National Volcanic Monument; **Contact:** Deschutes National Forest, Crescent Ranger District; **Notes:** NW Forest Pass or $5 day-use fee. Access road closed in winter. Dogs permitted on-leash. Privy at trailhead; **GPS:** N 43 42.39, W 121 14.17

The name of this hike has always intrigued me. Is it called the "Lost Lake" Trail because the lake itself is lost, or because hikers got lost trying to find one? Whatever the original intentions behind it, the moniker is still confusing. I'll clear it up for you: you should not encounter any lakes on this trail. If you do, it's not the lake that's lost—it's you. This trail traverses old forest before paralleling an obsidian flow up to the drier parts of the Newberry Caldera, where you'll explore some interesting pumice flats. This route is significantly less crowded than the nearby Big Obsidian Trail but affords similar views.

Quiet forests provide shade on hot days.

GETTING THERE

From Bend, take US Highway 97 south for 20 miles toward La Pine. Turn left for Newberry Caldera/Paulina and East Lakes near milepost 161, onto Paulina/East Lake Road 21. Drive about 15 miles and turn to the right into the Big Obsidian Trail parking lot. Park here, and then walk back toward the main road until you see the trail on your right.

ON THE TRAIL

Start up the path and keep straight on Newberry Crater Trail No. 58. Horses have stomped down the middle of the trail, making it kind of tricky to walk in. You'll probably see tracks where bikes have chosen to ride on the higher rim of the trail. That's probably the best place to walk, but just make sure you're sticking to the trail and not causing additional erosion.

At 0.5 mile, take a right onto Lost Lake Trail No. 58.2. In another 0.3 mile, the trail narrows and starts climbing. You'll gain nearly 800 feet over the next 2 miles. This secluded trail is sometimes covered with animal scat, so keep an eye out for bears,

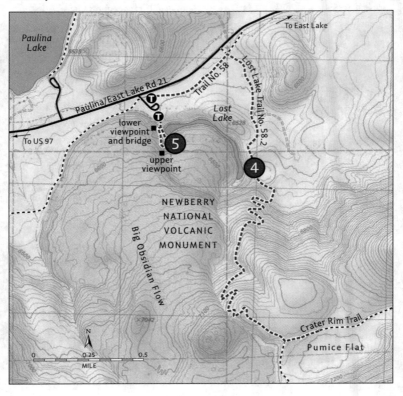

deer, or whatever else may cross your path. Don't go looking for trouble, but if you're hoping to see wildlife, early morning is your best bet.

From these forested switchbacks, you'll have a few sneak-peek views of the lava. The trail loops away from it at 1.25 miles and heads back into the trees. You'll appreciate the trees on hot days, as they provide shade during the parts of the hike where you're working the hardest. Within 1 mile, you'll reach a curvy switchback that, if you turn around, showcases Paulina Lake, all Three Sisters, Mount Bachelor, and plenty of lava flows. If a pretty view is all you came for, this is the best one. If you're ready to check out the unique Pumice Flat, however, continue upward.

After another great lava view at 2.6 miles, you'll reach a flat and windy ridge with weathered trees. After another 0.3 mile, turn left on the Crater Rim Trail for Pumice Flat. The flat comes into view within another 0.2 mile, which is a good stopping point.

If you've dragged kids along, here's a fun game/trick to try. My parents used to do this with my brother and me, and it definitely helped pass the time and curb our whining when we were too young to fully appreciate the value of a day spent hiking. Grab a small piece of obsidian on the way up. Pick up a bigger piece of pumice when you get to the flat, and ask the kids which one they think is heavier. The look on their confused faces when they pick up the feather-light piece of pumice will be priceless. Make sure to return both rocks on your way back down.

Still curious about Lost Lake? Well, it does exist, but it's nothing more than a small marshy pool at the base of the Big Obsidian Flow. If you really want to see it, you'll catch an aerial view of it on the left as you head up the Big Obsidian Trail (Hike 5).

5 Big Obsidian Flow

RATING/ DIFFICULTY	ROUNDTRIP	ELEV GAIN/ HIGH POINT	SEASON
****/2	0.8 mile	450 feet/ 6650 feet	June–Oct

Maps: USFS Deschutes National Forest, Newberry National Volcanic Monument; **Contact:** Deschutes National Forest, Crescent Ranger District; **Notes:** NW Forest Pass or $5 day-use fee. Access road closed in winter. Dogs not recommended. Privy at trailhead; **GPS:** N 43 42.39, W 121 14.17

If you only have time to make one stop at Newberry Caldera, this should be it. It's a popular spot because it's one of the most fascinating hikes in the state. The gnarly volcanic habitat here looks like something out of an old fairy tale. You half expect to find a dragon waiting just out of sight. You won't find anything quite that diabolical on this hike, but the trail is made of sharp, jagged, crushed obsidian, so use a bit of caution. The short distance and additional interesting features make this hike a great option for kids. Because of the rough surface, stairs, and general crowdedness, however, stroller use is not recommended.

GETTING THERE

From Bend, take US Highway 97 south for 20 miles toward La Pine. Turn left for Newberry Caldera/Paulina and East Lakes near milepost 161, onto Paulina/East Lake Road 21. Drive approximately 15 miles and turn right, into the Big Obsidian Trail parking lot.

Sharp but shiny obsidian slopes all the way down to Lost Lake.

ON THE TRAIL

Before you get too far down the trail, you'll be greeted with the first of several interpretive signs about the Big Obsidian Flow. Definitely stop to read up on the intriguing events that created this must-see attraction. It's pretty incredible that you're about to walk through what used to be piping-hot, swirling magma. Kids think that whole concept is especially intriguing.

Head up the metal stairs, and within just a few minutes you'll reach the lower viewpoint and panoramic vistas of a sparkling obsidian flow. This flow is actually one of the younger ones in the area, at just thirteen hundred years old. You'll see a mix of jet-black glassy obsidian and both gray and matte-black pumice. These composition differences resulted from the amount and size of bubbles in the magma when it cooled.

Continue across the bridge to the loop portion of this lollipop-shaped hike. Read about the geology and history posted on the informational plaques as you wind around to the upper viewpoint at 0.4 mile. From here you can really appreciate the uniqueness of this jagged but beautiful trail. Remember to "take only pictures, and leave only footprints." I know there's plenty to go around, and surely no one would miss that one piece, but no obsidian snatching, please.

Continue around the lollipop to return to the lower viewpoint. As you head back to the trailhead, look for a small lake over to the right as you reach the bottom of the metal stairs. You probably didn't notice it on the way up, but that's Lost Lake. Every August, thousands of frogs leave their grassy habitat at the small pond and migrate *over* the obsidian flow. Interestingly enough, no one knows why. Should your hike coincide with the great frog migration, watch out so you don't step on the little guys!

6 Cinder Hill

RATING/ DIFFICULTY	ROUNDTRIP	ELEV GAIN/ HIGH POINT	SEASON
****/3	6.75 miles	970 feet/ 7400 feet	July–Oct

Maps: USFS Deschutes National Forest, Newberry National Volcanic Monument; **Contact:** Deschutes National Forest, Crescent Ranger District; **Notes:** NW Forest Pass or $5 day-use fee. Access road closed in winter. Dogs permitted on-leash. Privy at campground; **GPS:** N 43 44.12, W 121 11.73

There are countless cinder cones spattered throughout Central Oregon as a result of the Newberry Volcano. As such, giving any particular one the official title of Cinder Hill seems almost pointless. But despite its indistinct name, Cinder Hill wows with a full panoramic view of the Newberry Caldera. Another bonus? Unlike some of the other viewpoints in the area, you can't drive to this one, since it's tucked away at the very end of the national monument. Hike this section of the Crater Rim Trail for the best views without the crowds.

GETTING THERE

From Bend, take US Highway 97 south for 20 miles toward La Pine. Turn left for Newberry Caldera/Paulina and East Lakes near milepost 161, onto Paulina/East Lake Road 21. Follow the road about 17 miles to its end, where it changes to Road 300. Continue north for 0.5 mile through the Cinder Hill Campground. Park in the day-use area near campsite 51.

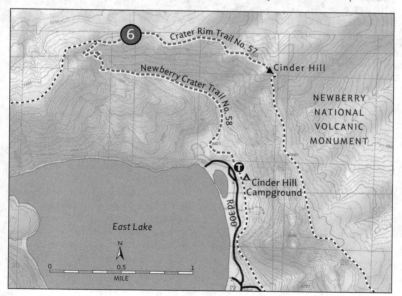

Standing atop Cinder Hill, with a clear view into the caldera, is a photographer's dream.

ON THE TRAIL

From the Cinder Hill Campground trailhead, take the Newberry Crater Trail No. 58 up a soft path into a forest of jack and lodgepole pines. Soon, you'll enter a sparser but more beautiful forest with stout ponderosas. They're spread out enough that you can see a decent distance, quite literally seeing the forest through the trees. If you see something moving off in the distance, it's possible that you've spotted a black bear. Well-maintained but somewhat lonely, this trail is a favorite for the local bears, who often use the path to travel down to the campground trash cans. Look closely and you may see their paw prints in the soft dirt path.

As you make your way through the low area next to the cinder cone, the path begins to lead up the cone's flank with gradual but inconsistent switchbacks. Some are quick, steep turns, while others are so long that you forget you're weaving back and forth. Near 2 miles, turn right at the junction to head toward the viewpoint on the Crater Rim Trail No. 57. The trail is well signed, but the marked distances are a bit inaccurate. The sign says you're 0.75 mile away from the viewpoint, but you still have a little over 1.25 miles to go.

The trail flattens out near the top, even sloping downhill for a few stretches. You'll likely think you've passed the viewpoint, or that it was such a pathetic through-the-trees view that you didn't even notice it had come and gone. No worries—you didn't miss it. Soon enough, you'll turn the corner and see a wide-open area just a little farther down the path. Continue on the trail and step out onto the exposed slope just past 3.3 miles, complete with unobstructed and stunning views of the 5-mile-wide Newberry Caldera.

The gaping hole left from Newberry's volcanic activity now houses two deep blue lakes: Paulina Lake and East Lake. From the top of Cinder Hill, you have perfect views of both, as well as Paulina Peak, Mount Thielsen, Diamond Peak, and expansive basalt and obsidian flows. This may be one of the best locations for photography in all of Newberry Caldera. Hit the trail early for the best chance of clear images without glare from the sun.

In between all of these landmarks, thick green forests blanket the landscape. In the summer, the rough red cinder is covered with itsy, fragile, magenta-colored flowers. Several downed trees offer spots to rest your legs while you admire the stunning views of the entire caldera. It can be chilly up here on breezy days. When you're ready (or cold), return the same way you came in.

7 Cougar Woods and the Big Pine

RATING/ DIFFICULTY	LOOP	ELEV GAIN/ HIGH POINT	SEASON
***/2	4 miles	50 feet/ 3260 feet	Year-round

Map: Oregon State Parks—La Pine State Park; **Contact:** La Pine State Park; **Notes:** Dogs permitted on-leash. Water and restrooms at picnic area; **GPS:** N 43 46.16, W 121 31.1

This lonely state park is often forgotten, as La Pine visitors are typically headed to Newberry Caldera. Just miles from the tiny town, La Pine State Park generally takes the backseat. While you won't find sweeping panoramas or high peaks here, you will find big ponderosas, a peaceful river, and convenient day-use areas. The easy trails and unique attractions are ideal for families and casual hikers.

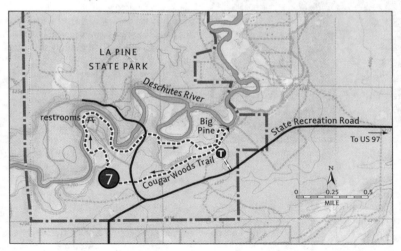

The Big Pine towers above the forest near the Deschutes River.

GETTING THERE

From Bend, take US Highway 97 approximately 20 miles south toward La Pine. Turn right at milepost 161 and follow the La Pine State Park signs. Drive 4.5 miles along State Recreation Road, following signs for the Big Pine. Then turn right onto a gravel road and drive another 0.7 mile to the trailhead at the Big Pine parking lot.

ON THE TRAIL

Ignore the large sign luring you to visit the Big Pine right away. You'll get there later. Because kids often think the towering tree is the most interesting part of the whole hike, it's worth stowing it in your back pocket until the very end to keep them engaged for the entire hike. Start instead by finding the Cougar Woods Trail on the back side of the parking lot, opposite the sign for the Big Pine.

Head into a pleasant forest, complete with the ever-present scent of powerful ponderosas. That Central Oregon smell never gets old! This easy dirt trail is gentle enough for kids, but it's also long enough that you won't feel like you're compromising with a "kid hike." Since mountain bikes are allowed, youngsters can even pedal along to keep up with the rest of the group. Stay on the trail as it crosses a park road at 0.75 mile before it curves right and gently descends to the river at 1.5 miles.

Sheltered by pine trees on either side, this picturesque section of the Deschutes River is extremely peaceful. Follow its lazy course just a bit farther until you reach a comfortable picnic area, cradled in a river bend along a sandy beach. If you pack a lunch (and I strongly suggest doing so), this is a great spot to relax, swim, and enjoy the spectacular Central Oregon sun. You'll likely find a few families doing just that.

Whether you stop at the picnic area or not, you'll need to find the return trail to complete the loop. Head away from the river and walk to the right, toward the restrooms.

The path connects just left of the restrooms, near another trail sign, and loops back down toward the river. Cross the road again at 2.75 miles, keeping straight and following signs for the Cougar Woods Trail. After another stretch on the soft path, you'll reach the parking lot at about 3.25 miles.

Finish off your La Pine State Park experience by checking out the Big Pine. Yes, there are trees *everywhere*, but this one is actually pretty impressive. The 0.7-mile paved loop leads to a five-hundred-year-old ponderosa near the river. This route is a great barrier-free option by itself, and it's a nice add-on to the Cougar Woods hike. After admiring this 162-foot giant, continue on the loop back to the parking lot.

8 Fall River Springs and Old Guard Station

RATING/ DIFFICULTY	ROUNDTRIP	ELEV GAIN/ HIGH POINT	SEASON
***/1	1.6 miles	50 feet/ 4310 feet	Year-round

Map: USFS Deschutes National Forest; **Contact:** Deschutes National Forest, Bend–Fort Rock Ranger District; **Notes:** Privy at guard station; **GPS:** N 43 46.39, W 121 37.24

This is the kind of stroll where your troubles melt away. It's short, simple, and completely free of chaos. No big hills or confusing directions—just the calm hum of Fall River on one side and sweet-smelling ponderosas on the other. This quick walk parallels the river as you head upstream to the springs and historical guard station. This trail is certainly short—more of a stroll than a hike, making it a great option for families. Spend a day here, enjoying lunch at a picnic table in view of the peaceful Fall River.

GETTING THERE

From Bend, take US Highway 97 approximately 16 miles south. Turn right onto Vandevert Road after milepost 155. In 1 mile, turn left onto South Century Drive, go 1 mile, and then turn right to stay on South Century

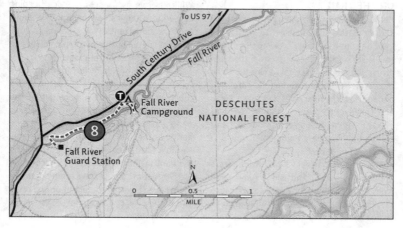

A large downed tree sits across the lazy Fall River.

Drive for just under 10 miles. Turn left at the signed Fall River Campground and park in the day-use area.

ON THE TRAIL

Leave the day-use area at the campground and take the designated trail upstream, indicated by the brown "trail" pointer. The trail is set back 50 feet or so from the river, giving you ample space to admire the thick puzzle-piece bark covering the fragrant ponderosas. The river itself is sluggish, clear, and shallow. It's very friendly in terms of children who want to splash around in it, but be mindful of anglers waiting patiently for a bite along the shore.

It's picture-perfect here. Wildflowers pepper the banks, and old water-logged trees lay right where they once fell. Because the Fall River is so shallow, the fallen trees sit just above the water line, forming zigzags up and down the creek. In 0.75 mile, the trail ends at the white and Forest Service–green guard station. The old shelter was built in the 1930s by the Civilian Conservation Corps. While its role as a Forest Service building ceased in 2003, it's now open to the public for recreational rental (www.recreation.gov). Respect any occupants by keeping quiet and not entering the guard station.

Skirt the right side of the guard station's fence, and descend about 75 feet to where the river's headwaters bubble out of the ground. This meadow area is very fragile, so tread gently. Head back to the guard station and take the trail back the way you came. Or, walk the fishermen's trail directly along the bank instead. If you feel like it, continue just 50 feet or so past the campground to a footbridge. The trails peter out on the other side of the river, so just admire the viewpoint from the bridge.

9 Fall River and Falls

RATING/DIFFICULTY	LOOP	ELEV GAIN/HIGH POINT	SEASON
***/3	5 miles	150 feet/4300 feet	Year-round

Map: Oregon State Parks—La Pine State Park; **Contact:** La Pine State Park, and Deschutes National Forest, Bend–Fort Rock Ranger District; **Notes:** Dogs permitted on-leash; **GPS:** N 43 47.63, W 121 31.85

Fall River is the kind of winding waterway that's so lazy and calm it hardly seems like a river at all. In some spots the water looks like it's barely moving, although it's certainly flowing quickly just under the surface. Interspersed among the peaceful segments are sections of mild white water and comfortable waterfalls. The trail starts off along a swifter section, with a visit to Fall River Falls, before connecting to the Deschutes River. You'll then visit the McGregor Memorial Viewpoint and finish with a stretch of trail through massive ponderosa pines before looping back to the parking area.

GETTING THERE

From Bend, take US Highway 97 approximately 16 miles south. Turn right onto Vandevert Road after milepost 155. In 1 mile, turn left onto South Century Drive, go 1 mile, and then turn right to stay on South Century Drive for 5 miles. Turn left onto West Deschutes River Road, toward La Pine State Park. In another 0.8 mile, *after* crossing the bridge over the river, turn left into the parking area.

ON THE TRAIL

There are plenty of places to start along this trail, but I like this spot. It's a maintained but quieter trailhead, away from La Pine State

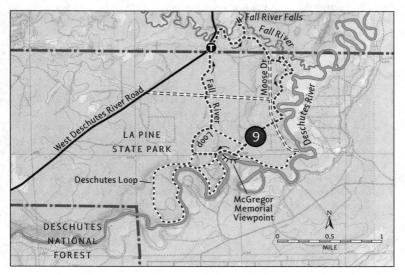

A hiker relaxes along the Fall River just beneath the waterfall.

Park's main entrance. From the parking area and the beginning of your loop, take the Fall River Loop east along the river. You'll get quite close to the water before bending away from it. At 0.4 mile, you'll reach a junction with the short 0.2-mile trail to Fall River Falls. Turn left. While the falls have just a 14-foot drop, the tumbling, rumbling white water is a stark difference from the peaceful river just above and below. Verdant meadows and lodgepole pines grow right up to the river's edge. It's one of the most scenic spots on the Fall River.

Go back to the main trail, continuing on the Fall River Loop as it follows the water, placid again as the bubbles settle after the falls. You'll hike along Fall River for 0.6 mile until you reach a little 0.4-mile roundabout side loop. Turn left onto this side trail to go back down to Fall River and then around to the Deschutes River. Larger than Fall River, the Deschutes makes several larger bends over the next stretch. After looping back to the main trail, turn left.

At 2.5 miles, you'll cross Moose Drive before continuing another 0.7 mile on the Fall River Loop to the McGregor Memorial Viewpoint and the Deschutes River (again). Continue on, keeping right on the combined Fall River Loop/McGregor Loop when it splits just 0.1 mile or so after the viewpoint. Cross the park road, and turn right in another 0.2 mile to stay on the main loop. It's only another 0.4 mile to your last junction, where you'll leave the McGregor Loop and stay left on the last stretch of the Fall River Loop.

This section of trail is mostly viewless but still gorgeous in its own way. This remote area is more forested and less frequented, so you'll probably have it all to yourself. Nothing wrong with that! You'll cross another park road at 4.25 miles and then one more at 4.75 miles, before finishing up the loop where you started.

EXTENDING YOUR TRIP

There are several other options for exploration here. Link up with the Deschutes Loop—a 3-mile addition—by taking a left after the McGregor Memorial Viewpoint. Follow along the curvy river for 1.5 miles before turning away from the river and connecting back to the McGregor Loop. Stay left here to jump back onto the Fall River Loop.

Opposite: Peering down into Lava Butte's crater

bend

If Central Oregon had a capital city, it would without a doubt be Bend. So named for the strange bend in the Deschutes River as it cuts through town, Bend used to be an old logging city. Now a tourist destination and launchpad for all types of recreation, it's the thriving hub that everything else in Central Oregon branches off from. It's a great place to stay if you're visiting, as it's more or less equidistant from every region in this book. With stunning views of the Cascades all over town, the lovely Deschutes River, plenty of interesting history, and a lot of lava, even the most urban zones in Central Oregon have their fair share of hiking opportunities.

10 Lava Cast Forest

RATING/ DIFFICULTY	LOOP	ELEV GAIN/ HIGH POINT	SEASON
**/1	0.9 mile	90 feet/ 5790 feet	May–Nov

Maps: USGS Lava Cast Forest, map at trailhead; **Contact:** Deschutes National Forest, Bend–Fort Rock Ranger District; **Notes:** NW Forest Pass or $5 day-use fee. Dogs permitted on-leash. Privy at trailhead; **GPS:** N 43 49.03, W 121 17.31

This hike is accessible in the sense that it's fairly close to Bend and its road is just off US Highway 97. But that particular road happens to be 9 miles of washboard gravel. In fact, the drive takes longer than the short hike does! So, skip it if that's just going to irritate you. And if you're looking for a good workout, this isn't the hike for you. But if volcanic flows are your thing, or you're looking for an easy day trip to get the kids outside, the Lava Cast Forest is worth checking out.

GETTING THERE
From Bend, drive US Highway 97 south for 11 miles to exit 153. Turn left at the fork, heading under the highway. Follow bumpy Lava Cast Forest Road 9720 for 9 uphill miles to the parking lot.

ON THE TRAIL
Find the trailhead on the far side of the parking lot. This hike is on a paved interpretive trail, so grab one of the flyers that correlates with signs along the path. If there aren't any left, take a picture of the information on the trailhead board and use it to follow along. Or, if you want to wing it without the info, that's fine too. Head left on the paved trail and into the black, otherworldly terrain.

Three different lava flows make up the 5-square-mile Lava Cast Forest Geological Area: the Lava Cast Forest Flow, the Cascade Flow, and the Forest Road Flow. All, however, originated from vents on Newberry Volcano. When these flows ran through the forest over six thousand years ago, they engulfed and collapsed just about everything in their paths. The lava cooled around the trees before they completely burned, leaving their trunks encased in stone and creating the lava casts, or tree molds, that you see today.

The lava casts look either like wells or tunnels, depending on if the tree was able to stand its ground against the lava flow or not. Go ahead and take a peek inside—it's pretty interesting! Even though this harsh territory is a bit like a tree graveyard, there has been a slow resurgence of life since the fiery flow. Evidence of this revegetation can be seen in the trees, wild currant, and Indian paintbrush that cling to life here. The sparse but colorful flora stands in glaring contrast to the black and gray lava rock that blankets the landscape.

One of the unique lava casts along the trail

The path is paved, but the surface is quite bumpy and does have a few gentle ups and downs. Follow the trail through the lava fields, looping around and finishing up at the parking lot just short of 1 mile. You'll pop out about 20 feet down from where you started. If you grabbed a flyer, make sure to put it back for other hikers to enjoy.

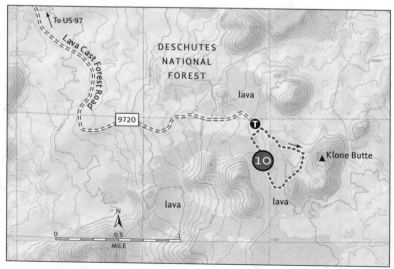

11 Lava River Cave

RATING/ DIFFICULTY	ROUNDTRIP	ELEV GAIN/ HIGH POINT	SEASON
***/3	2 miles	200 feet/ 4500 feet	May–Sept

Maps: USGS Lava Butte, map at trailhead; **Contact:** Deschutes National Forest, Bend–Fort Rock Ranger District, and Lava Lands Visitor Center; **Notes:** NW Forest Pass or $5 day-use fee. Open 9:00 A.M.–5:00 P.M., May–Sept. Dogs not allowed. Privy at trailhead; **GPS:** N 43 53.72, W 121 22.12

Catch a break from the summer heat by heading just a few miles out of town to the Lava River Cave. Formed by an eruption over eighty thousand years ago, this lava tube is believed to be the longest uninterrupted one in the state. Today, there's a flat but rocky 1-mile trail through the cavernous tunnels.

While lava tubes are everywhere in Central Oregon, this is the most family-friendly site. Safety railings, steps, and a self-guided interpretive path make it a very popular spot.

Here are a few tips to make your visit an enjoyable one: First, pack warm clothing, as it's a bit chillier underground. While the sudden thrust into cooler temperatures is a welcome reprieve on hot days, you'll quickly cool down and wish you'd brought a jacket. Second, sturdy shoes are a must, as the cave is rugged in parts. Third, bring your headlamp or rent a lantern at the trailhead. Hiking in the dark will surely end with some type of injury. Lastly, exploring the cave is slow going, so give yourself extra time for this trip. The unique experience is worth it.

GETTING THERE
From Bend, take US Highway 97 south for 9 miles toward La Pine. Take exit 151 for Cottonwood Road, and turn left to follow it

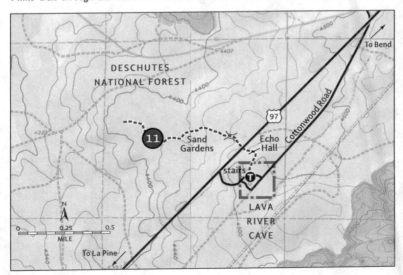

Light from above shines into the Lava River Cave's cavernous entryway.

through the underpass. Follow signs for Lava River Cave for about 1 mile and turn right into the parking area.

ON THE TRAIL

Step carefully down a small flight of rough metal stairs built atop a pile of lava to enter the cave. The temperature drops with each step before reaching a near constant 42 degrees Fahrenheit inside. During winter months, icy stalactites and stalagmites form, often sticking around until early summer, when they finally melt. Watch your step—the trail is gentle, but the surface is rough and often slippery.

Just 0.2 mile in, you'll reach the large atrium-like space called Echo Hall. The cave ceiling is about 58 feet above you, but voices are all around as they bounce off the cave walls—an eerie sound in the unfamiliar darkness. Continuing on, you'll head down another set of stairs and pass underneath US 97 near 0.3 mile, 80 feet above you. What a terrifying thought! Sometimes you can hear the hum of the cars above. Walk farther into the cave, crossing a small bridge. Shine your light around the cave to illuminate the wide variety of surfaces and shapes the lava took as it cooled.

Near 0.4 mile, the tube narrows a bit and gets noticeably shorter. In fact, you're actually in a tube within a tube! The interpretive signs explain how the unique two-tube tunnel formed. The cave is home to bats, who probably enjoy the inaccessible upper tube. While it's unlikely that you'll see these nocturnal fellas, you can still help keep them safe. In order to avoid spreading white-nose syndrome, avoid wearing or bringing any clothing or equipment that might have been used in a cave or mine outside the Pacific Northwest.

At 0.6 mile, you'll reach a protected area called the Sand Gardens. Did you notice the layer of sand forming on top of the rough lava rock? Over time, aboveground precipitation has slowly dripped volcanic ash and sand from the ceiling onto the cave floor. The Sand Gardens showcase the pinnacles that have formed from this constant water dropping within the cave. Visitors were less than gentle around this area in the past, so now the gardens are fenced off to protect the fragile spires from further destruction.

The amount of sand increases the farther into the cave you go. At 1 mile, you'll notice that the sand actually reaches the top of the cave. In the 1930s, two apparently non-claustrophobic men were curious how much farther the cave went on, so they dug out a little more. To this day, no one knows quite how far past the sand plug the cave continues, and it's now closed off to keep the public safe. Turn back the way you came when the thought of being so far belowground starts to creep you out.

12 Sun-Lava Path to Benham Falls

RATING/ DIFFICULTY	ROUNDTRIP	ELEV GAIN/ HIGH POINT	SEASON
***/2	5 miles	300 feet/ 4230 feet	Year-round

Maps: USGS Benham Falls, Sunriver Resort Pathway Map; **Contact:** Deschutes National Forest, Bend–Fort Rock Ranger District, and Lava Lands Visitor Center; **Notes:** Dogs permitted on-leash; **GPS:** N 43 54.83, W 121 26.20

This entirely paved trail links Sunriver Resort with Lava Butte, while also providing another way to access the Benham Falls area along the Deschutes River. Some locals are bummed out by the asphalt walkway in the middle of the otherwise natural setting. However, there are still plenty of dirt single-track trails in this area, such as the Black Rock Trail. Plus, I think that anything that encourages more people to be active and enjoy the great outdoors is a good thing. The Sun-Lava Path does just that and is an excellent barrier-free option.

While the entire Sun-Lava Path runs 5 miles between Sunriver Resort and Lava Butte, the whole stretch is a tad long and monotonous to do twice, out and back. So, this hike starts from Sunriver and then branches off, leaving the Sun-Lava Path to visit the wild and popular Benham Falls. While this second part is unpaved, it's mostly wide and gentle all the way to the falls. You can also start at Benham Falls and hike this trail backward. To do so, follow the directions to the Benham Falls west trailhead in Hike 14.

GETTING THERE

From Bend, take US Highway 97 south for 9 miles toward La Pine. Take exit 151 for Cottonwood Road. Stay right at the end of the off-ramp and proceed 2.4 miles on Cottonwood Road. At the roundabout, take the first exit onto East Cascade Road. Drive another 0.4 mile and take the first exit at another roundabout to stay on East Cascade Road. In 1.1 miles, turn right into the Forest Road 600 parking lot signed "River Take Out."

ON THE TRAIL

Start on the paved Sun-Lava Path, which winds through the north side of Sunriver Resort. Flanked by tall ponderosa pines, the route winds through a typical Central Oregon landscape. There's a bizarre dichotomy here: the paved path suggests civilization, but there are absolutely no houses or businesses around. In the summer, this trail can be busy. Expect to share the path with cyclists, runners, strollers, and dogs.

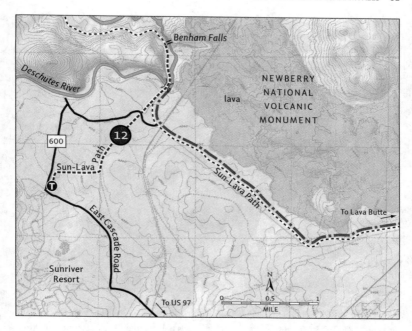

The path is mostly flat, with a few gentle ups and downs. You'll see distance markers every half mile. At 1.7 miles, you'll cross the road and reach a junction where the Sun-Lava Path skirts off toward the Lava Lands Visitor Center at the base of Lava Butte. Keep left toward Benham Falls, to where the paved path ends and a gravel path begins. Descend slightly to the river and go straight to cross the footbridge and continue on the Deschutes River Trail toward the Benham Falls west trailhead.

Just under the 2-mile mark, on the other side of the footbridge, follow the trail along the river. Though this part of the trail is unpaved and occasionally rocky, it's wide and very easy going. Ponderosas line both sides of the trail, and you can see an extensive lava flow on the opposite side of the river. At 2.4 miles, turn right at the brown hiker symbol to head 0.1 mile down to the semiprotected overlook above Benham Falls.

While not your typical cascading waterfall, these violent and twisting rapids are quite impressive as they force their way through the canyon. White water experts rate them class V+, which means they're pretty much impassable unless you're a pro. If you're lucky enough to see kayakers scouting the rapids, definitely stick around to watch! Head back the way you came when you're ready.

EXTENDING YOUR TRIP

The trail continues for 8 miles past the falls (see Hike 14). Or, should you decide you want to hike all the way to Lava Butte, you

The Deschutes River is calm here, just a half mile above Benham Falls.

certainly can. To do so, turn right at the junction to stay on the Sun-Lava Path for another 3.8 miles to the butte trails (also see Hike 13). This route is primarily uphill and significantly less crowded than the Sunriver part of the trail. You'll likely be sharing it with more cyclists than hikers.

13 Lava Butte's Trail of Molten Land

RATING/ DIFFICULTY	LOOP	ELEV GAIN/ HIGH POINT	SEASON
**/1	1.3 miles	115 feet/ 4635 feet	May– early Oct

Map: Lava Lands Map (available at visitors center); **Contact:** Lava Lands Visitor Center; **Notes:** NW Forest Pass or $5 day-use fee.

Dogs permitted on-leash. Monument closed in winter. Water and restrooms available; **GPS:** N 44 54.34, W 121 21.28

While it won't impress hardcore hikers, the Lava Lands area just a few miles south of town has some easy hikes and tons of information about one of Bend's most accessible volcanic landmarks. Kids will love the interactive displays at the visitors center and the gentle walk directly into the rough lava field. Complete your excursion with a drive up to the top of the butte and an up-close examination of the crater.

GETTING THERE

From Bend, take US Highway 97 south for approximately 7 miles toward La Pine. Follow

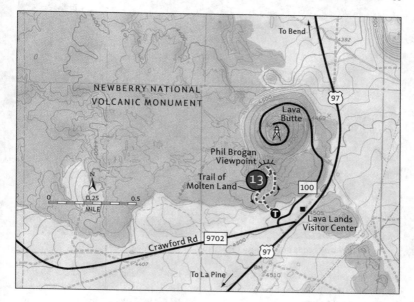

signs for Lava Butte, turning right into the pocket lane onto Crawford Road/Forest Road 9702 and then shortly afterward turning onto FR 100 to the parking lot.

ON THE TRAIL

From the Lava Butte parking lot, head toward the visitors center and follow signs for the Trail of Molten Land near the base of the lava. The paved interpretive loop travels through the rocky basalt flow with signs that explain Lava Butte's geology and interesting history. While the trail is technically barrier-free, the path is bumpy and steep in areas.

Follow the path and turn right at the first junction as you enter the lava fields, reading up on history along the way. Lava Butte is actually one of four hundred cinder cones that make up the Newberry Volcano. The lava that flowed from this particular cone

over seven thousand years ago affected the area in many ways, and you'll see evidence of it all around Bend in the form of waterfalls, caves, and tunnels.

At 0.3 mile, turn right to stroll for about 0.2 mile one-way to the Phil Brogan Viewpoint. From there, you can see how the Lava Butte flow covered approximately 10 square miles of pine forests. Beyond the lava and the surviving forests, Central Oregon's Cascades stretch across the horizon: Mount Bachelor, Tumalo Mountain, South Sister, Broken Top, Middle Sister, and North Sister.

Head back to the main trail, and take a moment to appreciate the few precious wildflowers that somehow have made their home in this desolate terrain. While there isn't much life on the rocky black basalt, all sorts of desert varmints hang out in the parking lot and at the top of the butte. Kids

This paved pathway heads directly into the lava on the Trail of Molten Land.

will definitely ask if they can feed the chipmunks, squirrels, weasels, and pikas that scurry around up here. They're cute little fellas, but for everyone's sake, please don't give them any snacks.

Loop back to connect with the first junction at 0.9 mile, and turn right toward the parking lot to finish the hike at 1.3 mile.

EXTENDING YOUR TRIP

There's plenty more to do at Lava Butte! At the kiosk on the way in, get a free permit for the winding drive to the top of the butte. Do this side trip before or after the Trail of Molten Land, depending on how long you have to wait for your assigned drive time. If it's too long, you can always hike to the top along the road, although it's a bit monotonous and not particularly safe due to car traffic. Either way, from the top of the butte, walk up the stairs to the fire lookout for sweeping views of the lava flow, Cascades, and surrounding areas. The casual 0.25-mile stroll around

the 150-foot-deep crater is another worthwhile activity. Get up close and personal with the gaping hole that formed when the butte erupted and the ponderosas that now grow within it.

14 Dillon and Benham Falls

RATING/ DIFFICULTY	ONE-WAY	ELEV GAIN/ HIGH POINT	SEASON
****/3	8 miles	400 feet/ 4150 feet	Year-round

Map: USFS Deschutes National Forest; **Contact:** Deschutes National Forest, Bend–Fort Rock Ranger District; **Notes:** NW Forest Pass or $5 day-use fee. Dogs must be leashed May 15–Sept 15. Privy at trailhead; **GPS:** N 44 0.03, W 121 13.48

🏠 *As this trail's namesake river winds through Bend, there are many places to step onto the Deschutes River Trail for a*

Big boulders along the path as it rises above the Deschutes River

refreshing fill of natural beauty. This stretch visits several waterfalls and culturally significant spots. While they are certainly beautiful, some of the falls are underwhelming. Rather than hiking back through the same territory on the way home, your time is better spent exploring the entire trail. Visit all the major sights with a one-way excursion by leaving another car at the Benham Falls west trailhead to shuttle you back.

If shuttling a car is too much bother, or if you're looking for a shorter hike, there are plenty of options. There are many entry points to this 8-mile trail segment, so you can pick your own adventure to a certain extent. Hike the trail in reverse, drive to each highlight by following signed turnouts off Conklin Road, or just wander without overthinking it. No matter how you spend it, a day on the Deschutes is sure to give your spirit a boost.

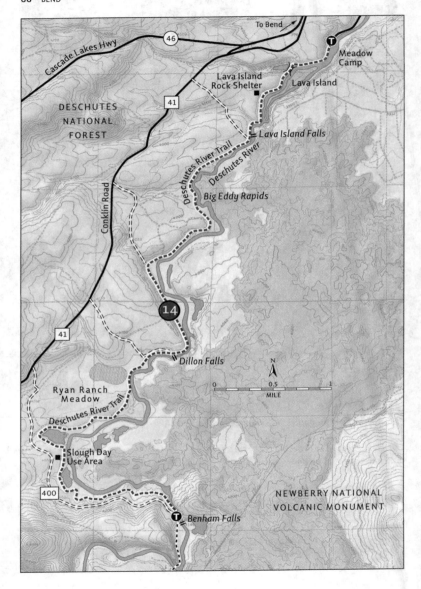

Cascade Lakes Hwy

To Bend

46

T Meadow Camp

Lava Island Rock Shelter

Lava Island

41

DESCHUTES NATIONAL FOREST

Lava Island Falls

Deschutes River Trail

Deschutes River

Big Eddy Rapids

Conklin Road

14

41

Dillon Falls

N

0   0.5   1
MILE

Ryan Ranch Meadow

Deschutes River Trail

Slough Day Use Area

400

T Benham Falls

NEWBERRY NATIONAL VOLCANIC MONUMENT

GETTING THERE

From Bend, take Cascade Lakes Highway/ State Route 46 for 6 miles west and turn left before Widgi Creek Resort, following signs for Meadow Camp (day use only). Drive 1.3 miles, passing through the Meadow Camp picnic area to where the road ends.

To drop a car off at the Benham Falls west trailhead, stay on Cascade Lakes Highway/ SR 46 another 1.5 miles past the Meadow Camp turnoff, and turn left onto Dillon Falls Road/Conklin Road/Forest Road 41 for Deschutes River Recreation Sites. Continue for 4 miles, and then turn left on FR 400 for 2.2 miles to the trailhead.

ON THE TRAIL

From the road's end at Meadow Camp, head upstream along the Deschutes River. While the water itself is wild, the surroundings are peaceful. Big ponderosas border the trail, and the path is soft and comfortable. The trail begins by rising gently from the parking area, traversing through the forest above the river before descending back down to a meadowy area. At 0.6 mile, you'll reach a junction. Going right takes you toward the nearby Seventh Mountain Resort, so instead turn left to keep on the Deschutes River Trail (DRT). You'll cross over a small body of water on an elevated land bridge, reaching the opposite side in 100 feet or so. Stay left here to continue on the DRT.

At this point, you're entering the Lava Island Falls reach. The falls themselves aren't all that unusual, but the surrounding area is. As the name implies, the lava flow split the water into two small passages separated by a now tree-covered island. When the water is frozen, animals often wander over to the island.

Nearby, at the 1.25-mile mark, you'll arrive at the Lava Island Rock Shelter. This intriguing cave outcropping has a long history of human habitation, which you can read about on an informational sign at the site. As you continue, you'll quickly pass the Lava Island trailhead and picnic area before passing Big Eddy Rapids at 2.5 miles. This is where most of the guided rafting trips begin. At this point, the river trail becomes slightly rougher but still very manageable for another 2.25 miles to Dillon Falls.

The winding trail and bending river make it a little tricky to get a good view of the falls. Without a railed platform, you'll have to scramble partway down a rocky outcropping to really get a decent picture of the waterfall, and even then it's lacking a bit. Still, the 15-foot waterfall is gorgeous as it tumbles into the rocky gorge.

Follow the trail along the day-use area road, cross the boat launch, and find the trail on the other side. Over the next stretch you'll cross through a meadow and colorful aspen grove and skirt a pond to the Slough Day Use Area at about 6.5 miles. In another 1.5 miles, you'll reach the largest waterfall in this stretch—Benham Falls.

Dense ponderosas line the banks around the rocky canyon just above and below the narrow gorge where the river rips through. While the actual drop is probably only 25 feet or so, the entire series of rapids runs closer to an impressive 100 feet. The striking gorge has just as much to do with this attraction's charm as the falls do, if not more so. A protected overlook gives you somewhere safe to perch and admire the whole scene. It's a picturesque spot, for sure. Find your self-shuttled car at the parking lot just 50 yards up the trail.

15 Shevlin Park

RATING/ DIFFICULTY	LOOP	ELEV GAIN/ HIGH POINT	SEASON
***/3	4.7 miles	680 feet/ 3860 feet	Year-round

Maps: USGS Shevlin Park, Bend Urban Trails; **Contact:** City of Bend Parks and Recreation; **Notes:** Dogs permitted on-leash. Water and restrooms at trailhead; **GPS:** N 44 4.97, W 121 22.67

Venture out to Shevlin Park for one of the best wilderness experiences that an urban park can offer. There are two main trails at this park. The first sticks mainly to the top of the canyon, heading down to the river only to climb up the other side and loop back around. The other parallels the river along the bottom of the canyon. As a nice introduction to the park, this route combines these two favorites—the Shevlin Loop Trail and the Tumalo Creek Trail—for a best-of-both worlds experience. These trails also connect to nearby mountain-biking loops, so you'll share the path with cyclists. There are plenty of trails to explore around here, and all have something different to offer. Pick up a trail map at the parking lot kiosk. That way, if you change course midway through, there's nothing to worry about. Whichever trail you take, you really can't go wrong at Shevlin.

GETTING THERE
From Bend, take Greenwood Avenue west. As you cross the river, the road becomes Newport Avenue and then Shevlin Park Road. Continue straight for 3.5 miles until you reach the park.

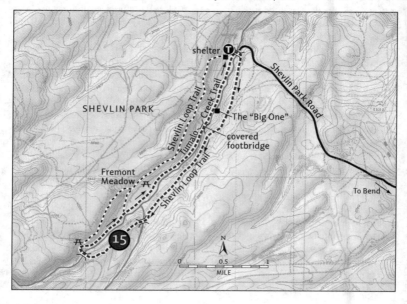

ON THE TRAIL

Walk toward the larch trees and follow signs for the Shevlin Loop Trail. At 0.25 mile, turn left before the shelter and follow the trail over the bridge. The gravelly path turns up a few switchbacks as it rises from the creek onto a plateau overlooking the creek and park. As you walk along a service road, the ponderosas are sparse. The wide openness of it all makes the sky look incredibly large.

Ignore the Tumalo Creek Trail sign at 0.8 mile and continue straight. Then, at 1.8 miles, turn right to leave the service road and head down toward the river. Two more quick rights and you'll cross a small footbridge and then go left to a sandy shoreline along the little creek. This makes for a great little spot to let your dogs get water. As you continue on, still following the Shevlin Loop Trail, you can hear the creek churning just down the trail. Walk over a little bridge to a small picnic area—a good halfway spot to eat a snack.

Soon you'll reach a strange intersection with a map, a lot of signs, and way too many options. You're connecting to a different trail here, so ignore the Shevlin Loop Trail going straight and instead head right to take the Tumalo Creek Trail. This gives you a chance to hike through the shady forests along the rumbling creek.

At 2.9 miles, you'll arrive at the popular Fremont Meadow picnic area. It can definitely be crowded during summer afternoons, but the amenities make it convenient for families. Continue straight along the interpretive trail, crossing a series of rudimentary footbridges over creeklets.

The path splits at 4.3 miles. Keep left to cross over a covered footbridge. You'll pass the "Big One," a 165-foot ponderosa pine, as you continue on. Near 4.6 miles, leave the

A happy hound gets a drink from Tumalo Creek.

path and turn left into the parking lot, arriving on the opposite side than you started from. If you go through an underpass and run into the small fishing pond, you've gone a bit too far and missed your turn.

EXTENDING YOUR TRIP

Skip the sometimes crowded second part of the loop by sticking to the canyon rim. Instead of taking the Tumalo Creek Trail, continue straight on the Shevlin Loop Trail. This will take you up the other side of the canyon before dropping back down to the park road near the parking area. This loop is 1 mile longer than the combined route described here.

16 Upper Tumalo Falls

RATING/ DIFFICULTY	ROUNDTRIP	ELEV GAIN/ HIGH POINT	SEASON
****/3	4 miles	700 feet/ 5560 feet	May– early Nov

Maps: USGS Tumalo Falls, Bend Adventure Map; **Contact:** Deschutes National Forest, Bend–Fort Rock Ranger District; **Notes:** NW Forest Pass or $5 day-use fee. Access road closed in winter. Dogs permitted on-leash. Privy at trailhead; **GPS:** N 44 1.91, W 121 33.98

One of the most popular and most accessible outdoor attractions in Bend, a trip to Tumalo Falls is almost always a crowded affair. If you're looking for a little more solitude near this busy hot spot, hike upstream to get away from the masses. The hustle and bustle of the tourist attraction fades away as you travel mostly alongside the creek just above Tumalo Falls. The shaded riverside path leads to several smaller, but just as gorgeous, waterfalls.

GETTING THERE

From US Highway 97 in Bend, take exit 139 and follow Reed Market Road west toward the Old Mill District. Stay straight for 3 miles, during which the road changes to Mount Washington Drive. At the Skyliners Road roundabout, take the third exit to turn left and continue for 8.8 miles. Turn onto gravel Tumalo Falls Road/Forest Road 4603 for another 2.5 miles to the trailhead.

ON THE TRAIL

From the main Tumalo Falls parking lot, head up the path to the falls. Visit them if you wish (see Appendix I), or just keep going past the hordes to the real fun. Manzanita and snowbrush line the dirt path as it heads upstream and into the woods. Before you get too far along, take a peek down the river and appreciate how the water just disappears, tumbling out of sight to create Tumalo Falls.

Continue on the soft and shaded trail, attributes that make this a comfortable hike even during hot spells. One of the great things about this trail is that it's equally beautiful in all types of weather. As the typical summer hiking season dies down, the foliage along the river morphs into glorious shades of crimson red, burnt orange, and canary yellow. Even when winter cold freezes the falls and covers the area in snow, you can snowshoe along this popular route. Note that the road does close with snowfall, so you'll have to trek in on foot.

At 1 mile, you'll reach the first little waterfall. Continue on after a quick look, as there's a bigger waterfall just a bit farther along at 1.1 miles. You're taking in an aerial view along a high ridge, so watch your step and don't get too close to the edge. Speaking of being careful right here, you also need to pay attention in general on this trail. While significantly less chaotic than the main attraction at Tumalo Falls, this is still a busy multiuse path. Mountain bikers are only allowed in the uphill direction, so you may not know they're coming until they're right behind you. Be ready to step off the path as they make their way uphill.

If you've brought dogs along with you, choose swimming spots carefully to make sure they don't get swept over any waterfalls. A good safe area is located near 1.3 miles. While you shouldn't allow pups to swim out too far, it'd be rude to deny them a nice sip and dip in the chilly runoff. Shortly afterward,

Find another stunning waterfall just upstream from Tumalo Falls.

at 2 miles, you'll reach the final upper falls along this route, a big cascading rumble in the otherwise calm forest. Take a moment to admire the beauty while sitting on one of the smooth barkless trees that lie like benches in direct view of the waterfall. When you're ready, turn back the way you came.

EXTENDING YOUR TRIP

There's no reason to turn around quite yet if you're not ready. Head upstream for more tranquility, a few elusive huckleberry bushes, and more little waterfalls. If you're up for it, keep on another 2 miles to Happy Valley—a lovely meadow and excellent picnic spot.

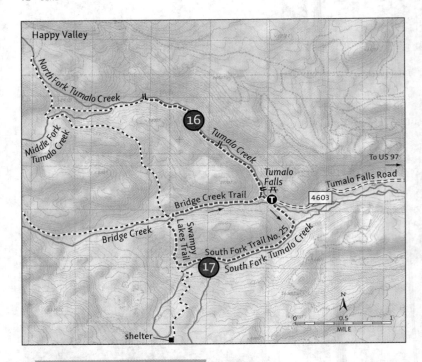

Happy Valley

North Fork Tumalo Creek

Middle Fork Tumalo Creek

16

Tumalo Creek

To US 97

Tumalo Falls

Tumalo Falls Road

T 4603

Bridge Creek Trail

Swampy Lakes Trail

Bridge Creek

South Fork Trail No. 25

South Fork Tumalo Creek

17

N

0   0.5   1
MILE

shelter

17 South Fork Tumalo and Bridge Creeks

RATING/ DIFFICULTY	LOOP	ELEV GAIN/ HIGH POINT	SEASON
***/3	3.7 miles	500 feet/ 5450 feet	June–Oct

Maps: USFS Tumalo Falls, Bend Adventure Map; **Contact:** Deschutes National Forest, Bend–Fort Rock Ranger District; **Notes:** NW Forest Pass or $5 day-use fee. Free permit in Bend Watershed Area. Access road closed in winter. Dogs not allowed. Privy at Tumalo Falls trailhead; **GPS:** N 44 1.91, W 121 33.98

⭐ *This may be the least hiked loop near Tumalo Falls. Because it starts off along a primary thoroughfare for mountain bikers, some hikers avoid this chunk of trail. Or maybe pedestrians are deterred because once you leave the South Fork Trail, you enter a segment where dogs aren't allowed. Once you connect to the Bridge Creek Trail, you'll enter the Bend Municipal Watershed Area where both animals and mountain bikes are prohibited. So if you never hike without your trusty pup, skip this loop. If, however, you want to hike without the distractions of bikes and four-legged friends, this gentle loop and less-traveled trail will make you happy. This feel-good trail is also a great reminder of what restoration efforts can do. The vegetation here was destroyed by fire, but conservation volunteers helped rejuvenate the area.*

GETTING THERE

From US Highway 97 in Bend, take exit 139 and follow Reed Market Road west toward the Old Mill District. Stay straight for 3 miles, during which the road changes to Mount Washington Drive. At the Skyliners Road roundabout, take the third exit to turn left and continue for 8.8 miles. Turn onto gravel Tumalo Falls Road/Forest Road 4603 for another 2.5 miles to the trailhead.

ON THE TRAIL

From the Tumalo Falls trailhead, walk back down the main road 0.1 mile and find South Fork Trail No. 25 on the downstream side of the bridge over Tumalo Creek. Leave the busy trailhead in the dust and descend to the creek for a scenic stroll along the stream. As a reminder, this portion of the trail is quite popular with mountain bikers who are connecting to other trails in the area. We're all just out here to enjoy the wilderness, so let's get along. Be on your best trail behavior and obey right-of-way rules to avoid conflicts.

The trail rises gradually and follows the creek most of the way. At 1.8 miles, you'll reach a junction with the Swampy Lakes Trail. Bikes must turn left here, but you'll turn right to hike toward Bridge Creek. In about 0.4 mile, you'll enter the watershed area. You'll need to fill out a watershed boundary permit at the kiosk. Make sure to note the special rules that apply to this area, which help protect Bend's water supply.

Bountiful manzanita bushes grace the sides of the Bridge Creek Trail.

In another 0.2 mile, you'll reach a junction with the Bridge Creek Trail. Turn right. Over the next mile, you'll pass two pretty waterfalls along Bridge Creek as you gradually descend through fir and spruce forests. Shortly after passing through the 1979 Bridge Creek Burn area, you'll reach the main Tumalo Falls Trail. Turn right for your final descent to the parking area.

EXTENDING YOUR TRIP

Instead of turning onto the Bridge Creek Trail, go left onto the Swampy Lakes Trail. You can follow this path for about 1 mile as it switchbacks through forest to the Swampy Lake Shelter. Head back to the junction and continue the loop, having added 2 miles to the trip total.

18 SW Canal Trails

RATING/ DIFFICULTY	LOOP	ELEV GAIN/ HIGH POINT	SEASON
***/2	3.3 miles	150 feet/ 3870 feet	Year-round

Map: Bend Urban Trails; **Contact:** City of Bend Parks and Recreation; **Notes:** Dogs permitted on-leash; **GPS:** N 44 0.56, W 121 21.10

If you're looking for an urban hike with fewer crowds than Shevlin Park and more variety than Pilot Butte, check out this lesser-known area. Nestled within the triangle-shaped chunk of land between the Deschutes River, the Brookswood Boulevard thoroughfare, and a residential area on the southwest side of Bend, the SW Canal Trails make an easy loop on their own, or you can use these paths as a gateway to other trails.

I'm more familiar with this area of Bend's urban trail system than any other. The first year I lived in Bend, I learned the city's layout by exploring on foot. One day on a run, I stumbled upon this trail. Its beauty floored me. This stretch of the Deschutes is a tumbling rush of white water. The high canyon walls and fragrant ponderosas are completely stunning, especially for something just feet away from a residential area. It's pathways like this that add to the quality of life here in Bend. I hope you find this route as refreshing as I did the first time I came upon it.

GETTING THERE

From downtown Bend, take Bond Street south for 1.7 miles to the Old Mill District. Continue for 2.5 miles on Brookswood Boulevard, passing through three roundabout intersections before turning right onto Sweetbriar Way. Take a left onto Snowbrush Drive and then a quick right on Pine Drive at River Canyon Park.

ON THE TRAIL

Park along the street adjacent to River Canyon Park. You're welcome to walk the park's short (seriously . . . it's about 0.1 mile) paved path, but you can definitely skip it. The views are better where you're headed anyway, so instead find the beginning of the trail on the right, at the end of Pine Drive. Skirt the gate and begin a quick descent, switchbacking once on your way into the canyon. At 0.1 mile, the access road splits. Instead of continuing straight toward the Central Oregon Irrigation District (COID) station, keep right on the trail as it heads toward the river.

Follow the gravel path over a small bridge that crosses the canal, which tumbles through the station and into a maroon pipeline that lines the canyon stretch of the trail. The COID tracks water patterns here in order to better manage the flow for the

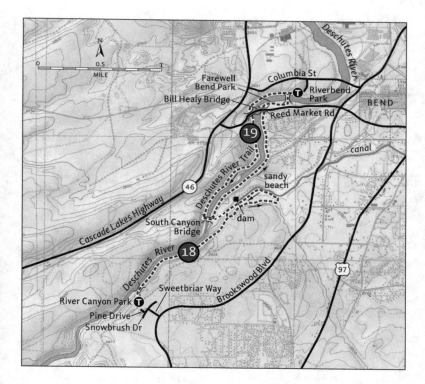

city's irrigation needs. This hike is on an access road, and it's not actually public land. Thanks to a joint-use agreement with COID, there's now public access to the canal ditch roads. COID vehicles do still need to access these trails each day, and you're a guest here. Make sure to step off to the side and give them a wave as they pass. Remember, we're lucky to have access to these trails!

The trail hugs the riverbank and parallels the rusty pipeline as it travels downstream for 1 mile. From here, the gravel road starts up a slight hill before splitting at 1.2 miles.

Instead of taking the main access road toward the left, turn right to head up the hill and away from the fenced canal. Look for an unofficial but clearly defined user path between the trees.

This part of the loop gives you a chance to get off the main trail. You'll climb a bit before looping around and curving left, meeting a junction with another user trail at 1.3 miles. Leave the current trail and jump onto this new one by heading left, taking the wide, flat, dusty path through pine forests and manzanita. At 1.4 miles, you'll continue straight for another 0.2 mile above a low

These irrigation canals are a hidden gem in Bend.

plateau. The little mounds and logs that look too perfectly placed to be natural are small human-made mountain-biking obstacles, although you probably won't see anyone using them.

As you continue on, you'll begin hiking alongside a set of powerlines. When you reach the point where houses sit at the top of a long slope to your right, you're almost to your next turn. When the trail T's with the canal at 1.6 miles, make a sharp left to get closer to the water and begin hiking upstream. If you have a pup with you, there's a great sandy spot here for her to get water and go for a quick swim.

In a quick 0.2 mile, the water gets very swift as it flows through a dam. Keep fol-

lowing the trail upstream, keeping generally parallel to the fence along the canal ditch. Despite the fence, this is a fun stretch of trail; you'll pass some interesting rock formations as you wind along the canal. You'll also pass a big ditch on your left, but there's nothing worth exploring down there. You'll come back to the junction with the main access road at 2 miles. Take the access road left to head back.

EXTENDING YOUR TRIP

From the access road, find the trail on the left just below you at approximately 1.1 miles. This trail provides a steep connection to the Deschutes River Trail (Hike 19). Explore to your heart's content.

19 Deschutes River Trail to South Canyon Bridge

RATING/ DIFFICULTY	LOOP	ELEV GAIN/ HIGH POINT	SEASON
***/3	3.6 miles	650 feet/ 3960 feet	Year-round

Map: Bend Urban Trails; **Contact:** City of Bend Parks and Recreation; **Notes:** Dogs permitted on-leash. Water and restrooms at Riverbend Park; **GPS:** N 44 2.55, W 121 19.24

You'll find this section of the Deschutes River Trail near the three iconic smokestacks that mark the Old Mill District in the heart of Bend. Like most of the Pacific Northwest, Bend's early livelihood was a thriving timber industry. Still the city's main landmark, Old Mill always has something going on. If I could, I'd be on this trail every day, and I'm not the only one! This loop is part of many locals' daily routine, attracting walkers, dogs, and runners. It's popular, but if you don't mind a little company, it's one of the best urban interpretive trails out there. This trail travels along both sides of the Deschutes River, connecting by way of the South Canyon Bridge at the turnaround point.

GETTING THERE
From US Highway 97 in Bend, take exit 139 and follow Reed Market Road to the Old Mill District. At the roundabout, take the first exit, turning right onto SW Bond Street. In 0.1 mile, turn left onto Columbia Street. Drive another 0.3 mile. At the four-way stop, turn left at SW Shevlin Hixon Drive into the parking area by the kayak structure.

ON THE TRAIL
From Riverbend Park, head upriver on the paved Deschutes River Trail (DRT). At 0.25

Rustic carved wooden trail pointers on the Deschutes River Trail

mile, where the pavement ends, you'll reach a junction at a footbridge. A barrier-free trail continues over the footbridge, where you can stroll back downriver toward Old Mill. For this hiking loop, however, go straight, following signs for the South Canyon Bridge onto a dirt trail. Continue along the river, keeping left to go under the Bill Healy Bridge and then up through the gates to the more "hike-like" section.

As you traverse along the riparian zone, look for signage about the local history, plants, and wildlife. Since most trail users are locals out for daily exercise, you'll likely have zero competition at the signposts. But the interpretive information is worthwhile reading and will give you a little background about the area.

Mind your trail manners and stay on designated paths. Several of the slopes on the right side of the trail are private property. Also, this popular trail is narrow in spots, so you'll likely have to step off to the side on occasion to let runners and other speedsters by. Listen up for friendly "On your left!" announcements so you aren't caught off guard.

At 1.25 miles, you'll climb above the river on a high ridge before heading back down to the water. Keep left at the signed junction, again following signs for the South Canyon Bridge. Keep on along the trail upriver until you reach the wooden South Canyon Bridge at 1.75 miles. Look up the canyon. At peak flow, the waters here are class IV rapids. Cross the footbridge and continue downriver on the other side. You'll cross through another gate within 0.1 mile.

Work your way downriver, weaving through trees and over rocky areas. After a short but steep descent, the trail returns to the river. Turn left at a signed junction to follow the DRT toward Farewell Bend Park,

walking over a boardwalk next to a small and discreet hydropower plant. Hit pavement at 3 miles and go underneath the Bill Healy Bridge again, this time on the opposite side of the water. Stay on the path nearest the river, and then turn left to cross over the footbridge next to the iron horse statue at 3.3 miles. Turn right on the paved path on the other side, and head back to the parking lot at Riverbend Park.

20 Pilot Butte

RATING/ DIFFICULTY	ROUNDTRIP	ELEV GAIN/ HIGH POINT	SEASON
****/3	2 miles	460 feet/ 4147 feet	Year-round

Map: Bend Urban Trails; **Contact:** Pilot Butte State Park and City of Bend Parks and Recreation; **Notes:** Dogs permitted on-leash. Privy and water at trailhead; **GPS:** N 44 3.46, W 121 16.74

Pilot Butte is one of the most identifiable geographical landmarks within Bend's city limits, and it's certainly a great stop. The cinder cone on the northeast side of town has two different spiraling paths up the hill—one for cars, and one for hikers—providing convenient urban excursions for all ability levels. From the butte's lofty vantage point, you'll have 360-degree views of the city and the Cascades that sit beyond it. The route described here is a solid 2-mile roundtrip on the nature trail, but if you're short on time, you can also drive to the top on the paved road (open April through October) to see the all-around views. Either way, please stick to defined trails. Overuse and a general disregard for trail signs has led to rogue paths and erosion.

GETTING THERE

In Bend, take Greenwood Avenue/US Highway 20 east of 3rd Street/US Highway 97 Business Route. In 0.7 mile, you'll see the first Pilot Butte signs, which indicate a left-hand turn for the paved road up the butte. For the hiking trailhead, continue 0.6 mile to the second set of Pilot Butte signs, turning left onto NE Arnett Way for 100 feet or so and then left on NE Linnea Drive. Drive 0.25 mile to the parking lot at the end of the road.

ON THE TRAIL

From the trailhead sign by the set of pull-up bars, take the paved trail toward the butte. In just a few yards, the paved path goes left to connect to the car route. While you *can* walk up that way, the Nature Trail is much better, as you'll be completely free from traffic worries. Therefore, continue straight on the unsurfaced Nature Trail.

The trail, either sandy or muddy depending on the weather, corkscrews around Pilot Butte to the summit. The 460-foot climb is steep in sections but mostly gradual. If you're huffing and puffing, you'll find nice resting benches every tenth of a mile or so, conveniently placed in prime scenic spots. Curious about the numbered posts along the way? They correspond to an interpretive plant trail. There are rarely brochures at the trailhead, but you can download one ahead of time from the Oregon State Parks website.

Most people don't know the interpretive trail exists, using the numbered posts instead as indicators of where they are on the hike. As you wind around the butte, it's a strange feeling. You almost feel like you're not making any progress, because the route is just a continual, slight left-hand turn—a similar feeling, perhaps, to being the slowest race-car driver in history. The view constantly

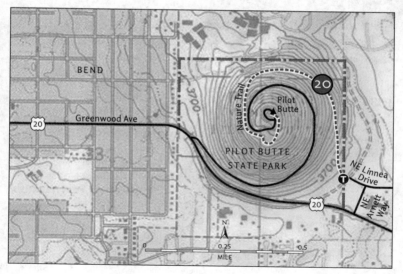

Sweeping views of Bend and the surrounding mountains from Pilot Butte

changes, which keeps things interesting, but it's still hard to know how much hike you have left. There are eighteen posts, so that should give you a general mid-hike gauge. From almost any point on the trail, you'll be able to see the entire city laid out before you, with a string of Cascades shining behind it.

The view is even better once you reach the top, at 0.9 mile. Walk to the center of the summit and up the steps to a large circular platform. Find the brassy compass in the middle that identifies the mountains and peaks in each direction. On perfectly clear days, you can see just about everything, from local buttes all the way to distant Mount Adams. You'll also find signs outlining the history, geography, and culture of Central Oregon.

The best way down is the same way you came up. Stop at the pull-up bars and crank out a few military-style exercises to round out your workout, if you wish.

Opposite: A Cascade Mountains showcase from the top of South Sister

upper cascade
lakes highway

Just outside of Bend, the scenic Cascade Lakes Highway/State Route 46 traverses the most photogenic region in all of Central Oregon. This area is decorated with sparkling blue alpine lakes in the shadow of high Cascade peaks, and there's little room for improvement. The Three Sisters Wilderness and its miles and miles of trails are only steps from the road. The incredible access is also this gorgeous area's only downside. Because snowfall blocks the highway in the winter, the major trailheads are packed nearly every day during the summer.

Still, there's a lot of terrain up here, so there's plenty of solitude to go around. Also, several trails take off from each trailhead, so a crowded parking lot isn't necessarily a guarantee that the hike itself will be busy. If you're concerned about crowds, time your hikes during off-peak days and hours. Alternatively, accept that you'll be sharing the trail with plenty of other adventure-seekers. You'll be in good company.

A new welcome station devoted to this scenic road and its recreation opportunities is located on Cascade Lakes Highway, just inside the Deschutes National Forest boundary a few miles west of Bend.

21 Tumalo Mountain

RATING/ DIFFICULTY	ROUNDTRIP	ELEV GAIN/ HIGH POINT	SEASON
****/4	3.5 miles	1400 feet/ 7775 feet	June– early Nov

Map: Green Trails No. 622 Broken Top; **Contact:** Deschutes National Forest, Bend–Fort Rock Ranger District; **Notes:** NW Forest Pass or $5 day-use fee. Privy at trailhead; **GPS:** N 44 0.11, W 121 39.94

🔘 🔶 🏠 *If a short workout with amazing views is what you're looking for, this is definitely the place! You'll have to work for the calendar-worthy vistas, but not too much. Well, not for too long. The route is a quick but steep 1.75 miles to the top, where you'll have unobstructed views of the Three Sisters, Broken Top, Mount Bachelor, and the lower deserts. You'll gain over 1000 feet on the ascent and there's very little shade, so get ready to sweat. Make sure to bring water—you won't find any on the trail.*

GETTING THERE

From Bend, take Cascade Lakes Highway/State Route 46 west for 21 miles. About 0.25 mile past Mount Bachelor's Sunrise Lodge, turn right into the Dutchman Flat Sno-Park and proceed to the parking lot.

ON THE TRAIL

Find the trail at the far end of the Dutchman Flat Sno-Park, on the right side. You'll immediately cross a snowmobile trail before heading up the slope into the trees. The way is forested for now, but you'll quickly leave the shelter of hemlock and fir and begin traversing the cinder cone's exposed hillside. Fortunately, this open space allows for summer wildflowers to bloom. Look for purple dwarf lupine adding pops of bright color to the scene.

Because this route is devoid of junctions, off-trail points of interest, or really anything else to distract you from your goal, it's pretty hard to get lost. The path is even lined with red cinder rock in many stretches, to keep you in your place. So, just put your nose to the grindstone and forge upward on the well-maintained trail to the summit of Tumalo Mountain.

Cascade views abound at the top of Tumalo Mountain.

Do be sure to take your eyes off the ground every now and then to look around. The best views are at the top, but you'll still get sneak peeks. About 1 mile in, these opportunities start increasing as you put more distance between yourself and the treeline. While

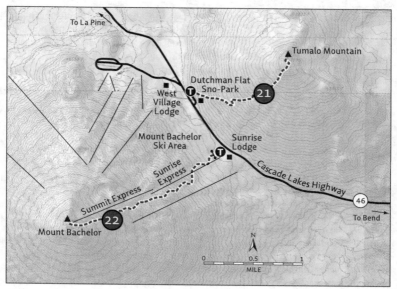

excellent in the summer, the views of the white peaks in the winter make this trail a favorite for snowshoeing as well.

In terms of treescape, you'll mostly find just a few resilient whitebark pine as you get closer to the top. Traversing the reddish cinder hillside on a series of switchbacks, you'll reach the summit near 1.6 miles. Continue across the plateau another 0.1 mile to explore. With views in every direction, it's easy to understand why this was a good place for a lookout tower long ago. It's gone now, but you can still do a bit of "looking out" of your own. Bring a pair of binoculars and take in the whole scene before retracing the same route down.

22 Mount Bachelor Summit

RATING/ DIFFICULTY	ROUNDTRIP	ELEV GAIN/ HIGH POINT	SEASON
***/5	6.2 miles	2765 feet/ 9065 feet	July– early Sept

Maps: USGS Mount Bachelor, Mount Bachelor Ski Trail Map; **Contact:** Deschutes National Forest, Bend–Fort Rock Ranger District, and Mount Bachelor Resort; **Notes:** No access during ski season. Restrooms and water at lodge; **GPS:** N 43 59.75, W 121 39.81

In many ways, I think hiking to the top of Mount Bachelor is sort of silly. It's a ski resort, for crying out loud. Hiking a treeless slope underneath a chairlift is hardly the plunge into nature that most people crave when they seek out a hiking adventure. The trail isn't even that great or well defined, and most people just pay to ride the Pine Marten Express Chairlift to the top. Meanwhile, you're slogging up a sweat for apparently no reason.

On the other hand, summiting Mount Bachelor makes sense. I totally get it. It's a 9065-foot mountain just begging to be climbed, and determined peak-baggers want to cross it off their list. They can't just ignore it because the hiking is slightly miserable. Hike this one if the feeling of satisfaction and achievement will make it worthwhile.

GETTING THERE
From Bend, take Cascade Lakes Highway/State Route 46 west for 21 miles. Turn left at Mount Bachelor's Sunrise Lodge. The gate will block you from entering the parking lot, so flip a U-turn at the turnout and park along the highway. Walk around the gate and head toward the Sunrise Express Chairlift at the base of the mountain.

ON THE TRAIL
All right, peak-baggers. You're at 6300 feet right now, heading for 9065 feet. It will be arduous, sweaty, and somewhat boring at times. But it will also be beautiful and quite satisfying. Let's do this.

Facing the mountain, find the Cat track on the right side of the Sunrise Express. After just about 100 yards, you'll run into a single-track trail heading up the hill. Go left on this path and follow it as it switchbacks up the mountain to the top of the chairlift. This is the "official" route up, but if snow blocks the trail, your best bet is to head toward the open chute on the Marshmallow ski run on the right.

Once you've reached the top of Sunrise Express, things get tricky. Instinct tells you to head toward the Summit Express Chairlift, but don't. Instead, find the green hiker sign at the top of Sunrise Express pointing toward the trail's next ascent. These signs get knocked down and/or stolen sometimes, so this one may be haphazardly propped up against a tree. Either way, the path is quite obvious once you know to look for it.

Though you'll feel like you're almost there, you still have about 1700 vertical feet to go. Note that the terrain above this point is unpatrolled, so make sure you're fit to go on. This is, without question, the toughest part of the climb. A switchback ascent will take you over jagged lava rock and across the wide-open space all the way to the top. Use caution when going across any remaining snowfields.

At the top of Summit Express, you are nearly there. It's just a short walk to the official summit on the right. From way up here you can see just about everything: the Three Sisters, Broken Top, Newberry Caldera, the expansive Deschutes River valley, Three Fingered Jack, Mount Jefferson, Mount Hood, Mount Adams, and a large array of Cascade lakes. Up close, make sure to check out the steep cirque bowl and the stately pinnacles guarding its upper rim.

You'll likely see other hikers here, several of which probably traversed over from the top of the Pine Marten Express. Wipe that smug look off your face—they don't care that you climbed the whole way up. Just enjoy the views and the burn in your legs before you head back down. (Riding the Pine Marten Express down is an option, but you have to buy a ticket at the West Village Lodge before your hike up.)

Make sure to come prepared. Unless you're planning on making a side hike to the upper lodge at the Pine Marten Express (which is only occasionally open anyway), bring enough water, food, sunscreen, and clothing for the hike. Also, leftover snowfields that mask the trail can cause hikers to make their own route to the top, in which case your own mileage may differ slightly. This is even more true if you decide to glissade down the snowfields on your return to the base. Have fun!

The Summit Express Chairlift marks the top of Mount Bachelor.

23 Todd Lake

RATING/ DIFFICULTY	LOOP	ELEV GAIN/ HIGH POINT	SEASON
***/2	1.7 miles	100 feet/ 6230 feet	June– late Oct

Maps: Green Trails No. 622 Broken Top, No. 621 Three Sisters; **Contact:** Deschutes National Forest, Bend–Fort Rock Ranger District; **Notes:** NW Forest Pass or $5 day-use fee. Free self-issue wilderness permit Memorial Day–October 31. Access road closed in winter. Dogs must be leashed July 15–Sept 15. Privy at trailhead; **GPS:** N 44 7.47, W 121 24.33

As you pass Mount Bachelor, Todd Lake is the first body of water on Cascade Lakes Highway. On any given summer day, outdoorsy folks pack up the kids, lunches, and all their nonmotorized lake toys for a full day of play at Todd Lake. It's certainly crowded here on nice days, and why shouldn't it be? An easy trail takes you around the scenic lakeshore and through fragile wild-flower meadows. This is a flat, easy-going, stress-free stroll, great for families and any-one who wants to experience the splendor of the Central Oregon wildflower display.

GETTING THERE
From Bend, take Cascade Lakes Highway/State Route 46 west for 23 miles to Todd Lake. Turn right on unpaved Forest Road 370 and drive 0.6 mile to the parking lot below the lake.

ON THE TRAIL
At forty-five acres, Todd Lake isn't the biggest of the Cascade Lakes, but it's stunning in its accessibility and simplicity. From the

Todd Lake is one of the most popular locations on the Cascade Lakes Highway.

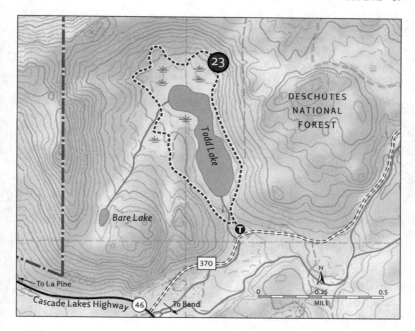

To La Pine

Cascade Lakes Highway (46)   To Bend

DESCHUTES
NATIONAL
FOREST

Todd Lake

Bare Lake

370

N

0   0.25   0.5
MILE

parking lot, take the popular beat-down dirt path up to the wilderness permit kiosk and trailhead. In a quick 0.2 mile, you'll reach the lake. The trail doesn't require any navigational skills, so you can take the 1.3-mile loop in either direction.

The forested trail takes you through picnic areas and around the lake, all while giving you views of the water and surrounding mountains. The lake sits at the base of Broken Top, so when you approach Todd's south end, you can see the mountain's jagged peak line breaking out above the trees. Alternatively, at the north end, you'll be able to see the tapered top of Mount Bachelor sloping down toward the lake.

A speckling of wildflowers adorns the lake's shore, but the real show is on the north end of the lake. There are so many varieties in this area that it's likely to be sparkling with color no matter when you visit. In early season, you can expect to see purple Jeffrey's shooting star and white marsh marigold. Midsummer brings knotweed, Indian paintbrush, elephant's head, various monkey flowers, mountain heather, Jacob's ladder, and white bog orchids. Butterflies flitting about make the scene even more magical. Flowers linger into autumn, although they are overshadowed by the changing colors of scattered alder and poplar trees.

The marshy conditions that make this subalpine meadow such a great place for wildflowers also make it quite soggy in early season. Until it dries out a bit, this area is commonly rife with mosquitoes and squishy for the feet. Either wear boots or accept that your shoes will get soggy. Or, just plan on washing the mud off with a quick dip in the calm lake waters, drying off in a sunny picnic spot before heading home.

24 Broken Top Saddle and "Hidden" Lake

RATING/ DIFFICULTY	ROUNDTRIP	ELEV GAIN/ HIGH POINT	SEASON
*****/4	7 miles	1400 feet/ 8300 feet	Aug–Oct

Maps: Green Trails No. 622 Broken Top, No. 621 Three Sisters; **Contact:** Deschutes National Forest, Bend–Fort Rock Ranger District; **Notes:** NW Forest Pass or $5 day-use fee. Free self-issue wilderness permit Memorial Day–Oct 31. Access road closed in winter. Dogs must be leashed July 15–Sept 15. Privy at trailhead; **GPS:** N 44 03.35, W 121 40.53

Sitting between Mount Bachelor and South Sister, Broken Top can be overlooked. Not quite "mountain-like" enough to stand out, its spiny form can just blend in with the Three Sisters. But Broken Top is all its own. The peak's unique history, colorful composition, jagged ridge, spectacular views, and hidden gems really shine on this hike. The trail winds through alpine terrain up to a spectacular lake, hidden in the shadow of Broken Top. Climbing to "Broken Saddle," the upper ridgeline on the right, also nets fantastic panoramic views of Central Oregon.

Once a secret, the "hidden" lake is now well known but is still unnamed. Parts of the trail are not maintained, which deters some of the crowds. There are few if any trail signs, but if you keep Broken Top in sight and follow

the well-defined user path, you should be good to go. This up-close and personal view of Broken Top is nearly too incredible for words. It will certainly give you a new appreciation for this oft-neglected wild peak.

GETTING THERE

From Bend, take Cascade Lakes Highway/ State Route 46 west for 23 miles to Todd Lake. Turn right on Forest Road 370 and drive 0.6 mile to the parking lot below the lake—but don't stop here. Continue on an extremely rough dirt road for 2.5 miles. Drive past FR 378 on your left and continue another 0.8 mile. Turn left on FR 380, signed for the Broken Top trailhead. In another 1.3 slow miles, you're there.

Note: Take it slow on this road. It's just under 5 miles, but it's rough, and the drive will likely take you more than half an hour. Two-wheel drive is probably fine, but a car with decent clearance is strongly recommended.

ON THE TRAIL

Start out on the "official" Broken Top Trail. This is one of the last trailheads to open in the summer, as its high elevation makes for later snowmelt. You'll likely encounter snow on the trail into late summer. The trail initially winds through forest before gradually gaining elevation as it climbs through desolate pumice fields, sparse patches of alpine grass, and weathered whitebark pines. At about 0.5 mile, you'll reach a large, and typically unmarked, fork near a sometimes-present creek runoff. Head to the right and continue straight uphill toward Broken Top's jagged ridge, which looms tall in the distance.

Beyond the junction, you'll reach Soda Creek as it runs down the slope. Channel

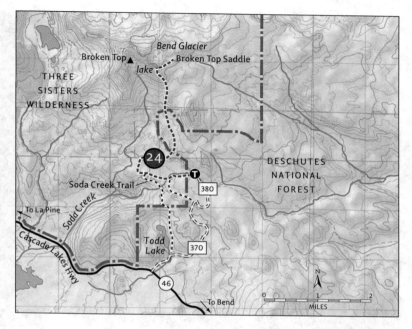

your Jack-be-nimble self, and tiptoe across rocks to the other side of the creek, where the path is a little more defined. Continue another 0.5 mile, as the trail leads through a calm meadow filled with shallow streams and a few tenacious wildflowers. Here you'll see the Soda Creek Trail coming in on the left. Stay right at this junction, and follow the trail another 1 mile through a snowfield to a ridge underneath a large moraine hill.

Take a minute to admire Broken Top's colorful face. See those deep red, yellow, and black stripes? Over time, layers of red cinder rock, yellow ash, and black lava slowly compiled, forming the peak into a smooth cone. That smooth surface was eventually busted up by violent volcanic eruptions and carved by glaciers, creating the incredibly

hostile, jagged, and beautiful landmark that remains today. With meadows and streams in the foreground and Broken Top in the background, this is a great spot to bust your camera and snap a few mantle-worthy photos.

Okay, you're nearly there. Look back toward the moraine hill and find the little notch in the slope where the creek flows from. As you crest the slope, feast your eyes on the milky green waters nestled in the shadow of the gnarly volcano—the hidden lake. A glacier holds fast to the rocky crags, and steep gravelly slopes lead all the way down to the shore. Because this gorgeous alpine lake is shadowed by Broken Top directly above it, large ice chunks float around on its surface, drifting with the breeze.

The gorgeous lake hidden just below Broken Top

From here, walk around the right side of the lake and take a quick stop at the very noticeable giant boulder sitting just a few feet in the water. If you're feeling spry, scramble to the top and have a buddy take your photo with Broken Top, the glacier, and the lake in the background.

The last ascent to Broken Top Saddle is well worth it. Follow the lakeshore path as it veers up a loose right-hand slope. With a little gentle scrambling, you'll reach the top of the pass and an unbeatable panorama of a whole string of Cascade volcanoes in just 0.7 mile. Traverse to the right along the red ridge and take in the ridiculously breath-taking view of South Sister, Middle Sister, North Sister, Mount Washington, Mount Jefferson, Mount Thielsen, and Mount Adams.

EXTENDING YOUR TRIP

If you want a few extra miles, or if you're wary of the bumpy forest road to the Broken Top trailhead, park at Todd Lake instead. Take the Todd Lake Trail for 2.5 miles (Hike 23), and then continue straight on the Soda Creek Trail for another 0.9 mile. Join up with the Broken Top Trail just past Soda Creek, turning left and following the remainder of the main hike's directions. Roundtrip, this route clocks in at around 14 miles.

25 Sparks Lake

RATING/ DIFFICULTY	LOOP	ELEV GAIN/ HIGH POINT	SEASON
★★★★/3	2.6 miles	160 feet/ 5495 feet	June–Oct

Maps: Green Trails No. 622 Broken Top, No. 621 Three Sisters; **Contact:** Deschutes National Forest, Bend–Fort Rock Ranger District; **Notes:** NW Forest Pass or $5 day-use fee; **GPS:** N 44 0.78, W 121 44.21

Ahh, Sparks Lake. A favorite of photographer Ray Atkeson, it's easily one of the most picturesque spots along Cascade Lakes Highway. It's also extremely accessible, which means you can snag amazing views without too much work. There are two intertwining loops in and around the lake area—the Hiking Trail and the barrier-free Ray Atkeson Memorial Trail. The route described here incorporates both loops, but you can easily do the barrier-free one on its own.

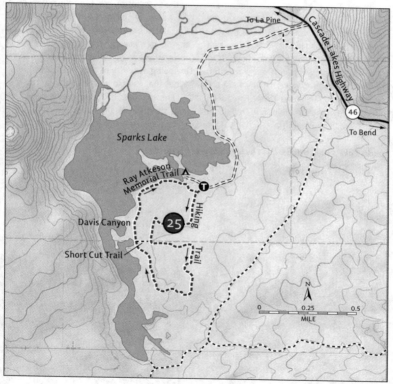

GETTING THERE

From Bend, take Cascade Lakes Highway/State Route 46 west for 23 miles. Turn left at Sparks Lake, just past Todd Lake at milepost 25. Stay left at the fork for 1.5 gravel miles.

ON THE TRAIL

Start on the Hiking Trail, heading left through weather-battered pine, hemlock, and cedar forests. The signage here is consistent, but there are so many intertwining trails that sometimes the pointers aren't quite clear. That said, start out on the correct track by following signs pointing toward the Hiking Trail. When you reach the sign pointing toward the Short Cut Trail, head east (left) to continue on the big loop via the Hiking Trail, traveling through more forested areas with peekaboo views. (If you want the barrier-free option, head right instead on the short Ray Atkeson Memorial Trail. It's a quick 0.6-mile roundtrip.)

The Hiking Trail loops back around, and you'll reach the Davis Canyon area, an interesting narrow lava slot canyon. Walk through the canyon, and then continue on the Hiking Trail on the opposite side. This is where you finally start to see a few views of the lake. As you continue on, the view only gets better. The Hiking Trail connects with the barrier-free trail at 2.25 miles.

This short paved trail is a memorial to Ray Atkeson, and it offers the best views of the whole hike. Mount Bachelor, Broken Top, and South Sister are the lake's backdrop. I like leaving this grand finale segment for last, but you can definitely do it first, or skip the longer Hiking Trail altogether. Along the path, read up on Sparks Lake's history, including evidence of the Great Basin Indian tribes that used to inhabit the area.

The sparkling lake, along with its rugged lava shoreline, really is breathtaking. Long ago, lava traveled over this area, making the

Sparks Lake's calm waters, lined by lava and green forests

lake much smaller and shallower than it used to be. A combination of volcanic and glacial activity formed what you see today. You'll likely see a few paddlers exploring the water.

Sparks Lake is largest in the spring, when snowmelt runoff is at its peak. It slowly dries up as summer fades away, shrinking to its smallest depth in late fall. Summer is a great time to visit, as there's still plenty of lake to admire, but the nearby lava fields and alpine meadows become more visible later on, creating a picture-perfect setting. Follow the barrier-free memorial trail back to the parking lot.

26 Green Lakes

RATING/ DIFFICULTY	ROUNDTRIP	ELEV GAIN/ HIGH POINT	SEASON
*****/4	9 miles	1000 feet/ 6500 feet	July–Oct

Map: Green Trails Three Sisters No. 621; **Contact:** Deschutes National Forest, Bend–Fort Rock Ranger District; **Notes:** NW Forest Pass or $5 day-use fee. Free self-issue wilderness permit Memorial Day–Oct 31. Access road closed in winter. Dogs must be leashed July 15–Sept 15. Privy at trailhead; **GPS:** N 44 01.77, W 121 44.13

Green Lakes is one of the most popular hikes in the Three Sisters Wilderness—and for good reason! This classic route has a mostly comfortable incline, easy-to-navigate trails, and ridiculously awesome scenery. There's such a wide variety of stunningly beautiful terrain that you'll never get bored. The majority of the hike follows Fall Creek, first through shaded forest and tumbling waterfalls, then alongside a lava flow canyon and through a colorful wildflower meadow. The grand finale reveals the chilly Green Lakes, sitting in an alpine basin at the base of South Sister and Broken Top. An afternoon spent hiking up to Green Lakes will no doubt satisfy every outdoor craving. This trail is my all-time favorite Central Oregon hike. Unfortunately, it tops other people's lists too. For more solitude, hike midweek or in the fall.

GETTING THERE

From Bend, take Cascade Lakes Highway/State Route 46 west for 26.5 miles. Turn right at the sign for the Green Lakes trailhead, into the parking loop.

ON THE TRAIL

Starting from the trailhead at the far end of the parking lot, head down the trail 200 yards or so, where the trail meets the creek. Swift but shallow, Fall Creek runs clear over multicolored rocks and pebbles, and the trail follows it almost the entire way up to the lakes. If you were to get lost, following this creek up or down (depending on where you're headed, of course) would be your best bet. Luckily, this popular trail is well signed, so there's very little chance of losing your way.

Cross the creek on the sturdy single-log footbridge, and follow the trail into a moderately dense forest. As you enjoy the shady reprieve from the hot summer sun, keep your eyes peeled for waterfalls on your right. You'll see plenty of them over the first few miles.

At about 1.6 miles, you'll reach a junction where the trail splits toward Moraine Lake (Hike 31). Keep right, taking Green Lakes Trail No. 17 along the river for another 0.5 mile. Cross the creek again, on a nearly identical log footbridge. From here, the trail winds around into a meadow, with views of South Sister and Broken Top looming in the

Snow lingers late into the summer at Green Lakes.

distance. In the summer, the meadow is dotted with red paintbrush, blue lupine, yellow composites, and pink monkey flower.

Head back into the trees for 1 mile or so of gentle switchbacks before dropping down into an incredibly unique oasis alongside Fall

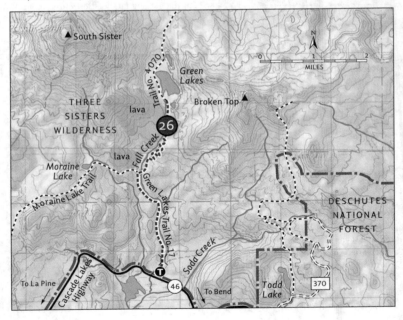

Creek. A grassy wildflower meadow sits in the foreground, but a massive lava flow flanks the far side of the creek, forming a one-sided canyon of sorts. Mostly gray, the sediment also gleams with pieces of glassy black obsidian. The desolate volcanic rock wall is a stark contrast to the lush meadow.

Continue along the crystal-clear creek on a mostly flat trail for the remainder of the hike. Head straight for the basin between South Sister and Broken Top, which you'll reach at about 4.4 miles. My go-to spot up here is the gravelly shoreline at the first lake just 0.1 mile off the trail on your right. It's often slightly quieter than the bigger lakes, and it has equally impressive views. From here, you'll have incredible views of Broken Top's jagged ridge on one side and South Sister on the other. When you're ready, head back down the way you came.

EXTENDING YOUR TRIP

Hike 1.8 miles over to Moraine Lake (Hike 31). Or, instead of stopping at the first little lake, head straight on Green Lakes Trail No. 4070 to see all three lakes over approximately 1.5 miles one-way.

27 Soda Creek and Lower Crater Creek Falls

RATING/ DIFFICULTY	ROUNDTRIP	ELEV GAIN/ HIGH POINT	SEASON
***/3	4.5 miles	400 feet/ 5960 feet	June– early Nov

Map: Green Trails Three Sisters No. 621; **Contact:** Deschutes National Forest, Bend–Fort Rock Ranger District; **Notes:** NW Forest Pass or $5 day-use fee. Free self-issue wilderness permit Memorial Day–Oct 31.

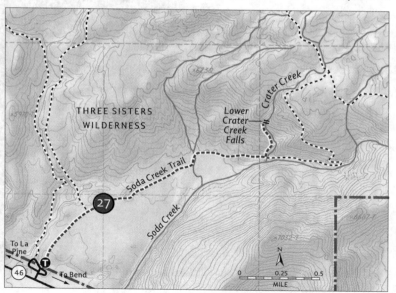

Access road closed in winter. Dogs must be leashed July 15–Sept 15. Privy at trailhead; **GPS:** N 44 01.77, W 121 44.13

Don't let the packed parking lot fool you—this is not a crowded hike! Most of those cars are here for the Green Lakes Trail that shares the same lot. While the trail to Green Lakes throws just about every amazing outdoor feature at you at once, this portion of the Soda Creek Trail has a more understated beauty. You won't find calendar-cover mountain views or brag-worthy elevation gain, but you will enjoy shaded forests and lush meadows before turning around at Lower Crater Creek Falls.

This relaxing, serene, and refreshingly simple hike is great for families.

GETTING THERE
From Bend, take Cascade Lakes Highway/State Route 46 west for 26.5 miles. Turn right at the sign for the Green Lakes trailhead. The Soda Creek trailhead is on the right side of the road as you drive into the parking area.

ON THE TRAIL
The hordes of people heading to gorgeous Green Lakes (Hike 26) go left, but you'll go right, crossing the road you came in on and finding the Soda Creek trailhead. Start off your leisurely stroll on the dusty Soda Creek

This lazy stream weaving through a green oasis is the perfect spot to relax.

Trail as it winds through a flat lodgepole pine forest and interesting lava rock piles.

You probably won't have the trail to yourself, but you won't be fighting for space either. Many hikers simply use this route as a connection to other trails in the area, often rushing up this trail without truly noticing the beauty before them. Instead, breathe deep and take it all in. This is the kind of hike that should leave you energized rather than exhausted.

At 1.4 miles, you'll reach a shallow serpentine stream lazily flowing through a lush green meadow. In early summer, this area is spattered with colorful wildflowers, including scarlet skyrocket and purple thistle. If all you're looking for is a place to relax in nature, this is an excellent spot to plop down.

Walk along the stream—a small tributary of Soda Creek—and then cross it just around the bend. Obey the posted signs by leaving the stream as it is. It's not deep, so you shouldn't need to, but please refrain from adding any rocks or logs. You'll cross another small tributary just beyond here. Take a moment to appreciate how the green patches next to the creek flourish in its path.

At this point, you'll start to gain a bit of elevation as the trail heads into the forest, about 200 feet over the next 0.5 mile. At 2 miles in, you'll bump into Crater Creek. Due to the swift flow and lack of footbridge, this creek is typically impassable. Turn around here, or do a bit of off-trail exploring to see Lower Crater Creek Falls.

Turn left to follow the west side of Crater Creek upstream for just under 0.25 mile. From here, you can see part of the 85-foot waterfall plunging through the basalt gulch. Enjoy this hidden gem before heading back to the main trail and retracing your route.

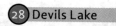

28 Devils Lake

RATING/ DIFFICULTY	ROUNDTRIP	ELEV GAIN/ HIGH POINT	SEASON
***/2	1.4 miles	50 feet/ 5555 feet	June–Oct

Map: Green Trails Three Sisters No. 621; **Contact:** Deschutes National Forest, Bend–Fort Rock Ranger District; **Notes:** NW Forest Pass or $5 day-use fee. Access road closed in winter. Privy at trailhead; **GPS:** N 44 2.07, W 121 45.92

Devils Lake is nothing like what you'd expect. Sure, there's a fair amount of lava, but it's way lusher, livelier, and lovelier than the name suggests. A gentle shoreline path weaves around the lake, offering spectacular views of this divine spot. A quick jaunt across the highway takes you to the scenic springs of Satan Creek, before you turn around and head back to the lake.

GETTING THERE
From Bend, take Cascade Lakes Highway/State Route 46 west for 29 miles. Turn left at milepost 28 for the Devils Lake trailhead, and follow the gravel road to the upper parking lot at the campground on the right.

ON THE TRAIL
The Devils Lake trailhead is a launching pad for several big-name hikes, so the serene lake sometimes gets left in the dust by hikers on their way to the high alpine country. But the lake stroll is short and oh so worth it, even if you just walk the beaten path long enough to catch a glimpse of the blue-green waters.

Find the "To Devils Lake" sign on the right side of the parking lot and follow the trail.

The enticingly bluish-green waters of Devils Lake

You'll shortly be on Devils Lake Trail No. 61, a gentle path that leads around the lake. The little treads that trickle off the main trail go to scenic camping spots, so leave them be if the spots look occupied.

As the trail skirts the lake's rim, you'll pass through, under, and around moss-covered trees. Moss everywhere, even cloaking the extensive blowdown on the slope to your right. The whole scene looks like it's been undisturbed for a long time, like you've stumbled into a remote secret spot rather than one of the most popular trailheads in Central Oregon.

Devils Lake is especially gorgeous in the early morning, when it sits still and silent in the brisk air. When the sun hits the water, it turns a stunning bluish-green color that makes it especially spectacular. The soft and shaded path is flat and easy, bringing you to the edge of Cascade Lakes Highway at 0.5 mile. From here, look both ways and skip across to the other side of the road.

Once across, walk to your right about 20 yards until you see the little side trail leading down toward the left. Follow this for less than 0.1 mile, down to where you'll see sparkling Satan Creek, springing out underneath Devils Garden, the tall gnarly mound of lava rock. If you look closely, you might even find a few faded pictographs on the black boulders.

These meadowy headwaters are exceptionally lush. However, Satan Creek's marshy haven is also a breeding ground for mosquitoes in early summer, so it's not the best place to park yourself for a break. Instead, retrace your steps back to the lake.

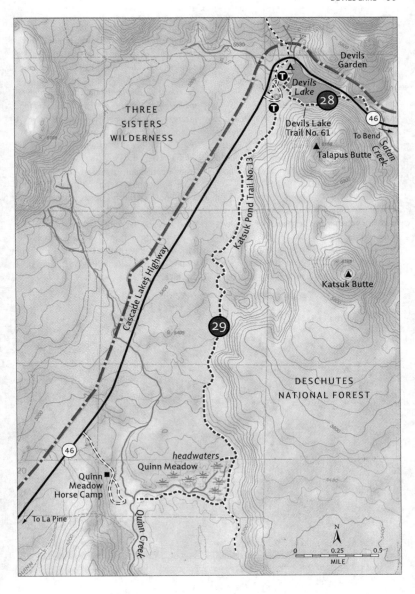

THREE
SISTERS
WILDERNESS

Devils
Garden

Devils
Lake

28

Devils Lake
Trail No. 61

To Bend

▲ Talapus Butte

Katsuk Pond Trail No. 13

Cascade Lakes Highway

Satan Creek

29

▲ Katsuk Butte

DESCHUTES
NATIONAL FOREST

headwaters
Quinn Meadow

Quinn
Meadow
Horse Camp

← To La Pine

Quinn Creek

N

0   0.25   0.5
MILE

29 Quinn Meadow

RATING/ DIFFICULTY	ROUNDTRIP	ELEV GAIN/ HIGH POINT	SEASON
**/3	7.8 miles	300 feet/ 5480 feet	July–Oct

Map: Green Trails Three Sisters No. 621; **Contact:** Deschutes National Forest, Bend–Fort Rock Ranger District; **Notes:** NW Forest Pass or $5 day-use fee. Access road closed in winter. Privy at Devils Lake trailhead; **GPS:** N 44 1.99, W 121 45.96

Hikes that don't knock your socks off are actually the best ones for breaking in a new pair of boots. You don't want to venture too far into the backcountry on a gear test without knowing you can depend on your new equipment to get the job done comfortably and effectively. The soft Quinn Meadow Trail has just enough ups and downs to put your new kicks to the test, and the destination is just boring enough (in a good way!) that you won't be sorry turning back if you get a bad blister. That said, this trail really is lovely, with plenty of lodgepole pine and interesting lava formations to make for a worthwhile day spent in the great outdoors.

GETTING THERE

From Bend, take Cascade Lakes Highway/State Route 46 west for 29 miles. Turn left at milepost 28 for the Devils Lake trailhead. Just 20 yards down the road is the Katsuk Pond Trail, on the right. Park on the roadside near the sign if there's a spot. Otherwise, park at the upper lot at Devils Lake Campground and walk along the road back to start this hike.

Forested segments of trail offer shade in the hot summer.

ON THE TRAIL

Start on Katsuk Pond Trail No. 13. Within just 0.1 mile, you'll reach the first of many lava rock piles, a common scene in Central Oregon. This trail is the main thoroughfare to the Quinn Meadow Horse Camp, which is largely evident by the big grassy manure mounds left every half mile or so. The path is more stirred up from horses than packed down from hikers. In fact, there's a good chance that the hiker-to-horse ratio on this trail is pretty even.

Continue on, tunneling through an open but narrow mini lava canyon. At 1.5 miles, you'll enter a considerably less exposed forested section. Nothing on this trail is exceptionally exciting, but an outing here is enjoyable. Pass a large flat open area at 1.8 miles and enter a forest of bare, dead standing logs—victims of a burn some time ago.

At 2.9 miles, you'll reach the tranquil headwaters of Quinn Creek. This is actually a great place to end your hike. It's by far the prettiest part of the trail, and it also happens to be the best place to stop for a picnic. Plop down on a rock while you enjoy your calm surroundings.

If you want to log a few more miles or just can't handle not knowing what's at the end of the trail, keep straight at a signed junction. You'll reach another junction at 3.2 miles. Follow the sign pointing to the right toward the horse camp. You'll have peekaboo views of South Sister as you continue on, passing marshy Quinn Meadow in 0.1 mile.

Continue on until the trail dead-ends at the horse ford at the swift creek. Although it's a scenic spot, the only reason to cross here is to see Quinn Meadow Horse Camp on the other side. Head back the way you came, taking time to enjoy the peaceful headwaters if you didn't do so on the way in.

30 South Sister Summit

RATING/ DIFFICULTY	ROUNDTRIP	ELEV GAIN/ HIGH POINT	SEASON
*****/5	11 miles	4900 feet/ 10,341 feet	Aug– early Oct

Map: Green Trails Three Sisters No. 621; **Contact:** Deschutes National Forest, Bend–Fort Rock Ranger District; **Notes:** NW Forest Pass or $5 day-use fee. Free self-issue wilderness permit Memorial Day–Oct 31. Access road closed in winter. Dogs must be leashed July 15–Sept 15. Privy at trailhead; **GPS:** N 44 2.4, W 121 45.54

If you're able-bodied enough to do so, it's my opinion that you must, at least once, climb South Sister. Many writers leave this route out of hiking guidebooks, or include it with caveats asserting that the views are just as good from lower vantage points. While there's some truth in that, don't let it deter you. Views alone can't beat the feeling of accomplishment earned from that final push to the summit. Because the ascent doesn't require technical climbing skills or equipment, anyone in decent shape can conquer this Cascadian volcano. Don't get me wrong—this trip is definitely strenuous. You'll gain nearly 5000 feet on the way up. It's not Everest, but it is the third-highest peak in Oregon. If you're a peak-bagger, it should be on your list. Why climb South Sister? In the words of mountaineer George Mallory, "Because it's there."

GETTING THERE

From Bend, take Cascade Lakes Highway/ State Route 46 west for 29 miles. Turn left at milepost 28 and proceed to the Devils Lake trailhead lower parking lot.

Hiking poles are certainly helpful on the South Sister descent.

ON THE TRAIL

From the north side of the parking area, take South Sister Climbers Trail No. 36. Begin a steep ascent through thick forest. Over the first 1.5 miles, you'll gain 1000 feet of elevation. This is gut-check time. If you can't handle this section, you probably shouldn't attempt to summit.

Continue for another 0.25 mile, where you'll reach a four-way junction. Keep straight on the Climbers Trail, leaving the forest and spitting out onto a subalpine plateau. With South Sister now in sight, you'll at least have extra visual motivation as you tackle the upcoming climb. From here, you'll also have a view of Broken Top to the east, the lava flow to the west, Mount Bachelor to the south, and several alpine lakes in various directions.

At 3 miles, you've climbed 1300 feet. As you continue to gain altitude, do a quick weather check. Storms can blow in at a moment's notice. Ambitious as you might be, play it safe and turn back if it looks like clouds are closing in. Summit storms aren't anything to mess around with. The mountain will always be here, so it's not the end of the world if you don't summit on your first try.

The trail leads along a ridge above Goose Creek and then really gets down to business. From here, you still have another 3200 feet to gain before reaching the crater. The climbing is grueling, so you'll be thankful for the flat area you'll reach next. At 4.5 miles, drop into the sandy moraine underneath Lewis Glacier. Cradled in this saddle is an aqua lake called Teardrop Pool. This silty cirque is Oregon's highest lake and possibly its most scenic. Take advantage of this little break to chug some water and eat an energy bar. You still have a fair amount of climbing to do.

Forge onward, taking the trail to the left up a steep cinder ridge. The loose scree

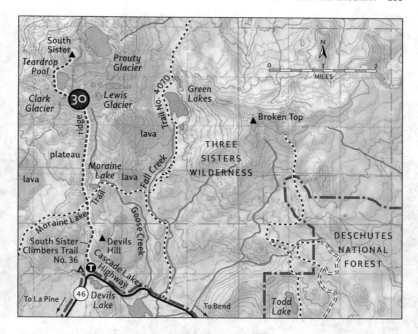

can be frustrating—a one-step-forward, two-steps-back feeling is hardly one you want to experience on such a demanding hike. Just be patient and try to keep the trail in sight as you scramble a steep 0.7 mile to the edge of the crater. This is a false summit, but you're nearly there. Follow the rim trail as it curves around the east face of the mountain for another 0.4 mile until you reach the official summit. If you choose to cross the glacier instead, use extreme caution.

You did it! From up here at 10,341 feet, you're basically smack-dab in a real-life topo map. Views abound in every direction, showcasing nearly the entire Cascade Range: Middle and North Sisters, Three Fingered Jack, Mount Washington, Mount Jefferson, Mount Hood, Mount Saint Helens, Mount Adams, the tip-top of Mount Rainier, and Diamond Peak. With most of the state (and beyond) laid out before you, the views are picture-perfect all around.

The wind up here will cool you down pretty quickly, so bring a light jacket if you want to spend any reasonable amount of time at the summit. As you come down from your top-of-the-world high, the descent seems to go on forever. In some ways, it's even tougher than the ascent. Take it easy—it won't be easier with a twisted ankle. Hiking poles are helpful here. When your body feels like it's going to give, the feeling of triumph will carry your tired legs the rest of the way. Revel in your accomplishment, giving yourself ample time to head down the mountain.

31 Moraine Lake

RATING/ DIFFICULTY	LOOP	ELEV GAIN/ HIGH POINT	SEASON
*****/4	7.5 miles	2050 feet/ 6715 feet	July–Oct

Map: Green Trails Three Sisters No. 621; **Contact:** Deschutes National Forest, Bend–Fort Rock Ranger District; **Notes:** NW Forest Pass or $5 day-use fee. Free self-issue wilderness permit Memorial Day–Oct 31. Access road closed in winter. Dogs must be leashed July 15–Sept 15. Privy at trailhead; **GPS:** N 44 2.10, W 121 46.1

One of the sparkliest jewels in the Cascade Lakes crown, stunningly beautiful Moraine Lake is a must-see. On this approach, you'll start on the Elk-Devils Trail,

The stunning hillsides above the Moraine Lake Basin, with South Sister beyond

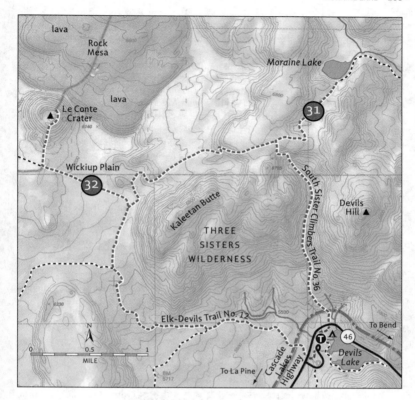

cross through Wickiup Plain to the lake, and then circle back to Devils Lake on the South Sister Climbers Trail. Besides visiting one of the most picturesque alpine lakes in the area, you'll also be rewarded with striking views of South Sister and the surrounding topography.

GETTING THERE

From Bend, take Cascade Lakes Highway/ State Route 46 west for 29 miles. Turn left at milepost 28 for the Devils Lake trailhead, and follow the road to the lower parking lot.

ON THE TRAIL

Start on Elk-Devils Trail No. 12. Within 0.1 mile, the trail reaches the trailhead kiosk, where you'll fill out your free wilderness permit. The trail is sandy with a lot of scattered rocks, making climbing a bit more difficult than it would be on a packed-down trail.

At 1 mile, head right to follow signs for Sisters Mirror Lake. At 2 miles, you'll reach another junction. This time follow signs for Moraine Lake, which will take you along the right-side trail. Keep right in another

0.4 mile to continue on between Wickiup Plain on your left and Kaleetan Butte on your right. As you head across the prairie, you'll encounter several strange junctions. They're all redundant connections between intertwining paths to Sisters Mirror Lake, Moraine Lake, the Pacific Crest Trail, and the Devils Lake trailhead. You'll reach such an intersection just 0.1 mile from the last one. Just continue to follow signs for Moraine Lake (in this case, to the right), and you'll be good to go.

The trail starts to climb a bit, the trees increasing with elevation, as you wind up a series of shaded switchbacks. This climb will definitely have you sweating by the time you pop back out into the sun at around 3.6 miles. The trail then flattens out while it traverses the terrain toward Moraine Lake.

In 0.25 mile, you'll reach a junction with South Sister Climbers Trail No. 36. You're headed straight, toward Moraine Lake, but it's worth taking notice of this spot. You'll return to this junction to close the loop back to the trailhead. For now, however, continue straight on the path to the lake.

You'll descend about 0.75 mile into the lake basin; this is where the scenery really opens up. The bones of the earth are laid bare, as shadows emphasize every little fold in the exposed hillsides. This slope is the moraine, a sandy ridge left by Lewis Glacier that the lake is named for. With South Sister standing firm in the background, it's a happy scene stretched out before you.

Go straight again when you enter the signed lake area, continuing down a steep grade to the glacier-carved basin at 4.6 miles. The stunning lake, cradled by the semicircle ridge around it, is one of the most beautiful places in Central Oregon. Watch the pebbles

on the lake bottom sparkle as the sun hits the clear water. While these alpine waters can be chilly, this is definitely an inviting place for a dip on hot summer days.

After a long, leisurely break at the lake, head back up the hill to the junction with the South Sister Climbers Trail at 5.4 miles. Turn left to take that trail a little over 2.1 miles down to the parking area, a steep but gorgeous descent through hemlock forest and past a few bubbling springs.

32 Le Conte Crater

RATING/ DIFFICULTY	ROUNDTRIP	ELEV GAIN/ HIGH POINT	SEASON
***/4	6.5 miles	1200 feet/ 6500 feet	July–Oct

Map: Green Trails Three Sisters No. 621; **Contact:** Deschutes National Forest, Bend–Fort Rock Ranger District; **Notes:** NW Forest Pass or $5 day-use fee. Free self-issue wilderness permit Memorial Day–Oct 31. Access road closed in winter. Dogs must be leashed July 15–Sept 15. Privy at trailhead; **GPS:** N 44 2.10, W 121 46.1

Central Oregon is filled with craters and buttes, but many of them are never visited. They sit quietly alongside the major trails, overshadowed by the big boys. One such volcanic mound is Le Conte Crater. This little fella's trails are endangered for a few reasons. The lack of maintenance means that trails are unclear, which leads to visitors trampling all over the place and causing erosion. A tricky situation, for sure. While Le Conte Crater isn't exceptionally unique, it's cool to step off the beaten path and put your footprints on something that is oft neglected. This hike is

Get off the beaten path and find the faint trail up Le Conte Crater.

also a nice add-on to some of the other trails in the area. Visit in early summer to see the little snowmelt pool at the top.

GETTING THERE

From Bend, take Cascade Lakes Highway/ State Route 46 west for 29 miles. Turn left at milepost 28 for the Devils Lake trailhead, and follow the road to the lower parking lot.

ON THE TRAIL

Start out on Elk-Devils Trail No. 12, following it about 0.1 mile to the wilderness permit kiosk. From here, the sandy trail leads through a mixed conifer forest before reaching a junction at 1 mile, where you'll turn right toward Sisters-Mirror Lake.

At the 2-mile mark, you'll reach another junction. Take the right-side trail across Wickiup Plain and parallel the western flank of Kaleetan Butte. In 0.45 mile, at the next junction, ignore the more established right-hand path to Moraine Lake (Hike 31), and instead turn left. There are a lot of intertwining trails around here, but you'll know you're headed the right way if you keep north and focus on Le Conte Crater—the grassy hill to the left (west) of South Sister.

The Le Conte Crater Trail to the top is technically an official trail, but it's not well marked or maintained. This part of the hike is more of a free-for-all. When you get to the base of the crater, it's a 400-foot scramble to the top. Watch your footing, as the rocky soil is loose underfoot. From up here, you'll have a nice view of the surrounding Rock Mesa flow. In early summer, you'll find a little snowmelt pool at the top. In the later months, red fall color graces the slopes. Return the way you came.

EXTENDING YOUR TRIP
For a varied return, hike a loop via South Sister Climbers Trail No. 36 (Hike 31).

Opposite: The top of Mount Bachelor behind Elk Lake

lower cascade
lakes highway

Cascade Lakes Highway/State Route 46 starts near Bend and curves around Mount Bachelor, stretching all the way south toward La Pine. While the entire highway closes in winter, there are two snow gates. This stretch is at a lower elevation that melts out more quickly, so the road and nearby hikes open sooner than the northern stretch. The trees also get denser and mossier the farther south along the highway you go. The wide variety of terrain surrounding the lower Cascade Lakes Highway makes this region happy grounds for all types of wildlife.

The lakes close to the highway here are just as scenic as the northern ones, but probably more recreational. Elk Lake, Cultus Lake, and Twin Lake all have lodges, with restaurants and activities throughout the summer. Stopping at one of these for a bite to eat is a nice way to cap off a long day hiking in the wilderness. Elk Lake is especially popular, especially with Pacific Crest Trail thru-hikers, who can get a hot meal just a mile off the lengthy trail. The new Cascade Lakes Welcome Station, just inside the Deschutes National Forest boundary a few miles west of Bend, is devoted to this scenic area and its recreation opportunities.

While the lakes close to the highway are very popular, hiking just a few miles from them yields remote landscapes, dense forests, and welcome isolation. Get ready to explore: there are hundreds of itsy lakes waiting to be discovered in this area.

33 Sisters Mirror Lake

RATING/ DIFFICULTY	ROUNDTRIP	ELEV GAIN/ HIGH POINT	SEASON
***/3	6.7 miles	600 feet/ 6000 feet	July–Oct

Maps: Green Trails Three Sisters No. 621, Geo-Graphics Three Sisters Wilderness; **Contact:** Deschutes National Forest, Bend–

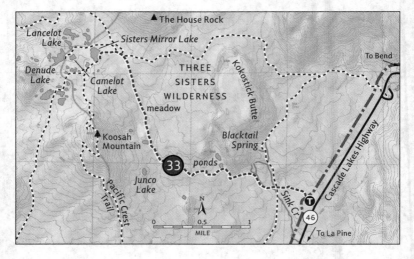

A faint trail passes through an open area before entering the forest.

Fort Rock Ranger District; **Notes:** Free self-issue wilderness permit Memorial Day–Oct 31. Access road closed in winter; **GPS:** N 44 1.63, W 121 0.73

🦴 ⚙️ *This stress-free route is an old standby. Many paths lead to Sisters Mirror Lake, but this one starts at a smaller trailhead with a little less traffic. You'll quickly enter the heart of the Three Sisters Wilderness, where you'll find a pocket of little alpine lakes. Sisters Mirror Lake is shallow, with a soft bottom, perfect for letting eager paws and little feet tromp around in. You can't see the Three Sisters from the lake, but don't let that dissuade you from visiting. You'll catch a few views on the loop back, but what's the rush? Bring a picnic and relax.*

GETTING THERE

From Bend, take Cascade Lakes Highway/State Route 46 west for 30 miles. About 1.3 miles past Devils Lake, near milepost 29, turn right into the small Sisters Mirror Lake trailhead parking lot.

ON THE TRAIL

Load up on bug spray and hit the trail! You'll start by entering a dense pine and hemlock forest, passing a few small lava flow areas to keep the scene interesting. In just under 0.5 mile, you'll head straight at the junction, passing over a small trail connecting to others in the area. You'll cross over the sometimes-dry Blacktail Spring outlet before tiptoeing through the lichen-lined Sink Creek.

Overall, this hike is fairly flat, but it climbs

a bit here as it continues into the woods. At 1.6 miles, you'll approach two small ponds in the shadow of a large rocky outcropping. Continue on, passing Junco Lake on the left and heading into a large meadow. In the summer, this pasture is colored with heather and sprinkled with paintbrush. As you make your way through the meadow, you'll hit the Pacific Crest Trail (PCT) at 3.2 miles. Turn left to hike the PCT to Sisters Mirror Lake.

On this approach to the lake, the trail looks a bit more like a user path. Small grassy patches find root in the empty soil as the snow clears each year, before foot traffic tramples them down. Make every effort to stay on the trail to avoid causing erosion. The forest soon thins out, bringing you face to face with a rich meadow and its still lake.

Sisters Mirror Lake isn't that big, but it's beautiful. The water here is also fairly shallow. In late summer, rocks that aren't quite large enough to be boulders still sit well above the surface, even in the middle of the lake. You can see the lake's only mountain view by taking the shoreline path to the southwest side, where you'll catch the tip of South Sister's reflection in the water. The House Rock sits just in front of South Sister. Soak it all in and follow the same route back to the trailhead.

EXTENDING YOUR TRIP

If you're keen on exploring before heading home, there are several inviting lakes in the area. To reach them, backtrack on the PCT. *Before* you reach the junction with the trail you came in on, take the teensy user path on the left. Within 0.2 mile, you'll reach another barely noticeable fork. Head right to pass a few little ponds before reaching Lancelot Lake in 0.1 mile. Or, head left for a 0.3-mile

spree past Bounty Lake and Camelot Lake to Denude Lake. Get back to the PCT, and hike left briefly before turning right to retrace your path to your car.

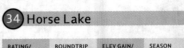

34 Horse Lake

RATING/ DIFFICULTY	ROUNDTRIP	ELEV GAIN/ HIGH POINT	SEASON
***/3	8.6 miles	700 feet/ 5325 feet	July–Oct

Maps: USGS Elk Lake, USGS Packsaddle Mountain, Geo-Graphics Three Sisters Wilderness; **Contact:** Deschutes National Forest, Bend–Fort Rock Ranger District; **Notes:** Free self-issue wilderness permit Memorial Day–Oct 31. Access road closed in winter. Privy at trailhead; **GPS:** N 43 59.03, W 121 48.68

The beginning stretch of this route is popular, as the Pacific Crest Trail (PCT) lies just 1.5 miles from the trailhead, and Elk Lake is a popular pit stop for thru-hikers. But this route mostly avoids the beaten-down PCT path, so you'll have a little more room to breathe. There's a lot to explore back here, but all the tangled up connecting trails can make an otherwise relaxing day a little stressful. This out-and-back gets you to Horse Lake with the least amount of navigating, although loops or combinations with other hikes are definitely possible.

GETTING THERE

From Bend, take Cascade Lakes Highway/State Route 46 west for 32 miles. Just across from the Elk Lake Resort turnoff, turn right at the "Trailhead" sign and drive 0.25 mile to the parking area.

Horse Lake glimmers behind the shoreline's dense growth.

ON THE TRAIL

Head up the dusty path and into the trees. Within 150 feet, you'll reach your first junction. Head right on Horse Lake Trail No. 2 and soon cross the Three Sisters Wilderness boundary. Like you'd expect on a trail with such a name, the Horse Lake Trail will probably have a few mounds of manure to step around along the way.

Within the first 1.5 miles, you'll cross the PCT and continue straight, now on Trail No. 3516. You'll begin a slow ascent here, gaining a little less than 250 feet over the next mile. The slope is definitely still gradual enough for you to maintain conversation and enjoy the journey.

At 2.5 miles, the single-track trail carves through a serene grassy meadow, speckled with little yellow and purple wildflowers in season. From here, you'll begin a gradual descent. In 0.8 mile, at the 3.3-mile mark, you'll reach a crossroads with the Sisters

Mirror Lake Trail. Head left. In another 0.3 mile, you'll reach the signed Horse Creek Trail. Turn right, descending again toward the heavily wooded lake area.

Look down to your left and you'll see Horse Lake between the trees. Despite taking the most direct route to this lake, you still have some low-key bushwhacking to get to the water's edge—there's no official trail. Near 4.1 miles, choose a spot to step off the trail. No particular place is necessarily better than another. Climb over logs and brambles and make your way about 0.2 mile to the shore.

What a gorgeous spot! The largest lake in the area, Horse Lake is completely surrounded by greenery. This marshy area is a mosquito haven in early summer, so bring bug spray or be prepared to outrun the hungry little pests. Follow the faint shoreline trail along the water if you like, or just turn around and take the same route home, following signs for Elk Lake.

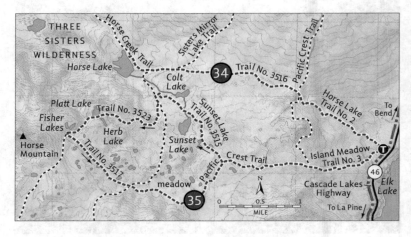

EXTENDING YOUR TRIP

Make a loop by connecting with the trails described in Hike 35. Head back up the Horse Creek Trail to your last junction. Turn right, crossing Horse Creek and connecting to Sunset Trail No. 3515 just north of Colt Lake. Keep right to visit the little lakes surrounding Horse Mountain, or stay left to pass between Sunset and Colt lakes and connect to the PCT near Island Meadow.

35 Horse Mountain Lakes

RATING/ DIFFICULTY	ROUNDTRIP	ELEV GAIN/ HIGH POINT	SEASON
***/4	9.5 miles	600 feet/ 5200 feet	July–Oct

Maps: USGS Elk Lake, USGS Packsaddle Mountain, Geo-Graphics Three Sisters Wilderness; **Contact:** Deschutes National Forest, Bend–Fort Rock Ranger District; **Notes:** Free self-issue wilderness permit Memorial Day–Oct 31. Access road closed in winter. Privy at trailhead; **GPS:** N 43 59.03, W 121 48.68

This lake basin is a gorgeous place to visit, and the thick tree cover and swimming opportunities make for a nice escape on hot days. Getting to the basin, though, involves a somewhat tricky loop with many confusing junctions. There's a healthy mix of painfully obvious trails and faint little backcountry connector trails. The farther you go, the more opportunities there are for getting mixed up. Every lake looks similar, and the heavy forest makes it difficult to see peaks that would help you determine your general location. Despite the navigational difficulties, if you stay on track, you'll make your way past Sunset and Colt lakes, traipse along a string of little lakes near Horse Mountain, and finally loop back on the Pacific Crest Trail (PCT) through Island Meadow.

GETTING THERE

From Bend, take Cascade Lakes Highway/State Route 46 west for 32 miles. Just across from the Elk Lake Resort turnoff, turn right at the "Trailhead" sign and drive 0.25 mile to the parking area.

ON THE TRAIL

The trail is dusty at the start, well worn from day hikers, trail runners, and weary PCT travelers. I suspect that a good amount of the beat-down is due to horses, of course. The benefit of frequently used trails is that they're often well signed. This is true here, at least in the beginning. Within 150 feet, turn left toward the signed Island Meadow Trail No. 3. Just beyond this point, you'll pass into the Three Sisters Wilderness at 0.2 mile.

Enter a dense, mossy grove of trees at around 0.3 mile before rounding a corner into an old burn area at 0.5 mile. While still very sparse, new life is beginning to flourish as little trees fill the space around dead ones. A clearing on the left showcases views of South Sister and Mount Bachelor. At your feet, low-level brush and ground cover poke onto the narrow trail, but not enough to obstruct it. At 1 mile, you'll collide with the PCT. Stay left.

Take a break from the sun exposure and head into the shade. The trail begins to descend farther into the trees at around 1.7 miles. At 2.1 miles, you'll begin to skirt a boggy meadow on your left. You'll reach a junction at the meadow at 2.25 miles. Take note of this spot, because your loop will bring you back here. For now, go right on Sunset Lake Trail No. 3515.

Follow the narrow trail through the meadow and past a marshy pond just beyond the trees on the right at 2.5 miles, followed by Sunset Lake on your left shortly thereafter. You'll pass over an often-dry creek bed at 3.25 miles, littered with moss and twigs. Stay right to keep on the Sunset Lake Trail, and then pass another meadow near 3.5 miles. If you'd like, look for a little user path around here to get to the somewhat-hidden Colt Lake to your right, just beyond the trees.

An old tree sign identifies this area's main attraction—the Pacific Crest Trail.

Signage in here starts to get a little less predictable. At 3.5 miles, go left, likely signed for Dumbbell Lake. Walk about 0.2 mile before reaching another junction, taking a right onto Trail No. 3523 and heading deeper into the forest. Within the next 1.5 miles, you'll pass a bevy of scenic lakes hidden among the trees. Platt Lake, Herb Lake, and East and West Fisher lakes are all worth a look! About 0.25 mile past the Fisher Lakes on your right, turn left onto Trail No. 3517 at 5.25 miles. You'll pass among even more tiny unnamed lakes on your way to connect with the PCT at 6.4 miles.

Continue straight on an approximately 2-mile stretch of the PCT that passes through the sometimes buggy, but always peaceful, Island Meadow before reaching the first PCT junction you encountered, at 8.5 miles. Stay right to exit the PCT and walk the final mile back to your car.

36 Elk Lake

RATING/ DIFFICULTY	ROUNDTRIP	ELEV GAIN/ HIGH POINT	SEASON
**/3	1.5 miles	80 feet/ 4930 feet	May–Nov

Maps: USGS Elk Lake, Geo-Graphics Three Sisters Wilderness; **Contact:** Deschutes National Forest, Bend–Fort Rock Ranger District; **Notes:** NW Forest Pass or $5 day-use fee. Access road closed in winter. Dogs not allowed. Privy at trailhead; **GPS:** N 43 57.79, W 121 48.35

This little lakeside jaunt is perfect if you're spending a day at the Beach Picnic Area. Take a break from the water and hit the trails. While a few paths head around the lake's east side, those miss out on the mountain views that make Elk Lake such a pretty place to hang out. Instead, follow the path between the shore and the highway. This way you'll gain a few extra views of gorgeous

Elk Lake, with the stunning Cascade backdrop as a nice bonus.

GETTING THERE
From Bend, take Cascade Lakes Highway/State Route 46 west for approximately 35 miles. About 2 miles past Elk Lake Resort, make a hard left into the Beach Picnic Area and drive the road to the parking lot.

ON THE TRAIL
Starting from the shore at the Beach Picnic Area, find the path on the left side. This is a strange trail. It doesn't go all the way around the lake, and you won't find it on your map. Yet at the same time, it seems to be much more than a user trail, and it even appears to be sporadically or sectionally maintained. One moment the trail is lined with rocks and logs to make sure you don't lose your way, and the next it seems to end without reason. Either way, it's easier to appreciate Elk Lake's fabulous views away from the picnic area's chaos.

One of Elk Lake's most popular picnic spots

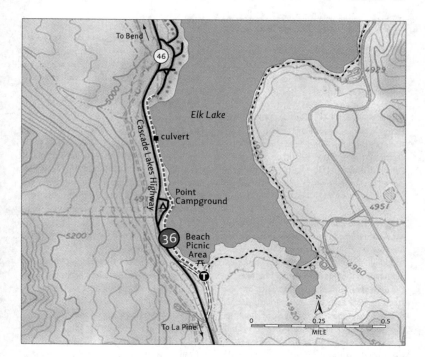

The trail, obvious for now, heads quickly into the forested area along the shoreline. As you depart from the sandy beach, the path's surface changes to something akin to sawdust. Shift your gaze above the boats buzzing along in the blue water to admire Mount Bachelor's cone, either white or brown depending on snow coverage, sitting perfectly in the background. Both Broken Top and South Sister can also be seen from here. Within 0.25 mile, you'll pass through the Point Campground and day-use area.

On the other side of the campground road, the trail gets a little jumbled. If you have trouble finding it, just look for the most open and bare space between the highway and the lake and go for it. At 0.6 mile, no matter which "path" you're on, you'll run into a culvert drainage area and a pile of large boulders. Use both hands to steady yourself as you make your way across the 20-foot pile of rocks. Once you reach the other side, you'll find an actual path—not just a *trail*, but an elevated, completely flat, perfectly symmetrical, apparently intentional path. Very strange!

Walk down this trail for about 0.2 mile, enjoying the calmness within the trees that line the path and form a sort of grove around you. At 0.75 mile, it's best to turn around. Go any farther and you'll start to hit private lakeshore property. Head back to the beach area, and cool off with a dip in the lake.

37 Blow and Doris Lakes

RATING/ DIFFICULTY	ROUNDTRIP	ELEV GAIN/ HIGH POINT	SEASON
***/3	4.75 miles	400 feet/ 5365 feet	July–Oct

Maps: USGS Elk Lake, Geo-Graphics Three Sisters Wilderness; **Contact:** Deschutes National Forest, Bend–Fort Rock Ranger District; **Notes:** Free self-issue wilderness permit Memorial Day–Oct 31. Access road closed in winter. Privy at trailhead; **GPS:** N 43 57.15, W 121 48.12

A hike to Blow and Doris lakes is a great option if you want to go on a nice day hike but don't want to spend the entire day trekking. You'll get to visit two of countless alpine lakes that sit deep within the forest on the Six Lakes Trail. Because it's such an easy stroll to Blow Lake and only slightly farther to Doris Lake, the trail can be busy. Don't let that take away from the fact that this chunk of wilderness is gorgeous and, if timed right, surprisingly peaceful.

GETTING THERE

From Bend, take Cascade Lakes Highway/ State Route 46 west for about 35 miles. About 2 miles past Elk Lake Resort and just after the Beach Picnic Area (after milepost 34), turn right at the "Trailhead" sign to a large parking area.

ON THE TRAIL

Head out on the gentle Six Lakes Trail. You'll soon enter a forest with a balanced mix of dead and living trees. Healthy pines dominate the scene among the old burn stumps, but a few noble firs sprinkled here and there will have you dreaming of the perfect Christmas tree even in the middle of summer. Within a short 0.1 mile, you'll enter the Three Sisters Wilderness, and then at 0.2 mile you'll cross a rudimentary footbridge over a usually dry creek. While there's probably water here in early spring, the creek bed is clogged with so many downed trees and debris that I'd be surprised if you could get to it.

At just under 0.5 mile, you'll round a switchback, giving you a nice peekaboo view of Mount Bachelor off to your left. Continue

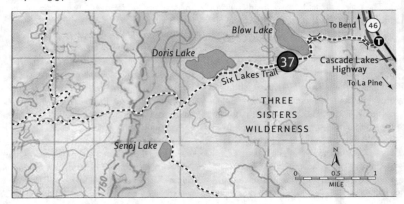

Doris Lake's wooded shoreline and calm waters

on, crossing another footbridge at 1 mile and reaching Blow Lake just a bit farther at 1.1 miles. The main trail continues to the left, but take any of the little side trails to the right to visit the lakeshore before heading on. It's a pretty little lake, with a few pleasant spots to

sit and enjoy. This is a good turnaround spot if you're hiking with kids, netting you 2.25 miles roundtrip. Otherwise, continue on to Doris Lake.

Beyond Blow Lake, the trail gets shadier as you enter thicker forest. The ground cover here is gorgeous in autumn, turning bright yellow and then changing to dark crimson as the season progresses. The way flattens out near a big rocky area to your left at about 1.5 miles before starting to climb again.

At 2.2 miles, you're close to Doris Lake, but the forest is thick enough to obscure it from view. The path is a little wider here, which is one of the signs that you're getting close. As you crest the hill, you'll finally see the pretty lake lower down on your right. The first path down to the lake is at 2.3 miles, on the right. This is a great access point, but feel free to continue around the lake until you find the place that makes you happy. Enjoy a picnic or a quick swim before turning around.

EXTENDING YOUR TRIP

This is a short hike, so it's worth adding a bit more to the trip if you're feeling up to it. Continue on the Six Lakes Trail for about 1 mile until you reach a junction. Stay left and hike another 0.6 mile to Senoj Lake. You can access way more than six lakes in this area, so bring a map and explore!

38 Lucky Lake

RATING/ DIFFICULTY	ROUNDTRIP	ELEV GAIN/ HIGH POINT	SEASON
****/2	2.7 miles	410 feet/ 5215 feet	June–Oct

Maps: USGS Lucky Lake, Geo-Graphics Three Sisters Wilderness; **Contact:** Deschutes National Forest, Bend–Fort Rock Ranger District; **Notes:** NW Forest Pass or $5 day-use fee. Free self-issue wilderness permit Memorial Day–Oct 31. Access road closed in winter. Privy at trailhead; **GPS:** N 43 54.27, W 121 46.52

Lucky Lake is a hike that will, without a doubt, make your dog happy. The trail isn't too long, but it's still steep enough to ease those restless legs. This comfortable hike leads to a calm alpine lake that is perfect for both chasing sticks and cooling off. On top of all that, the trail is soft underfoot and shaded overhead. It truly is a pooch's paradise. Human folk will think it's pretty amazing too. Lucky Lake makes for a nice add-on to another excursion in the area—or enjoy it all on its own.

GETTING THERE

From Bend, take Cascade Lakes Highway/ State Route 46 west to near milepost 38.5. Turn right for the Senoj Lake trailhead, and then turn right again to park in the hiker parking lot (horse trailers turn left).

ON THE TRAIL

From the Senoj Lake trailhead, head off in the direction of Lucky Lake. The trail is level at the beginning, skirting some marshy areas and passing under a set of powerlines within the first mile. Shortly past this area, the horse trail merges with the hiker trail. Dogs are allowed off-leash on this trail, but use your best judgment depending on your dog's temperament around livestock. You'll need to be cautious of horses that you may encounter along the way.

At around 0.25 mile, the trail begins to climb, although the grade is consistently inconsistent. It's the kind of trail that cycles between flat and steep every 0.2 mile or so. There are plenty of downed trees on either side of the trail, and a few massive stumps remind us of the monstrous ones that used to stand tall here. Amid the downed timber, colorful wildflowers pepper the landscape with vivid purple and crimson. At 1.3 miles, you're

Big stumps mark where huge trees once stood.

already at the lake. Eager dogs can hop right in the water at the trail's end.

Lucky Lake is clear with a sandy bottom, which makes it perfectly picturesque. It's warmer than many of the other Cascade lakes, making it ideal for swimming. "More!" you say? The surrounding hills even shelter the lake from the wind, which makes getting out of the lake more comfortable. Lucky, lucky you. Unfortunately, these conditions also make it easier for mosquitoes to linger. In early summer months, make sure you pack the DEET.

As if the serene glimmering lake wasn't enough, the shore also provides views of both South and Middle Sisters. If you want

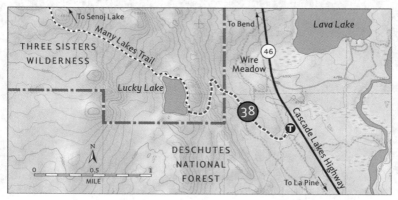

to find your own private picnic spot to enjoy the lake, continue on the loosely defined lakeside trail. The whole loop around the lake adds an extra 1.3 miles. Head back when you're ready.

EXTENDING YOUR TRIP

If you feel like knocking more Cascade lakes off your list, there are plenty to choose from, although they might be a bit far for pups. Stay on the Many Lakes Trail for another 5.5 miles to Senoj Lake. Still haven't had enough? In another 1 mile past Senoj, you'll hit the Six Lakes Trail, which leads to even more lakes than that, as well as another trailhead (see Hike 37).

39 Blue Lagoon

RATING/ DIFFICULTY	ROUNDTRIP	ELEV GAIN/ HIGH POINT	SEASON
***/2	1.35 miles	10 feet/ 4790 feet	June–Oct

Maps: USGS Elk Lake, Geo-Graphics Three Sisters Wilderness; **Contact:** Deschutes National Forest, Bend–Fort Rock Ranger District; **Notes:** Access road closed in winter; **GPS:** N 43 54.4, W 121 46.25

While plenty of trails in the area reward hikers for enduring long and difficult routes, some stellar views are

The magical waters of Blue Lagoon

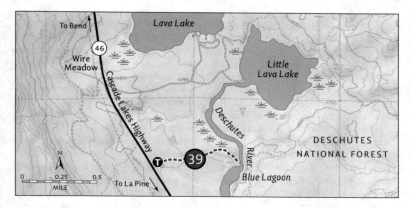

more easily obtained. In fact, sometimes the simplest paths lead to the most beautiful places. It's even better when you get to sit and enjoy the beauty without the distraction and noise from crowds and big groups. Such is the case with Blue Lagoon. This short walk takes off from an unmarked trailhead, leading to a colorful oasis near the source of the Deschutes River.

GETTING THERE
From Bend, take Cascades Lakes Highway/State Route 46 west for 40 miles. The unmarked trailhead is on the left, about 0.5 mile past the Lava Lake turnoff.

ON THE TRAIL
From the parking area, follow the simple signage pointing you toward the Deschutes River. It's rather sneaky of those Forest Service trail markers to give the destination such a vague name when it leads to such a spectacular place. Despite the lack of fanfare at the trailhead, you'll quickly see why this is a destination worth visiting.

The dirt trail starts out through a cluttered young jack pine forest, but the trees turn sparse as you skirt a large meadow. This is a short and peaceful stroll, making it great for kids and casual hikers. The trail is mostly flat but descends ever so slightly over the first 0.25 mile as you make your way toward the Deschutes River.

In just 0.5 mile, you'll reach the river and the aptly named Blue Lagoon. See? The trail sign doesn't give this spot enough credit! Right here along the Upper Deschutes, just south of where it flows from Little Lava Lake, the banks widen and create a large aqua pool. Surrounded by a grassy shoreline, the turquoise water glitters in the sunlight. The water is so clear that you can see old logs sitting along the sandy bottom.

This dazzling spot is a great place to throw a stick for your dog or plop down with a good book. It's the kind of hike you take when you need to just *be*, without the stress of planning or packing for a longer excursion. You'll probably see more people in the water kayaking than on the actual trail. Enjoy the serene escape of Blue Lagoon for a while before ambling back to your car.

40 Teddy Lakes

RATING/ DIFFICULTY	ROUNDTRIP	ELEV GAIN/ HIGH POINT	SEASON
***/3	7.8 miles	750 feet/ 4970 feet	May–Nov

Maps: USGS Irish Mountain, Geo-Graphics Three Sisters Wilderness; **Contact:** Deschutes National Forest, Bend–Fort Rock Ranger District; **Notes:** Free self-issue wilderness permit Memorial Day–Oct 31. Access road closed in winter. Privy and water at campground; **GPS:** N 43 50.43, W 121 50.06

Not far from the hustle and bustle of Cultus Lake lie two quiet tree-lined bodies of water. Larger than you'd expect from something that so few people talk about, *Teddy Lakes are certainly worth the trip. A comfortable trail follows the Cultus Lake shoreline before gaining a bit of elevation to the Teddy Lakes area. After a refreshing quiet time at Teddy Lakes, switch things up— embrace the chaos and stop for an after-hike ice cream at Cultus Lake.*

GETTING THERE

From Bend, take Cascade Lakes Highway/ State Route 46 west for 46 miles. At Cultus Lake Resort, turn right on Forest Road 4635 and proceed for 1.7 miles. Stay to the right on gravel FR 100, reaching Cultus Lake Campground in 0.3 mile. Then keep right at the fork and drive another gravelly 0.6 mile, passing the Winopee Tie Trail sign and continuing to the road's end at the Winopee trailhead on the left side.

A rain-drenched trillium near Cultus Lake

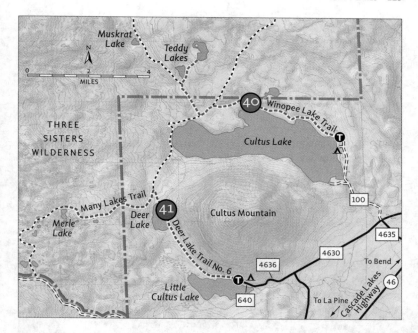

ON THE TRAIL

Start on the Winopee Lake Trail, keeping right at 0.1 mile to hike along Cultus Lake. From the shoreline, you'll have prime views of all kinds of water recreation. As you continue, however, the noises quickly fade away, allowing you to pick up noises that weren't quite as clear at the lake. Birds happily chirp, trees creak, and woodland creatures pitter-patter about. Unfortunately, you'll also hear the mosquitoes buzzing in your ears. Keep the vibe serene and idyllic by loading up on repellent before hitting the trail.

The trail climbs gently, giving you just enough of a workout to keep warm, but not so much that you'll be uncomfortable when the sun beats down through the somewhat sparse lodgepole pine forest. Keeping Cultus Lake on your left, you'll start to climb away from the water near 1.75 miles. At 2.4 miles, keep left at the junction, and then turn right in another 0.2 mile to stay on the Winopee Lake Trail. In another 0.25 mile, you'll enter the Three Sisters Wilderness.

You'll reach another junction at 3.3 miles. Turn right here for the final 0.6-mile stretch. The trail passes South Teddy Lake almost immediately. There's no official trail to the water, but it's a mere 100-foot log hop to the lake edge. Both lakes are gorgeous, but North Teddy has an easily accessible shoreline—a desirable feature—so continue on. The trail ends at 3.4 miles at the water's edge.

North Teddy Lake is the perfect place to soak up the solitude and take a little swim.

There are no rocky spots to dry off on, but there are plenty of downed trees along the wooded shoreline to use as perfect little benches. Water dogs will love to chase sticks in the calm lake. Finish up by retracing your path to the trailhead, making sure to keep left at that last junction before the parking lot.

EXTENDING YOUR TRIP

Add another lake to your trip with an extension to Muskrat Lake. From Teddy Lakes, hike back to the main Winopee Lake Trail and turn right. Proceed for 1.4 miles to Muskrat Lake and an old dilapidated log cabin. Turn around and take the Winopee Lake Trail all the way back to your car.

41 Merle Lake

RATING/ DIFFICULTY	ROUNDTRIP	ELEV GAIN/ HIGH POINT	SEASON
***/4	8.75 miles	880 feet/ 5295 feet	Apr–Nov

Maps: USGS Crane Prairie Reservoir, USGS Irish Mountain; **Contact:** Deschutes National Forest, Bend–Fort Rock Ranger District; **Notes:** Privy at trailhead; **GPS:** N 43 48.27, W 121 52.06

I'm surprised that this trail isn't more popular. Sure, you have to log a few miles on a beat-up forest road to get here, and yes, there are more scenic trails nearby. But

A prime camp spot at Merle Lake

there's something perfectly calming about walking an empty trail through dense forest. You'll start at Little Cultus Lake, make a quick visit at Deer Lake, and then reach scenic Merle Lake. Another bonus? This last lake is calm and often visitor-free, even at the height of summer. I didn't even know it existed until recently. Thanks to the random couple on the trail who tipped my parents off to this stunning lake!

GETTING THERE

From Bend, take Cascade Lakes Highway/ State Route 46 west for 46 miles. At Cultus Lake Resort, turn right on Forest Road 4635 and drive 0.8 mile. Then turn left onto FR 4630 and drive 1.7 miles before turning right onto FR 4636. In 0.5 mile, turn right onto FR Spur 640. Park on the left in 0.25 mile, near the campsite at the far end of the campground. You'll find the trail's entry point on the right as you walk toward the lake.

ON THE TRAIL

Starting along the north shore of Little Cultus Lake, go right to take Deer Lake Trail No. 6 into the trees. While thick pine and hemlock forest obscure the lake view most of the way, you'll catch glimpses every now and then of colorful tents dotting the shoreline campsites. A smattering of wildflowers thrives just off the trail among the trees, especially in late spring and early summer.

The Deer Lake Trail is soft and simple, changing very little over the course of the hike. It rambles through the forest, which is fairly quiet except for the birds, trees creaking in the breeze, and the occasional mountain biker cruising down the trail. Although your view from within the trees is limited, the path at this point is rounding the west flank of Cultus Mountain.

This trail has significant blowdown each winter. As the seasons turn and things dry up, wildfire season approaches. The old downed trees and brush always make me nervous, especially with all the campgrounds (and campfires) nearby. The overgrowth and downed wood would be mere kindling for a wildfire, but it does make the entire hike feel all the more wild and uninhabited.

In just 1.75 easy miles, you'll reach the southernmost end of Deer Lake. Considering the lack of fanfare getting here, the lake is larger than you might expect. The trees are thick along the shore too, but there are good clearings in relatively regular increments. From here, continue around the lake until you hit a junction at 2.3 miles. Turn left onto the Many Lakes Trail, then cross into the Three Sisters Wilderness.

The trail begins to climb from here. It also gets slightly less maintained. You'll find the ground a little rougher and the trail narrower. Pass underneath a rocky slope at 3.5 miles, and continue past a few marshy ponds. At 4.3 miles, you'll see scenic Merle Lake. Continue another 30 yards or so around the lake, where you'll find a nice spot on the left with a stunning view of the lake. This is an awesome spot to eat lunch and take a swim before turning back the way you came.

42 Osprey Point and Billy Quinn Gravesite

RATING/ DIFFICULTY	ROUNDTRIP	ELEV GAIN/ HIGH POINT	SEASON
**/1	0.9 mile	100 feet/ 4500 feet	June–Oct

Maps: USGS Crane Prairie Reservoir, Geo-Graphics Three Sisters Wilderness; **Contact:** Deschutes National Forest, Bend–Fort Rock

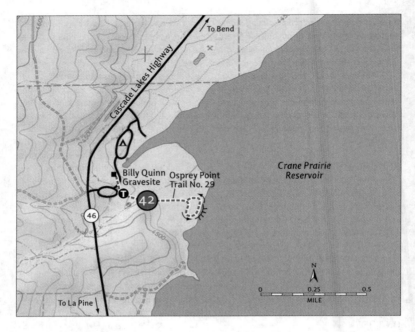

District; **Notes:** NW Forest Pass or $5 day-use fee. Privy at trailhead; **GPS:** N 43 47.15, W 121 48.09

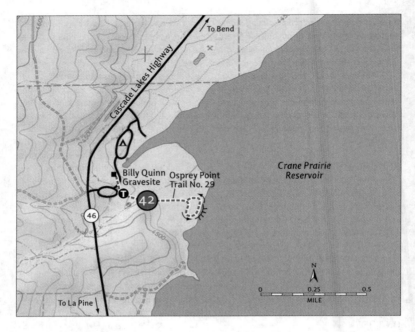 *There's not much to this trail, but its simplicity is what makes it truly refreshing. This quick hike takes you to the historic Billy Quinn Gravesite before continuing on to Osprey Point on the western shore of Crane Prairie Reservoir. The lake is well known among fishermen for its oversized rainbow and brook trout, as well as largemouth bass. The abundant fish attract an array of nesting and migrating avian species, so bring binoculars. The grave-site is a reminder of the area's history, as well as how far civilization has come in such a short period of time.*

GETTING THERE
From Bend, take Cascade Lakes Highway/ State Route 46 west for 46 miles. Just past Cultus Lake, turn left for the Osprey Point Observation Site. Proceed to the parking lot.

ON THE TRAIL
Before heading to the Osprey Point Observation Site, start with a little side trip. From the trailhead on the north side of the parking loop, near the picnic table, turn left off the main trail onto the short and simple Billy Quinn Trail. In just 0.1 mile, you'll reach a small but peaceful gravesite with interpretive signage detailing a tragic 1894 hunting accident. Billy was only twenty-five years old when he passed away here at Crane Prairie before the doctor could make it over from

Clouds cast shadows on the Crane Prairie Reservoir.

Prineville. Pause to give thanks for modern-day transportation, and then head back and turn left to continue on the main Osprey Point Trail No. 29.

This flat path travels through a mixed conifer forest for about 0.3 mile. You'll see both lodgepole and ponderosa pines and Engelmann spruce, as well as seasonal wildflowers here and there. At 0.3 mile from the trailhead, you'll arrive at an intersection and the beginning of a short loop. As you turn right, notice how things get marshier. The diverse habitat around the lake is what makes it such a haven for various types of insects, fish, birds, amphibians, and other wildlife.

As you round the corner in the loop, you'll have a nice view of the reservoir, where you can do a bit of bird-watching. It's believed that over half of the ospreys in the state of Oregon nest here at Crane Prairie. You'll feel like you're watching a nature show when you see these hunters dive into the water to grab fish with their claws. Be on the lookout for great blue heron, bald eagle, double-crested cormorant, various goldeneyes, Eurasian wigeon, and even more bird varieties. If you hit the trail during the quiet dawn or dusk hours, there's a chance you'll even see beavers and Rocky Mountain elk.

The loop to the observation area and around to the main trail is just a short 0.1 mile, linking back up with the main trail at 0.4 mile from the trailhead. From here, simply take the Osprey Point Trail back.

43 Lily and Charlton Lakes

RATING/ DIFFICULTY	LOOP	ELEV GAIN/ HIGH POINT	SEASON
***/3	5.25 miles	900 feet/ 6000 feet	Late June–Oct

Maps: USFS Deschutes National Forest, Geo-Graphics Three Sisters Wilderness, Bend Adventure Map; **Contact:** Deschutes National Forest, Bend–Fort Rock District; **Notes:** Privy at trailhead; **GPS:** N 43 44.94, W 121 58.20

While Charlton Lake lies pretty close to Willamette Pass near Waldo Lake, you can get to it via a few bumpy back roads off the Cascade Lakes Highway. The final road to the trailhead is long and slow, but once you're here, it's a mere hop, skip, and a jump to Charlton Lake. Pack a lunch and spend the day hiking, swimming, and enjoying the great outdoors. Try the pleasant loop to the smaller Lily Lake before a quick jaunt to hang out on the shores of Charlton Lake.

GETTING THERE

From Bend, take Cascade Lakes Highway/ State Route 46 west for 49 miles to where South Century Drive enters from the left. Turn right onto unpaved Forest Road 4290/5897 and drive 9 bumpy miles. Park at the Charlton Lake trailhead where the path crosses the road.

A wooded forest with a soft trail is perfect for dogs.

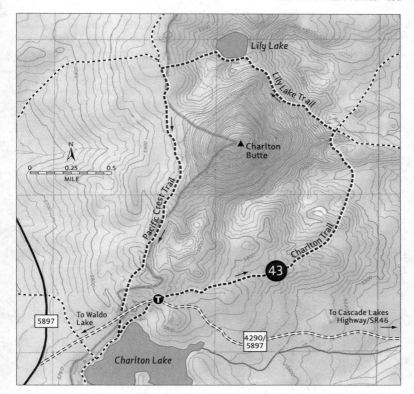

ON THE TRAIL

From the right side of the forest road, find the Charlton Trail heading north and away from the lake. This trail leads through dense forests and, in the summer, a lot of bugs. You'll cross a small and sometimes dry tributary of Charlton Creek before continuing around the eastern side of Charlton Butte to a four-way junction at 1.7 miles.

Turn left onto the Lily Lake Trail. In less than 0.75 mile, you'll reach the southern shores of a small lake. You'll see the destruction from forest fires around most of the lake, although there's a treed section on the southwestern edge that somehow escaped the burn. Lily Lake is a good spot to stop for a snack or make a refreshing jump into the cool pool on hot days before continuing on.

When you're ready, hike past the lake to a junction with the Pacific Crest Trail (PCT) at 3 miles. Turn left onto the PCT. The trail climbs as it loops around the western side of Charlton Butte, but it doesn't make any attempts to actually summit it. If you spontaneously feel the urge, you can take one of several side trails that lead up the 6300-foot butte.

The PCT meets the road at 4.9 miles. Grab lunch and a blanket out of the car, and carry them across the road, following the trail down a hundred feet or so to say hello to Charlton Lake. When you're ready, turn left to walk along the western shoreline. Find a spot to have a little picnic and enjoy the lake. At the end of a fun day, follow the trail back up to the road and begin your bumpy ride home.

Opposite: Flatiron Rock is one of the more intriguing lava formations in the Badlands.

the badlands
and horse ridge

When west-side trails in the Cascades are snowed-in or just too crowded, head east. Not far from the northern edge of Bend, you'll find the Badlands—one of Oregon's newest wilderness areas. Plagued by off-highway vehicle erosion until just recently, the region now flaunts miles and miles of Saved Trails across volcanic pressure ridges. The terrain is flat and barren except for ancient junipers and abundant sagebrush, making it feel more desertlike than most regions in Central Oregon. The new wilderness area stretches from the little town of Alfalfa on the north to US Highway 20 on the south.

Farther south, but still east of Bend, the China Hat and Horse Ridge area provide even more fun hiking trails. Much work has been done to protect overused routes here, including relocating trailheads and rerouting trails to keep the area beautiful. Little buttes, hidden lava caves, and other interesting landmarks are begging to be explored.

44 Bessie and Kelsey Buttes

RATING/ DIFFICULTY	ROUNDTRIP	ELEV GAIN/ HIGH POINT	SEASON
***/4	10.5 miles	1200 feet/ 4995 feet	Year-round

Map: USFS Deschutes National Forest; **Contact:** Deschutes National Forest, Bend–Fort Rock District; **GPS:** N 43 57.06, W 121 15.66

In the strange no-man's-land quadrant off China Hat in southeast Bend, you'll find an array of little buttes. You probably wouldn't be able to distinguish one from another in a photo lineup, but that's okay. Start to get to know these mounds with this long day hike from Bessie Butte to Kelsey Butte and back. There's just enough climbing to keep things interesting, but otherwise it's a fairly uneventful route. This is a nice long hike to explore when higher-elevation trails are

This trail gains 470 feet on its way up Bessie Butte.

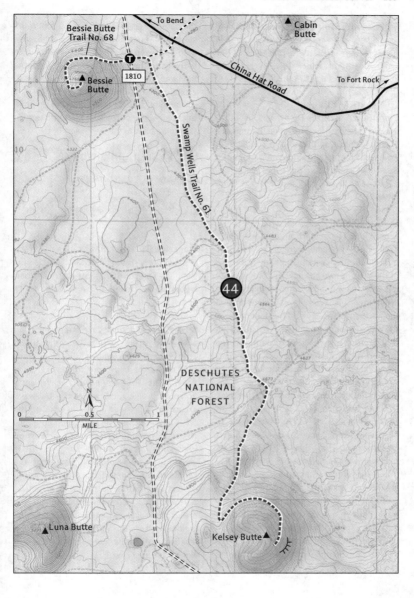

To Bend

▲ Cabin Butte

Bessie Butte Trail No. 68

China Hat Road

To Fort Rock

T

1810

▲ Bessie Butte

Swamp Wells Trail No. 61

44

DESCHUTES NATIONAL FOREST

N

0   0.5   1
MILE

▲ Luna Butte

Kelsey Butte ▲

still snowed-in. This trail is shared with moun-. tain bikers and horses, so brush up on your right-of-way etiquette before hitting the trails. Bessie Butte in particular is a nice place to watch sunrises and sunsets.

GETTING THERE

From Bend, take US Highway 97 south 2 miles and take exit 143 for Baker/Knott Road. Turn left onto Knott Road and continue for 1.5 miles, and then turn right onto China Hat Road. In 4.5 miles, turn right onto gravel Forest Road 1810 and park in the Bessie Butte lot on the left.

ON THE TRAIL

Cross FR 1810 and start out on Bessie Butte Trail No. 68, heading straight toward the butte. You could save this summit for the end of the hike, but we all know that would make it way too easy to back out. Best to just grind it out now. This 0.75-mile trail winds around the northern slope of the 4768-foot butte all the way to the top, gaining 470 feet along the way. From the summit, look south and see if you can spot Kelsey Butte just a few miles away. That's where you're headed next.

Come back down Bessie Butte and cross FR 1810 to pick up a trail on the other side. In about 0.25 mile, you'll hit a junction with Swamp Wells Trail No. 61. Turn right to hike south for 3.7 miles. The sights aren't overwhelming, but they're comforting in that sprawling-lonely-terrain kind of way that hikers are so addicted to. The winding, meandering path strolls through ponderosa forests and scented bitterbrush. The single-track path is muddy after rain and dusty during dry spells. It's frequently marked with both bike tracks and hoofprints.

Near the 5.2-mile mark, you'll come to the base of Kelsey Butte. The 300-foot climb starts out gradually, becomes tough, and then gets even steeper as it circles 0.8 mile partway up the butte. At 4.5 miles from the trailhead, you'll reach a scenic overlook with views of the Cascades and several of the surrounding buttes. While not the summit, this is a good spot to call it quits and retrace your route back to the trailhead.

45 Pictograph Cave

RATING/ DIFFICULTY	ROUNDTRIP	ELEV GAIN/ HIGH POINT	SEASON
**/4	5 miles	200 feet/ 4450 feet	May–Sept

Maps: USFS Deschutes National Forest, USGS Kelsey Butte; **Contact:** Deschutes National Forest, Bend Fort–Rock District; **Notes:** Cave closed Oct–Apr; **GPS:** N 43 55.04, W 121 9.25

🏠 ❌ *Pictograph Cave is one of many caverns within the larger Arnold Lava Tube System, and it stands in stark contrast to the more touristy caves around Bend. This isn't a paved, conveniently accessed, well-signed, or easily traversed excursion. Nope—you'll have to work a little bit if you want to visit Pictograph Cave. But the cave is an impressive structure with an interesting history, so it's worth a visit if you're feeling adventurous. Note that the cave is closed from October through April to protect hibernating bats. This is a remote, partially underground hike in a seldom-used area, so it would be wise to bring a buddy. The trail to the cave is 4 miles roundtrip, with a maximum of 1 mile more if you choose to explore the dark cavern (bring a headlamp).*

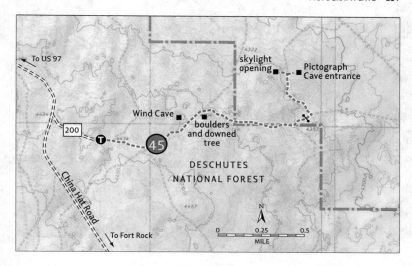

GETTING THERE

From Bend, take US Highway 97 south for 2 miles, and take exit 143 for Baker/Knott Road. Turn left onto Knott Road and continue for 1.5 miles, and then turn right onto China Hat Road. Drive 10.6 miles, the final 2.4 miles on gravel. Then turn left onto Forest Road 200 for Wind Cave. Continue another 0.2 mile to the blockade.

ON THE TRAIL

Walk around the blockade and hike 0.6 mile along the road to Wind Cave. This cave is permanently closed; don't attempt to enter it. Let this serve as a reminder that these caves are precious and under constant threat of being shut down. It's truly a privilege to be able to explore these caves, so obey all rules and common decencies so access isn't taken away.

When you hit Wind Cave, the road comes to an end at a turnaround loop. The trail leaving the road isn't marked, so it's essential that you pay attention in order to start out on the right path. Speaking from experience, taking the wrong turn will get you hopelessly lost in the desert. So, locate the big boulders and large downed tree on the left side of the turnaround loop. Two trails diverge from this point. Take the trail heading to the *right* here, even though it looks like you should go straight. Continue on this old dirt road for 0.9 mile. Pass through the gate and turn left. Step over the barbed wire and continue on. The trail will parallel another barbed-wire fence on your left.

In another 0.2 mile, the path reaches a junction between Pictograph Cave's two openings. Head left first for a quick 250 feet to the first opening, which shouldn't really be called an entrance, as you can't go in this way. It's a large skylight opening with an amazingly thin roof. Stay a ways back.

The entrance into Pictograph Cave

Next, head back to the junction and continue toward the second opening, at the 2-mile mark. Put away your camera, water bottle, or anything else you're carrying. You're going to need your hands for this part. Climb down into the cave. Directly in front of you, look for the faded Native American etchings that the cave was renamed for. Back in the late 1950s, however, it was called Stout Cave and housed a dilapidated moonshine distillery.

There are two tube branches here. Turn left, taking the path that connects to the skylight opening. Despite the large opening at the end of the tunnel, it's pretty dark in here. Make sure you have a headlamp, and watch your footing on the rough ground. You'll soon enter a spacious cavern and then clamber up and down a bit to get to where the skylight shines above, approximately 0.1 mile from the pictograph wall.

Head back to the main junction and take the right-hand tube. Again, the footing is

quite unstable and unforgiving, so check your foot placement before committing to each step. This tunnel extends much farther into the darkness. About 0.5 mile in, turn around. Carefully scramble out of the cave and retrace your steps back to your car.

46 Flatiron Rock

RATING/ DIFFICULTY	ROUNDTRIP	ELEV GAIN/ HIGH POINT	SEASON
***/2	6 miles	None/ 3755 feet	Year-round

Map: BLM Oregon Badlands Wilderness; **Contact:** BLM Prineville District; **Notes:** Privy at trailhead; **GPS:** N 43 95.771, W 121 05.186

Smack-dab in the middle of the state, the Badlands are Central Oregon's newest wilderness area. The area sits atop the Columbia River Basalts, so it's mostly flat with a spattering of interesting lava features. This relaxing trail winds gently through a fragrant juniper desert until it reaches an unusual formation called Flatiron Rock. Because the area is so vast, the trail is unlikely to feel crowded, even on busy days. This hike lacks major views, making it a good choice when the mountains are obscured by overcast weather. Less-perfect days also help beat the desert heat; the old junipers provide very little shade. No matter when you visit, make sure to pack plenty of water, as there aren't any sources on the trail.

GETTING THERE

From Bend, drive east on US Highway 20 for 16 miles. Turn left at milepost 16 for the Flatiron Rock trailhead.

ON THE TRAIL

At the trailhead, take a picture of the map if you brought your camera or phone. The trail itself is soft, sandy, and forgiving, but it can be directionally confusing at times. Several user trails lead to dead ends, and trail markers are few and far between, so you'll want to stick to the main paths. Start off by turning right to take the Flatiron Rock Trail. After 1.2 miles, you'll reach a signed junction with the Homestead Trail. Keep left to stay on the Flatiron Rock Trail, which continues straight for another 1.8 miles.

This hike is a great introduction to the Badlands Wilderness. Stately and weathered juniper trees, some over one thousand years old, line the landscape while fragrant sagebrush fills in the gaps. Magenta and yellow

Ancient junipers line the easy Badlands trails

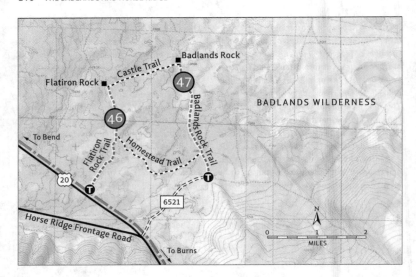

wildflowers add a pop of color to the desert landscape. Several igneous outcrops hint at the area's history. Other than lively anthills that dot the sandy path, there is very little activity. It feels like time stands still in this old, arid desert.

At 3 miles, you'll arrive at Flatiron Rock. Take the trail spur to the left to explore the lunaresque formation. Flatiron Rock itself isn't necessarily anything to write home about, but it does have several interesting elements, such as arches and peepholes in the hardened lava. With dark clouds in the air and crows cawing above you, meandering through the desolate formation has an eerie feel to it. On sunny days, however, scrambling to the top of the rock will give you cheerful views of the Cascades against a big blue backdrop.

After exploring the rock, come back out to the main trail. Again, the signage here is confusing. The Flatiron Rock Trail technically continues on past the rock formation, but it stops abruptly at private property. For this reason, make Flatiron Rock your turnaround spot. Head back the way you came in, savoring the wide-open sky and gnarly junipers in this lesser-known area in Bend's backyard.

47 Badlands Rock

RATING/ DIFFICULTY	ROUNDTRIP	ELEV GAIN/ HIGH POINT	SEASON
***/2	6 miles	None/ 3615 feet	Year-round

Map: BLM Oregon Badlands Wilderness; **Contact:** BLM Prineville District; **GPS:** N 43 95.387, W 121 01.476

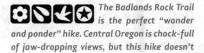 *The Badlands Rock Trail is the perfect "wander and ponder" hike. Central Oregon is chock-full of jaw-dropping views, but this hike doesn't*

really have any. That's okay, because some-times all you need from a hike is solitude and a peaceful, quiet stroll, to be alone with your thoughts. This desertlike and deserted hike heads through old juniper forests to a large rocky outcrop.

GETTING THERE

From Bend, drive east on US Highway 20 for 17 miles. Turn left at the signed Badlands Rock trailhead, just past milepost 17 at Forest Road 6521, and follow the road approximately 1 mile to the parking lot.

ON THE TRAIL

Before following the path into the desert, take a quick peek at the posted map at the trailhead to get your bearings. It's a tad confusing in the Badlands. When you're ready, proceed on the flat and gentle but gritty trail. The rough sandy soil is made up of volcanic ash and eroded lava from the Mount Mazama eruption over seventy-five

hundred years ago at what is now known as Crater Lake.

Approximately 0.25 mile in, you'll reach an intersection. Continue straight to stay on the Badlands Rock Trail. Ignore the random paths that jut out in every direction, unless you're up for some aimless wandering; most are just user paths with no actual destination.

As you hike, look for faint animal tracks in the sandy path. There's a wide variety of wildlife in the Badlands, including bobcats, black-tailed jackrabbits, mule deer, elk, pronghorns, cottontail rabbits, coyotes, and marmots. The area is also home to more than one hundred bird species, including golden eagle, sage grouse, prairie falcon, ravens, and hawks.

These trails can be popular in the summer, but you'll likely still have plenty of solitude as you continue toward Badlands Rock. You'll know you're getting close to the large out-cropping when you start to notice an increase in lava rock in the otherwise sandy path.

You'll find plenty of ancient juniper and lava formations in the Badlands.

After consistent views of gnarled juniper trees, wild sagebrush, and scattered wildflowers, you can't miss the rock; it's the only elevated thing in sight. This rough, igneous pressure ridge was created during the lava flow that formed the Badlands. When you reach the rock at 3 miles, circumnavigate it by following a narrow path around its base. Or scramble up the steep lava piles to the top for a nice view.

The rock piles are sharp and not necessarily steady, so keep your hands free just in case. It would also be wise to avoid attempting the scramble with young children or dogs. When you're ready, turn around at the rock and amble back through the desert the same way you came in.

EXTENDING YOUR TRIP

Consider returning to the trailhead via an alternate route that includes Flatiron Rock (Hike 46) by looping around on the Castle Trail. At Badlands Rock, turn onto the Castle Trail and go 1.1 miles to connect to Flatiron Rock Trail. Turn left and continue 1.8 miles until you reach a junction. Take the Homestead Trail to the left, which will lead you 2.1 miles back to the parking lot, for a loop total of 8 miles. Be aware that if you somehow miss your connection with the Homestead Trail, you'll end up at the Flatiron Trailhead instead—a few miles from your car.

48 Dry River Canyon

RATING/ DIFFICULTY	ROUNDTRIP	ELEV GAIN/ HIGH POINT	SEASON
****/3	4.8 miles	575 feet/ 3700 feet	Sept–Jan

Map: BLM Oregon Badlands Wilderness; **Contact:** BLM Prineville District; **Notes:** Closed Feb–Aug; **GPS:** N 43 56.25, W 121 01.04

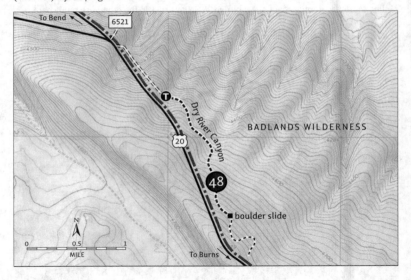

A fun little hole in the cliff walls within Dry River Canyon

This hike follows a now-dry ancient river that once cut through this canyon. The river flowed north from iced-over Lake Millican before emptying into the Crooked River. Today you can hike down into the gorgeous rocky canyon—well, at least for a few months of the year. The canyon closes annually from February usually through August to give breeding wildlife a chance to get off to a good start; check with the Bureau of Land Management. This stunning gorge features wildlife viewing opportunities, incredible rock walls, and intriguing topographical history—more than enough "wow" factors to make it well worth your while.

GETTING THERE

From Bend, drive east on US Highway 20 for 17 miles. Turn left at the Badlands Rock trailhead just past milepost 17. Stay to the right, toward the Oregon Department of Transportation storage area, and drive another 0.9 mile past the kiosk to the trailhead at the end of the road.

ON THE TRAIL

Start by walking south on the main road, keeping right at the first junction. This double-track road travels about 0.3 mile to a simple campsite at the mouth of the gorge, where it then narrows to a more primitive single-track trail along the canyon floor. Native American petroglyphs have been found in this area, but now the rocks are covered with more modern etchings. Respect the space and refrain from putting your own mark here.

If you look around, you'll notice mostly juniper and sagebrush around you. Strangely, you'll pass two large ponderosas that have somehow survived this arid landscape—the first at 0.9 mile and then another at 2.2 miles. As you admire the scenery, keep an eye out for wildlife in the sky, on the rocks, and on the ground. Falcons, sheep, mountain goats, and rattlesnakes all call this canyon home.

At 2.4 miles, the trail hits a wall at a large boulder slide. This is a good spot to turn back.

EXTENDING YOUR TRIP
You can continue by rock-hopping across the large boulders. After scrambling almost 100 yards, you'll connect to the remainder of the trail, which descends for another 100 yards or so. At the bottom of the canyon, you'll land on a much softer sandy trail that leads another 0.75 mile up the canyon. Admire the colorful lichen-covered walls and turn around to head back to the trailhead.

49 Horse Ridge via Sand Canyon

RATING/ DIFFICULTY	ROUNDTRIP	ELEV GAIN/ HIGH POINT	SEASON
***/4	7 miles	1200 feet/ 4885 feet	Year-round

Map: BLM Horse Ridge; **Contact:** BLM Prineville District; **GPS:** N 43 56.78, W 121 2.59

⭐ *Horse Ridge is located near the Badlands Wilderness, just across US Highway 20. While this prominent ridge is primarily a winter mountain-biking destination, there's no reason why you can't hike it. It's steep and sandy, so it will definitely get your legs*

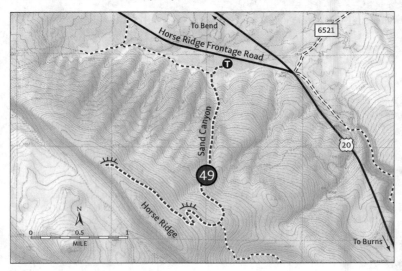

The trail is flat before reaching Sand Canyon.

burning. Luckily, the ridgetop is a great breezy place to eat a picnic and take in a few scenic views. While trail etiquette gives hikers the right-of-way over bikers, pedaling uphill in sand is more frustrating and demanding than walking in it. If a mountain biker is huffing and puffing behind you, do the nice thing and just step off the trail so the biker can maintain momentum. Hey, what goes around, comes around!

GETTING THERE

From Bend, drive east on US Highway 20 for 15 miles. Turn right onto Horse Ridge Frontage Road. Continue 0.7 mile to the new Bureau of Land Management Horse Ridge west trailhead on the side of the road.

ON THE TRAIL

From the trailhead, go right. This trail system is set apart from the Horse Ridge

145

Research Natural Area so as to improve wildlife habitat conditions. The trail starts out quite comfortably as it heads into the juniper desert. Savor this quick 0.25 mile of flat ground, because it's all uphill once you get to Sand Canyon. This is a fairly exposed route, so the climb is best tackled when it's not too hot out.

You'll reach a junction near 0.3 mile. There are so many little side trails that many junctions are unsigned. Head straight here, continuing to the Sand Canyon climb. There's no way around it; this is a tough ascent. For one, it's steep. You'll gain 1000 feet over the next 1.8 miles. Two, the sand is so punishing that your legs will want to scream with every step.

At 2.1 miles, you'll reach the top of the canyon. Turn right to head across the ridge. There are a few more ups and downs along this stretch, but they're hardly worth mentioning after your previous climb. You'll also pass several viewpoints, closing out with the best one at the trail's end at 3.5 miles. Enjoy lunch at the top of the ridge while admiring the surrounding views. A few little trails continue, but they're unreliable. Instead, turn back the way you came. The sand is easier on the way down!

50 Pine Mountain

RATING/ DIFFICULTY	ROUNDTRIP	ELEV GAIN/ HIGH POINT	SEASON
***/4	4 miles	1000 feet/ 6500 feet	May–Oct

Map: USGS Pine Mountain; **Contact:** Pine Mountain Observatory; **Notes:** Restroom at observatory; **GPS:** N 43 28.36, W 120 33.81

Pine Mountain Observatory's dome blends into the fog.

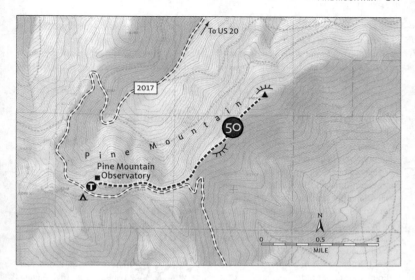

The same unobstructed views and clear Central Oregon skies that make Pine Mountain an excellent place for the University of Oregon's observatory create ideal conditions for a day hike. While the observatory near the hike's start is quite fun for kids, the overall trail to the summit may not be. The trail isn't very clear, so you can expect a fair amount of routefinding on your steep ascent to the summit. On foggy days, the ridge may be entirely invisible, so it's best not to attempt this trip in inclement weather. Mileage may vary depending on the particular route you choose along the way. Bring directional skills, warm clothing, your own water, and a pair of binoculars to zero in on views all the way across Central Oregon.

GETTING THERE

From Bend, drive US Highway 20 east for 26 miles. In 0.25 mile after passing the old Millican General Store at milepost 26, turn right toward Pine Mountain Observatory on County Road 2017. The road changes to gravel and turns right as the road becomes Forest Road 2017, winding and climbing 8 miles to the observatory. Park on the right side of the road near the campsites.

ON THE TRAIL

Cross FR 2017 and walk toward the observatory buildings on the opposite side. Walk through the marked "quiet zone" gate and continue toward the small hill just beyond the observatory domes. As you pass the large silver dome on the concrete pad, find the small path heading up the knoll.

This path is the closest thing to an established trail on the whole route, and it ends just up the hill from the observatory. Climb 0.1 mile to the windy hilltop, which is mostly empty except for a few wind-bent pines and a rocky wall to block the wind. The trail starts to peter out here, but find it again just past a smaller stone circle sitting among sagebrush. Descend about 0.25 mile to a forest road. Turn left and walk along the road for 0.6 mile. When the road suddenly turns right to go downhill near the 1-mile mark, go left, leaving the road and following the faded trail onto a saddle within an old-growth ponderosa forest.

In about 0.5 mile, you'll reach a craggy peak that is oft thought to be the Pine Mountain summit. It's not, but it does have excellent views. Scramble to the tip-top if you wish, or just head around its right side, descending again to another saddle at approximately 1.7 miles. This next 0.3-mile stretch to the top of Pine Mountain is your last climb. Once at the top, nothing more than a single pine tree and a small wooden summit marker stand in the way of the panoramic views.

Enjoy the scene before heading back the way you came, perhaps timing your trip to visit the observatory. It's open to visitors on Friday and Saturday nights in the summer. For a kid-friendly visit, arrive late in the day and explore the trail just long enough to see the changing sunset colors before heading back to the observatory for stargazing.

51 Tumulus Loop

RATING/ DIFFICULTY	LOOP	ELEV GAIN/ HIGH POINT	SEASON
**/2	4.5 miles	50 feet/ 3500 feet	Year-round

Map: BLM Oregon Badlands Wilderness; **Contact:** BLM Prineville District; **GPS:** N 44 2.82, W 121 01.92

The entire Badlands feels remote, but the Tumulus Trail is a little more so. The trailhead is farther

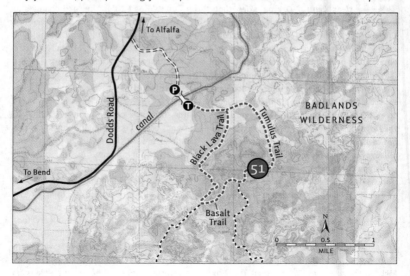

A stately old juniper in the Badlands Wilderness

from the highway than others in the area, so you'll have plenty of privacy. The Tumulus Trail is one of the longer official paths in the Badlands and extends far into the desert until it connects with the Dry River Trail. This hike adds a little variety with a loop that connects the Tumulus, Basalt, and Black Lava trails.

GETTING THERE

From Bend, drive east on US Highway 20 for 9 miles. Turn left on Dodds Road. At milepost 6, turn right onto a dirt road. Continue for 1 mile, staying right at the fork, to the parking area. Cross the footbridge to the trailhead on the other side of the canal.

ON THE TRAIL

From the trailhead, take off on the Tumulus Trail. You'll reach your first junction in just 0.5 mile. You can hike this loop either way, but head left to stay on the Tumulus Trail for the next 1.5 miles. The trail is named for the abundant tumuli in the area—one of the many results of the lava flows that occurred throughout the Badlands' history. Look for these miniature canyon cracks along the entire route.

At 2 miles, you'll start to loop back west by turning right on the Basalt Trail. The trail continues through wide-open old-growth juniper forests. These hardy trees are able to thrive in the ashy soil, which mostly consists of windblown leftovers from the long-ago Mount Mazama eruption. Junipers also require very little water, so they do quite well in this high-desert climate.

After 0.65 mile on the Basalt Trail, you'll reach a junction with the Black Lava Trail. Turn right for the final 1.35 miles back to the Tumulus trailhead. The entire Badlands area looks pretty similar, so try to keep your bearings. It's easy to get disoriented and turned around after taking side trails, but even the main intersections are occasionally unsigned. Come prepared with plenty of water and navigational skills.

Opposite: Alpine meadows and views of the Three Sisters at Camp Lake

sisters and mckenzie pass

US Highway 20 runs through downtown Sisters, a transportation corridor that links the town with Bend to the south and with highways running west over the Cascade passes to the valleys on the other side. Easy to get to, Sisters is also easy to get out of. This quaint town boasts some of the best views and best access to trails in the whole state, making daily escapes to the outdoors simply a part of the everyday lifestyle for both locals and visitors.

The Three Sisters Wilderness and its high peaks, lakes, rivers, and forests are just a few steps away. In season, you can also explore scenic McKenzie Pass off State Route 242—the entire highway is now on the National Register of Historic Places. The Oregon Department of Transportation closes this scenic road every winter, but when it opens back up in mid-June, your options for exploration nearly double. Even if you don't make it up SR 242 for hiking, it's worth the trip just for the drive.

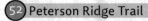

52 Peterson Ridge Trail

RATING/ DIFFICULTY	LOOP	ELEV GAIN/ HIGH POINT	SEASON
**/2	4.7 miles	200 feet/ 3400 feet	Year-round

Maps: Green Trails No. 590 Sisters, Sisters Trails Peterson Ridge Trail System; **Contact:** Deschutes National Forest, Sisters Ranger District, and Sisters Trail Alliance; **Notes:** Water and restrooms at Village Green Park; **GPS:** N 44 17.05, W 121 32.98

The Peterson Ridge Trail System is what happens when dedicated volunteers come together to preserve and grow an area for a whole community. Planned, constructed, and maintained by the Sisters Trail Alliance, this trail network includes over 20 miles of multiuse paths, just outside of Sisters. The beauty of Peterson Ridge is the "choose your own adventure" setup. It's a

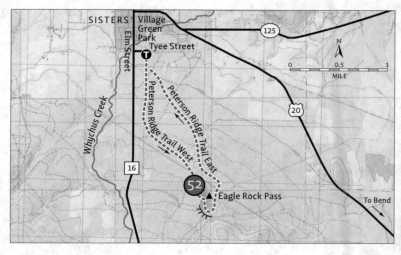

Peterson Ridge's brushy landscape

ladder-like system with a series of connections between two parallel trails. The route described here makes for a comfortable walk, but feel free to explore and create a loop of your own.

GETTING THERE

From US Highway 20 in Sisters, head south on Elm Street for 0.5 mile, and then turn left on Tyee Street. You'll find the small parking area on the right. If this lot is full, backtrack 0.4 mile along Elm Street and park at Village Green Park.

ON THE TRAIL

Start out on the main Peterson Ridge Trail (PRT). Each junction is signed with a number between 1 and 34, which coordinates with the trail-system map and makes it easy to

navigate. Starting at Junction 1, stay right to take the PRT West toward Junction 3.

The majority of the PRT is used by mountain bikers, but these reaches are popular with other users due to their proximity to town. The paths are mostly dirt single track, so the way is quite comfortable underfoot for all pedestrians: hikers, runners, or walkers. You'll see ponderosa pine, lodgepole pine, manzanita, and yellow arrowleaf balsamroot just off the path throughout this entire hike. Continue on the mostly flat trail, staying right past Junctions 3, 5, 7, 9, and 11.

At 1.9 miles, shortly after Junction 11, stay left to follow the track up a quick but steep ascent of Eagle Rock Pass. Reach the top of the rocky butte at 2.2 miles. Stop here to admire views of the Cascades—the Three Sisters look enormous from this close! Head down from the rocky pass and continue for 0.4 mile, staying left at Junction 14.

From here, you'll begin your loop back, this time taking the PRT East. This trail runs parallel to the one you came in on for another 1.8 miles. Make sure to stay right at Junctions 12, 10, 8, 6, and 4. At 4.4 miles, you'll reach Junction 2, where you'll stay left to close the loop and walk the final 0.3 mile back to the Tyee Street trailhead for 4.7 miles roundtrip. If you parked at Village Green Park instead, your total will be closer to 5.5 miles.

53 Logjam Falls

RATING/ DIFFICULTY	ROUNDTRIP	ELEV GAIN/ HIGH POINT	SEASON
***/3	3.5 miles	550 feet/ 3800 feet	Year-round

Map: Green Trails No. 590 Sisters; **Contact:** Deschutes National Forest, Sisters Ranger District; **GPS:** N 44 14.11, W 121 33.72

❌ ⭐ *How can a trail be saved and endangered at the same time? The Whychus Creek area has seen many altera-* *tions over the past few years. Some have been negative, such as when vandals disturbed scenic riparian areas by displacing several large boulders. These actions are certainly unfortunate, but they pale in comparison to the positive ones. The Deschutes Land Trust, the Forest Service, local Bureau of Land Management, and hardworking volunteers are dedicated to keeping this area beautiful and usable. Between land being added to the Whychus Canyon Preserve, dams being removed for fish migration, and new trails being added, the area is flourishing. This hike follows one of the newer trails to Logjam Falls—a pretty little waterfall nestled not far up the creek.*

GETTING THERE
From US Highway 20 in Sisters, head south on Elm Street, which turns into Three Creeks Road/Forest Road 16. Take this road for 4.2 paved miles from Sisters, and turn right into a small trailhead area marked with a brown hiker sign.

ON THE TRAIL
From the parking area, walk around the locked green gate blocking the service road.

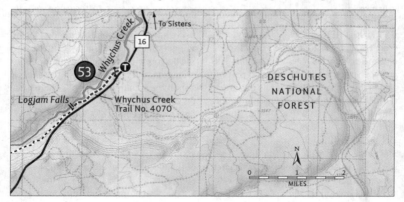

A scenic little spot along Whychus Creek

Ignore the gravel drive and instead turn right onto Whychus Creek Trail No. 4070. The flawless sign speaks to how new this trail is. Speaking of which, if you're using an old map, there are a few important things to note. Because this trail is relatively new, it probably won't be on the trusty old map that you've had in your backpack forever. Second, Whychus Creek was called Squaw Creek up until 2006, so check for that too.

The trail is steep and rocky at the start, descending through happy ponderosa pine and manzanita forest on the way to the river. Within just 0.1 mile, you'll reach Whychus Creek and turn left to follow it upstream, passing an old irrigation ditch. While the creek is clear and shallow here, it's still quite swift. The banks are lined with rocky outcroppings, and several sections are covered with bright green moss.

There's a lot to admire on this trail. Because it's for foot traffic only, and with a small parking lot, hopefully you'll have the solitude to really enjoy it. At 1 mile, you'll see the South Sister poking its head up behind the creek. This spot has a neat little rock wall—an example of yet another geologic formation to thank the nearby Three Sisters volcanoes for. From here, you'll leave the river's scenic banks and begin ascending, using a few rugged steps to make your way past a lava flow.

Keep climbing, eventually leveling out onto a flatter manzanita plateau. Look for wildflowers up here, such as arrowleaf balsamroot and a few other varieties depending on the time of year. At 1.5 miles, you'll notice that the trail gets significantly more challenging. Rough switchbacks lead just underneath the bottom of a rugged rockslide for a short but steep descent back down to the river.

Turn left to walk upstream. You'll reach Logjam Falls at 1.75 miles, and it's certainly aptly named. Big bundles of downed trees lie mangled in the middle of the river, giving the water something to rush over. Over time, I would expect this waterfall to change. Old logs will dislodge, and new ones will get jammed in, altering the course of the creek and changing the dynamic of the waterfall. Either way, it's a pretty little spot. The big rock overlooking the gorge is a nice place to take in the view. Turn back when you're ready.

EXTENDING YOUR TRIP

To keep exploring the wild and scenic Whychus Creek, continue on for another mile. You'll meet the junction with the Metolius Windigo Trail at 2.75 miles. In another 0.25 mile, you'll arrive at the northern trailhead at the end of FR 880. Return the way you came.

54 Whychus Creek Falls

RATING/ DIFFICULTY	ROUNDTRIP	ELEV GAIN/ HIGH POINT	SEASON
****/3	6 miles	700 feet/ 5350 feet	Late June–Oct

Maps: Green Trails No. 590 Sisters, Geo-Graphics Three Sisters Wilderness; **Contact:** Deschutes National Forest, Sisters Ranger District; **Notes:** Free self-issue wilderness permit Memorial Day–Oct 31; **GPS:** N 44 10.64, W 121 40.01

With the exception of minor reroutes to prevent erosion, most trails remain generally the same over time. Not this one. If you're using an outdated guidebook or map to get to the Whychus Creek Falls trailhead, you'll be very confused. Not only have the names of the river and waterfall changed within the last ten years, but the trail has nearly doubled in length due to road closures after the 2012 Pole Creek Fire. The good news is that the longer length should give you a little more solitude on your outing while also protecting this gorgeous area from overuse. Visit these popular falls for an excellent day hike just outside of Sisters. As postfire rehabilitation progresses, expect additional changes to this trail. Please obey all posted changes and closures.

GETTING THERE

From US Highway 20 in Sisters, head south on Elm Street, which turns into Three Creeks Road/Forest Road 16. Take this road for 7 miles from Sisters and turn right for Whychus Creek on gravel FR 1514. After 3 miles, the road forks. Stay right for another 2 miles, and then turn left on FR 600. Proceed another 1 mile to where the road is blocked.

ON THE TRAIL

Walk around the road blockage to start down the trail. The aftermath of the Pole Creek Fire necessitated closing a stretch of the road to vehicles for safety and trail restoration, so nowadays you have to walk 1.4 miles to the old trailhead. From the road, you'll see damage from the fire. While the burnt trees are eerie, they do allow for a better view of the creek than before, which shines like a literal silver lining despite the somewhat grim circumstances.

Now at the old trailhead, head down the original trail toward Chush Falls. Interestingly enough, there's still a healthy mixed conifer forest here. The path is flat and largely nontechnical, but you will cross two small creek offshoots along the way. You'll reach Chush Falls at 2.5 miles. Beginners and families with kids should view the waterfall from the safety of the overlook, while the

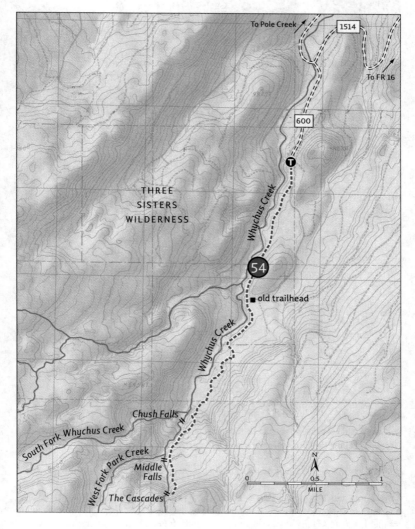

more adventurous may choose to wander to the base of the falls.

To visit the other falls, walk around the "Trail End" sign and continue on the unofficial but well-established user path as it travels upriver. You'll soon pass Middle Falls.

Once you get past the burn, you enter a healthy forest.

While pretty, these falls are probably the least interesting of the three, so just keep on. The trail gets a big snaggly here, so you may have to duck under branches and hunt for the trail a bit. As long as you stick to the most established paths and keep the river within earshot, you'll be good to go.

About 0.5 mile from the Chush Falls overlook, you'll reach the upper falls, otherwise known as the Cascades. This waterfall is higher, more forceful, and more beautiful than its lower brothers. A lunch in this scenic spot is a nice way to cap off your hike before you head back.

55 Park Meadow

RATING/ DIFFICULTY	ROUNDTRIP	ELEV GAIN/ HIGH POINT	SEASON
***/4	10 miles	700 feet/ 6100 feet	July–Oct

Maps: Green Trails No. 622 Broken Top, No. 621 Three Sisters; **Contact:** Deschutes National Forest, Sisters Ranger District; **Notes:** NW Forest Pass or $5 day-use fee. Free self-issue wilderness permit Memorial Day–Oct 31. Access road closed in winter. Privy at trailhead; **GPS:** N 44 7.05, W 121 37.73

  Hit hard by the 2012 Pole Creek Fire, the Park Meadow Trail is a little dull for the first couple of miles. Okay, it's very dull. There's not a lot of life left amid the burn, but once you reach Park Meadow, it's all worth it. Up here, lush fields, sparkling ponds, and stunning mountain views await. If you time your hike with wildflower season, you'll even be greeted with colorful blooms dotting the meadow and lining the creek's banks.

GETTING THERE

From US Highway 20 in Sisters, head south on Elm Street, which turns into Three Creeks Road/Forest Road 16. Take this road for 14 paved miles from Sisters and then another 0.3 mile on gravel before turning into the trailhead area on the left.

ON THE TRAIL

Follow the trailhead signs for Park Meadow and immediately enter the Pole Creek burn area. The Park Meadow Trail gives you an up-close view of the fire damage as it leads through a charred and mostly lifeless forest. The early segments of the trail follow a dusty snowmobile route that's marked by blue and yellow diamonds on the burnt trees. The lack of tree cover allows for a few peekaboo views of the mountains, the first of which you'll see at 0.5 mile.

At 0.9 mile, you'll reach a strange pocket of trees that wasn't entirely destroyed by fire before you head back into total destruction. Fences have closed off particular areas that need to be restored, which is almost laughable since the entire area desperately needs

This single purple lupine stands out in the dead forest.

help. There's really no reason to wander off the trail here anyway. It's easy to get lost in the burn, and the trees will likely continue to topple over for the next few years.

At 1.2 miles, the trail narrows as it leaves the snowmobile route in favor of hiking paths. Despite the desolation, the scorched remains are beautiful in a solemn kind of way, like an old cemetery on a gray, rainy day. Soon enough, you'll start to see a few signs of life. At 2.1 miles, you'll cross a tiny dribble of a creek that has an increasing number of green patches lining its perimeter. Follow signs straight ahead toward Park Meadow, entering into the Three Sisters Wilderness at 2.3 miles and reaching the swiftly flowing Snow Creek.

In another 1.75 miles, you'll cross Why-chus Creek. Continue through the burn until

4 miles, when you'll reach the edge of the burn area and head into a green forest—a welcome change. Hike for another mile on the dusty trail and finally reach Park Meadow.

If this spot was pretty before the fire, it looks even more stunning and vibrant now that you've witnessed what could have been had the blaze made its way up here. Sitting underneath Broken Top, Park Meadow is simply gorgeous. If you're looking for that perfect photo of South Sister with its re-flection in the water, you can find it at the small tarn on your left near the edge of the meadow. Since the hike in wasn't exactly pretty, make up for it by spending some extra time here. Bring a lunch, plop down near the creek, and stay awhile before heading back.

56 Little Three Creek Lake

RATING/ DIFFICULTY	ROUNDTRIP	ELEV GAIN/ HIGH POINT	SEASON
***/2	1.3 miles	50 feet/ 6790 feet	July–Oct

Maps: Green Trails No. 622 Broken Top, No. 621 Three Sisters; **Contact:** Deschutes National Forest, Sisters Ranger District; **Notes:** Access road closed in winter. Privy at campground; **GPS:** N 44 6.05, W 121 37.85

It's remarkable that this area didn't get burned by recent fires. The Pole Creek burn stopped just short of the lake area, allowing the beautiful habitat to remain intact. This itsy alpine lake sits

underneath spectacular Tam McArthur Rim and is hidden among the trees not far from the larger and more accessible Three Creek Lake. Hang out at the big lake for the recreation, but visit the little one for quiet time.

GETTING THERE

From US Highway 20 in Sisters, turn south on Elm Street, which turns into Three Creeks Road/Forest Road 16. Follow the road for 14 paved miles from Sisters, and then continue about 1.5 miles on gravel to Three Creek Lake. Turn right at the Driftwood Campground and drive 0.5 mile on the campground road, all the way to where it ends at the back edge of the campground. Parking is limited at this unofficial trailhead.

Quiet Little Three Creek Lake

ON THE TRAIL

While it's not the *official* trailhead, Driftwood Campground's backyard is a great place to begin your hike. Start with a brief and soft uphill stretch from the parking loop. Don't worry—this is the steepest part of the hike. The rest of the trail is seriously nonthreatening, with nothing more than a few gentle ups and downs.

The dusty trail passes through fir, hemlock, and lodgepole pine, as well as a scattering of wildflowers. At around 0.5 mile, you'll approach a small, shallow, unnamed lake. This diminutive pond is pretty, but it's not your final destination. Keep heading northwest along the trail for another 0.1 mile, and you'll see the chilly green lake you came here for.

Little Three Creek Lake is indeed little, but that doesn't take away from its beauty.

Tam McArthur's colorful walls make a lovely backdrop, stealing so much attention that you hardly notice the evidence of forest fire to your right. Grassy areas slope gently down to the shoreline, and old logs stand tall like ship masts in the water. It's a charming and gorgeous spot.

Walk along the water's edge a bit farther to curve around the bend of the lake. At 0.6 mile, you'll see a quiet, shady spot with scattered rocks and logs to sit on, right along the shoreline. This is a good place to stop and skip a few rocks in the gentle water before turning back.

Should you find yourself in the right place at the right time, you might get to witness the annual toad metamorphosis—something kids find especially fascinating. Watch your step for teensy toads as they morph from tadpoles, grow legs, and hop into the

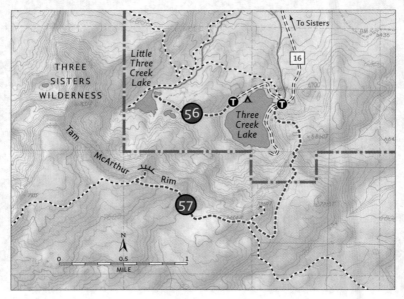

forest. While the timing depends on weather and snowpack, the show typically occurs in late summer.

EXTENDING YOUR TRIP

If you want to make this hike a bit longer, start from the official trailhead. Instead of driving to the end of the campground road, park at the trailhead on the right, *before* reaching the campground. This trailhead is located just a short distance down the Driftwood Campground Road, across from the Tam McArthur trailhead. This route brings you to the lake from the other end, for a 3.5-mile roundtrip hike.

57 Tam McArthur Rim

RATING/ DIFFICULTY	ROUNDTRIP	ELEV GAIN/ HIGH POINT	SEASON
*****/4	5.2 miles	1400 feet/ 7730 feet	Late July–Oct

Maps: Green Trails No. 622 Broken Top, No. 621 Three Sisters; **Contact:** Deschutes National Forest, Sisters Ranger District; **Notes:** Free self-issue wilderness permit Memorial Day–Oct 31. Access road closed in winter. Privy at trailhead; **GPS:** N 44 6.05, W 121 37.34

My oh my. Tam McArthur's enthralling rim demands your attention. Sitting high above the Three Creeks basin, the face-to-face view of the 500-foot cliffs would be stunning enough on its own, but there's more. If you can handle the steep climb to the top of the ridge, you'll be rewarded with some of the best views in the entire state. Nearly all of Oregon's Cascades are visible, and you'll have bird's-eye views of the lakes below as well. Thankfully, the Tam McArthur hike isn't very *long, so you'll only suffer a little bit before topping out on the windswept rim. Steep terrain can be a real ankle breaker going down too, so don't rush on the way back.*

GETTING THERE

From US Highway 20 in Sisters, turn south on Elm Street, which turns into Three Creeks Road/Forest Road 16. Follow the road for 14 paved miles from Sisters, and then continue about 1.5 miles on gravel to Three Creek Lake. The trailhead and parking area are on the left side of the road.

ON THE TRAIL

The trail leaves the road and enters the forest, climbing right from the get-go. Hey, when you have 1400 vertical feet to gain in just 2.6 miles, you can't waste any time. Within 0.5 mile, you'll reach the first set of switchbacks. You'll pass through several more switchbacks over this first mile, snagging a few peekaboo views of the Three Creek lakes below.

Next, the trail traverses a plateau. This flatter surface is a welcome change after that big ascent! Twisted whitebark pines and a few wildflowers dot the otherwise barren landscape. Head across the pumice fields toward the rocky overhang jutting out from the ridge. At 2.1 miles, you'll approach the final 0.5-mile climb to the signed end of the trail. Turn right at an unmarked fork and take the fairly well-worn path toward the cliff edge and a stunning viewpoint.

It's hard to catch your breath when the view just takes it away! From here you can see a never-ending spine of Cascades: Broken Top, South Sister, Middle Sister, North Sister, Mount Bachelor, Mount Washington, Three Fingered Jack, Mount Jefferson, Mount Hood, and Mount Adams.

Tam McArthur Rim stands tall behind Three Creek Lake.

Bring binoculars and look for the region's lakes and rivers, too. Paths continuing past this point are not officially maintained, so follow them at your own risk. Retrace your steps down when you're ready.

58 Camp Lake

RATING/ DIFFICULTY	ROUNDTRIP	ELEV GAIN/ HIGH POINT	SEASON
*****/5	13.5 miles	2200 feet/ 6980 feet	July–Oct

Maps: Green Trails No. 622 Broken Top, No. 621 Three Sisters; **Contact:** Deschutes National Forest, Sisters Ranger District; **Notes:** NW Forest Pass or $5 day-use fee. Free self-issue wilderness permit Memorial Day–Oct 31. Access road closed in winter. Privy at trailhead; **GPS:** N 44 11.25, W 121 41.99

The Camp Lake basin is one of the most gorgeous scenes in all of Central Oregon. While the Pole Creek Fire in 2012 marred much of the lower forests, the higher alpine areas were unaffected. Camp Lake is one of several high-altitude watering holes that make up Chambers Lakes. It sits directly underneath the South and Middle Sisters, providing incredible views of both peaks. Camp Lake is a great overnight spot, as its name implies. But it's also a great destination for a long day hike, so pack a lunch and make it an all-day excursion.

GETTING THERE
From Sisters, go west on State Route 242 for 1.5 miles. After the high school, turn left on Forest Road 15 and drive 5.6 miles. The road then turns into FR 1524; proceed for another 5.3 miles to the trailhead.

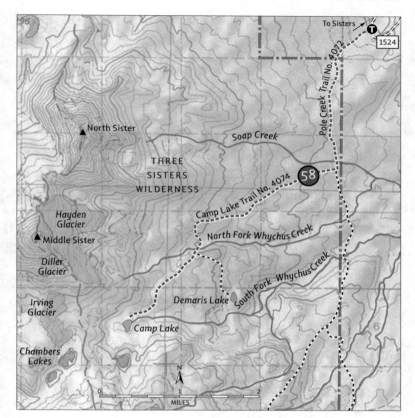

ON THE TRAIL

Start by heading south on Pole Creek Trail No. 4072. You'll bump into the wilderness permit kiosk quite quickly, so fill out the form and continue on your way. The trail is wide and sandy here, often frequented by horse travelers. Since it's a long hike, start early in the day to limit your encounters with large equine groups, as well as to keep the sun and mosquitoes off your back.

This first portion of the hike is a bit dreary. The Pole Creek Fire started right here, so be prepared for almost complete destruction. Luckily, this doesn't last *too* long. The trail ascends gradually through the burn and reaches a junction with the Green Lakes Trail at 1.4 miles. Stay to the left.

While you're not out of the burn just yet, the beauty around you gradually increases. The sparse forest affords a nice little view of the North Sister—just a preview of what's to come. Descend a bit before reaching the

Hikers at the summit of Middle Sister, just above Camp Lake

next junction at 2 miles, near Soap Creek. Cross the rocky stream and turn right on Camp Lake Trail No. 4074.

The slow and steady ascent resumes here, winding out of the burn and into sparse forest. You'll bump into two outflow forks from Whychus Creek. Cross the first just before the 4-mile mark and the second 0.5 mile later. When you cross to the other side, you'll reach an intersection with the Demaris Lake Trail. Stay right to continue toward Camp Lake.

Over the next few miles, you'll notice that the terrain is starting to change significantly. The burn has long since been left behind, and now you're starting to see rocky meadows, wildflowers, fields of pumice, and outstanding views of the Cascades that surround you. As you approach the lake area

at 6.3 miles, you'll see a sign indicating that fires are not allowed. The lake is less than 0.5 mile up the trail.

Camp Lake's charming blue waters sit right between the South and Middle Sisters. Lush meadows stretch out on all sides toward the sandy moraine and lingering glaciers above. You're at just under 7000 feet here, so there's very little shelter from the wind. The weather-bent pines around the lake are perfect evidence of that!

Many visitors set up camp here in hopes of summiting Middle Sister the next day. Others fill up their water bottles and forge on without an overnight. Both are great options, but bringing a lunch and just enjoying the view from here is equally pleasant. Head back the way you came when you're ready.

EXTENDING YOUR TRIP

Feel like summiting that big Middle Sister? Good call. From the lake, follow the trail as best as you can. There are several different routes to the top, and the best ones depend on snowpack. No matter where you go, you'll cross a few glaciers. Be careful up here, as crevasses can be hidden until late summer. Play it safe by roping up and proceeding cautiously. After topping out above the glaciers, the "trail" turns into a steep ascent over big piles of lava rock. You'll encounter everything from big boulders to loose, slippery shale. The going is slow, but each step is worth it if getting to the top is what you're here for. The total mileage depends on what route you take across the glaciers, but you should plan on an 18-mile day with upward of 5000 feet of elevation gain.

59 Black Crater

RATING/ DIFFICULTY	ROUNDTRIP	ELEV GAIN/ HIGH POINT	SEASON
****/4	7.5 miles	2540 feet/ 7250 feet	July– early Nov

Maps: Green Trails No. 622 Broken Top, No. 590 Sisters; **Contact:** Deschutes National Forest, Sisters Ranger District; **Notes:** Free self-issue wilderness permit Memorial Day– Oct 31. Access road closed in winter; **GPS:** N 44 17.08, W 121 45.96

Some may say to avoid Black Crater, as the near constant climbing and hot exposed areas are brutal in the summer. Personally, I don't mind a sweaty slog, since it calorically pays for a milkshake

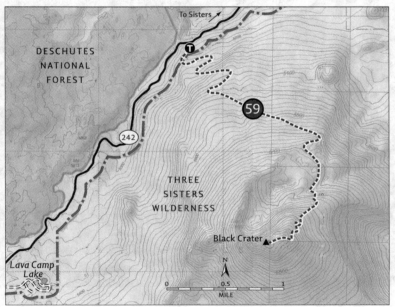

or beer when you get back to Sisters. At least half of the fun of hiking is the exercise. Granted, you can definitely get similar views for less work, but if you're looking for a workout, Black Crater is for you. The trail is steep, but it's mostly soft and easy to follow. Kind people who have previously hit the trail have left several hiking sticks at the trailhead for the rest of us. Grab one of these tossed-aside staffs for a little extra stability on the scree fields near the summit.

GETTING THERE

From Sisters, go west on State Route 242 for about 14 miles. Turn left into the Black Crater parking area, marked by a hiker symbol, between mileposts 80 and 81.

ON THE TRAIL

There's no warm-up on this trail. After leaving the parking lot, the Black Crater Trail begins to climb almost immediately. Fortunately, this portion of the forest is typically

You encounter a lava rock slope just a quarter mile up the trail.

chillier than the rest of the trail, as it sits in the shadow of the crater and rarely sees any sun. If you're hiking early in the season, that also means this section may have a bit of snow, even if the rest of the hike has thawed. Continue on the trail and forge ahead into the mossy woods.

At 0.2 mile, the trail skirts underneath a rocky slope on the right. Just after this, around 0.25 mile, take a glance to your left to check out a nice little overlook with views of Mount Washington and a lot of lava from the Belknap Flow. Keep climbing steadily through diverse forests filled with pine, fir, spruce, and hemlock.

Near 2 miles, the trail flattens out a bit, giving you a chance to catch your breath and peer through thinned-out trees for a couple of miniature viewpoints. The trail reaches the top of the ridge and then crosses through a glacier-carved valley with a colorful array of late-summer wildflowers, including the two signature Three Sisters Wilderness blooms: purple lupine and bright red Indian paintbrush.

The exposed sections of volcanic scree that you approach next aren't much fun, especially with the climb you have coming up shortly. With the valley now on your right and a big cirque on your left, the trail travels straight up the crater. You'll have a bit of help from some swervy switchbacks, but you'll still feel the climb. With just under a mile to go, you'll gain another 700 feet.

Finally, at 3.75 miles, reach the small summit ridge and the twisted whitebark pines that have, over time, adapted to the violent winter winds. Spin around and take in the 360-degree views. You'll catch the typical Central Oregon cast—the Three Sisters—as well as front-and-center views of Mount Washington. On clear days, you may even be

able to see all the way north to Mount Hood. This is one of the best spots for viewing the expanse of lava from the Belknap Flow.

Like many old fire-watch locations in the area, the lookout tower is long gone. If, however, you're desperate to get just a bit higher, use your hands to scramble up the small craggy pinnacle at the summit. This extra push is definitely not a necessity; the views are awesome without it. You'll also notice that the trail continues a bit farther, but don't be tempted to follow it. It's a flighty and unmaintained path that frequently disappears or leads you in the wrong direction, which makes it a very unreliable way to get back down. Instead, make it an out-and-back hike by heading down the same way you came.

60 Matthieu Lakes

RATING/ DIFFICULTY	LOOP	ELEV GAIN/ HIGH POINT	SEASON
****/3	6 miles	800 feet/ 6040 feet	July–Oct

Maps: Green Trails No. 622 Broken Top, No. 590 Sisters; **Contact:** Deschutes National Forest, Sisters Ranger District; **Notes:** Free self-issue wilderness permit Memorial Day–Oct 31. Access road closed in winter; **GPS:** N 44 15.64, W 121 47.27

The Matthieu Lakes loop is one of the most popular routes at McKenzie Pass, and for good reason. Two stunning lakes with completely different scenery sit just a few miles from the trailhead, making for an easy day hike with a great payoff. The soft trail is perfect for dogs, as are the multiple splashing opportunities. The trail even passes a few historical and cultural

A perfect little pinecone from Matthieu Lakes' mixed conifer forests

landmarks, including the Pacific Crest Trail, the old Oregon Skyline Trail, and Scott Pass. Although a few parts are steeper than the total elevation gain would suggest, this hike is a mostly moderate excursion. There's no excuse to stay at home!

Many an Oregonian has butchered the pronunciation of this hike's name. Close to Matthew, but not quite, the trail and lakes were named after Francis Xavier Matthieu—a French pioneer who helped found the Oregon Territory back in the mid-1800s. The lakes were named for him in 1924, just five years after his death. If you want to honor his memory, work on your French accent. When you say Matthieu correctly, you'll drop the h and sound a bit like you're sneezing.

GETTING THERE

From Sisters, go west on State Route 242 for 14.5 miles. Just past milepost 78, turn left for Lava Camp Lake and the Pacific Crest Trail. Drive about 0.25 mile on the gravel road and turn right into the parking area.

ON THE TRAIL

Start by taking Lava Camp Lake Trail No. 4060 to the right. It's a soft, beaten-down path, scattered with pine needles. As you approach a wall of lava rock within the first 0.25 mile, you'll meet a junction with the Pacific Crest Trail (PCT). Turn left to go south on the PCT, where you'll begin a slow, moderate climb. There are other ways to access this portion of the trail, such as

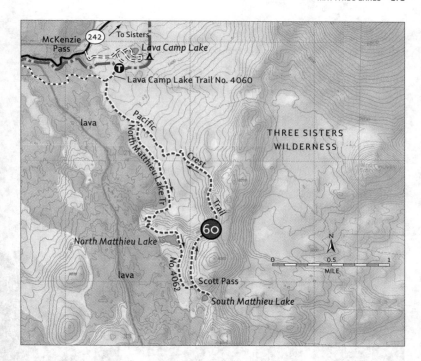

coming in on the PCT entrance near Dee Wright Observatory (see Appendix I), but the hot lava rock via that approach isn't very paw-friendly.

After 0.7 mile on the PCT, you'll reach another junction and the beginning of the loop portion of this hike. Stay to the right on the fork for North Matthieu Lake Trail No. 4062. The path hugs the edge of the large lava flow field and climbs past a few little ponds. With both wildflowers and huckleberries scattered about, it's a very pleasant forest.

In 1.3 miles, after viewing it from above, you'll reach North Matthieu Lake's thickly treed shore at 2.3 miles. Bright blue dragon-flies zoom about, matching the color of the sparkling waters. The lake is stocked every other year with trout, and it also has a charming little island. An unofficial but fairly established trail leads around the perimeter, but continue on the main trail to head to South Matthieu Lake.

This is the steepest portion of the hike. Switchbacks ease the 0.7-mile climb, but you'll probably be huffing a bit. This is actually a section of the old Oregon Skyline Trail—the precursor to the PCT. After making your way through mixed conifer forest, you'll pop out onto a rocky crest with Cascade views. The trail then intersects with the PCT again.

This spot is of particular historical interest. You're at the saddle of Scott Pass, which was one of the original wagon routes over the Cascade crest. Turn right—South Matthieu Lake is just around the bend. The lake is smaller and more exposed than its northern cousin, but its views are even more beautiful. North Sister looms beyond the water. Enjoy a swim in the cold lake with weary thru-hikers and day trippers alike.

The return side of the loop is a quick and easy descent, but it's not boring. You'll still have Cascade views and intriguing volcanic rock to keep you entertained. Turn around to double back on the PCT to your last junction, and then take the right fork to stay on the PCT for 2.1 miles to the next junction. Another 0.7 mile on the PCT will bring you to the junction with the Lava Camp Lake Trail. Turn right for the final 0.25 mile to the trailhead.

61 Little Belknap Crater

RATING/ DIFFICULTY	ROUNDTRIP	ELEV GAIN/ HIGH POINT	SEASON
***/4	5.3 miles	1100 feet/ 6305 feet	July– early Nov

Maps: Green Trails No. 589 Three Fingered Jack, No. 590 Sisters; **Contact:** Willamette National Forest, McKenzie Ranger District; **Notes:** Free self-issue wilderness permit Memorial Day–Oct 31. Access road closed in winter; **GPS:** N 44 15.62, W 121 48.57

Pass this gnarly stump on the way into the lava.

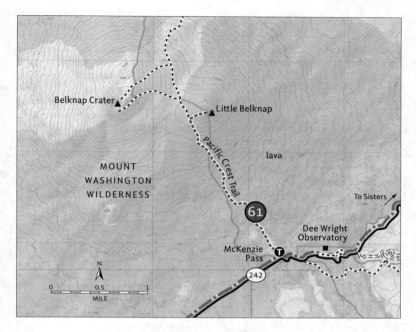

The trail to Little Belknap will have you feeling like you're walking on the surface of the moon. Just barely within the Mount Washington Wilderness, you'll walk a portion of the Pacific Crest Trail as it stretches from McKenzie Pass north toward Santiam Pass before branching off to the crater. The trail takes you through the brutal lava flow to the summit of Little Belknap and panoramic views. The barren rock is sharp underfoot, so best to leave the pups at home for this one. Properly outfit your own feet, too.

GETTING THERE

From Sisters, go west on State Route 242 for just over 15 miles, about 0.5 mile past Dee Wright Observatory. Turn right for the Pacific Crest Trail trailhead.

ON THE TRAIL

The trail starts out by heading north on the Pacific Crest Trail (PCT), winding through a comfortable and shady forest with plenty of ferns providing ground cover. Enjoy the soft path, because it won't last for long. After just 0.35 mile, you'll cross a section of lava that's 100 yards or so—merely a sample of what's to come. You can see Dee Wright Observatory from here. Back on the dirt, the trail follows the edge of a small island within the lava. This knoll is one of two little mounds that were elevated enough to avoid the fiery flow. After a little over 0.25 mile, say good-bye to the soft earth and step back onto the rough lava rock at 0.75 mile.

While this hike can be hot and unforgiving, given the lack of shelter and rough terrain underfoot, it's really quite beautiful. Directly in front of you, you'll see both Belknap Crater and Little Belknap, as well as Mount Washington, Three Fingered Jack, and Mount Jefferson. Turn around and you'll catch glimpses of North and Middle Sisters. Surrounding all, of course, is an endless sea of black rock.

All this lava flowed directly from Belknap Crater and Little Belknap a few thousand years ago, clearing everything in its path and creating today's lunar landscape. With the exception of a few trees struggling to survive in the unforgiving habitat, it's rocky all around.

At just under 2.5 miles, you'll reach a junction and a signed side trail to Little Belknap. The PCT continues on toward Santiam Pass, but you'll take a right on the Little Belknap Trail instead. Along this 0.25-mile stretch to the summit, you'll pass by several open lava tubes. The horizontal tunnels are fun to explore, but keep kids and pets away from the vertical ones. Some have 30-foot drops. Either way, flashlights come in handy for studying these unique lava caves. Notice how cold air flows out of these tubes, even in the summer heat.

The path is generally easy, but the final scramble to the top does get a bit steep, so you'll want your hands free for the ascent. Once you reach the 6305-foot summit, you'll be greeted with 360-degree views of the Cascades and the expansive lava flow. A small wind shelter forms a semicircle around a bench, giving you the perfect excuse to pack a lunch and enjoy some time at the top.

EXTENDING YOUR TRIP

Continue on the PCT to head to the (Big) Belknap Crater summit, and look into the old volcano's gaping cavity. Past the Little Belknap junction, you'll enter the forest within 0.25 mile—a welcome change from the painful lava rock. Over the next 0.25 mile, you'll see several unmarked side trails that lead through the trees and bushwhack to the top of the crater. The first trails lead to the steeper southern and eastern slopes. The later routes take you to the northern slopes, which are a bit easier to climb. Depending on which route you take, this off-trail extension adds about 2 miles roundtrip.

62 Hand Lake Shelter

RATING/ DIFFICULTY	ROUNDTRIP	ELEV GAIN/ HIGH POINT	SEASON
***/1	1 mile	100 feet/ 4800 feet	July–Oct

Maps: Green Trails No. 589 Three Fingered Jack, No. 621 Three Sisters; **Contact:** Willamette National Forest, McKenzie Ranger District; **Notes:** Free self-issue wilderness permit Memorial Day–Oct 31. Access road closed in winter; **GPS:** N 44 13.47, W 121 52.32

There are so many big-name hikes off McKenzie Pass that it's easy to miss this one. In fact, it was a few years before I even knew it was here! The trailhead is a nondescript lot on the opposite side of the road from the trail. If they had marked the trailhead with a photo of the view from Hand Lake instead of a simple brown hiker symbol, I assure you this short hike would be a lot more crowded.

GETTING THERE

From Sisters, take State Route 242 west for 19 miles. Between mileposts 72 and 73, look for the brown hiker symbol at the gravel

You can find various pine tree species on this trail.

pullout on the left side of the road. After parking, look both ways and cross the highway to the trailhead.

ON THE TRAIL

Start out on the super easy Hand Lake Trail. While the Three Sisters Wilderness borders the trail, lake, and shelter on each side, this route sits in a strange little peninsula of the southernmost tip of the Mount Washington Wilderness. This hike is also just on the cusp

of the lusher valleys on the west side of McKenzie Pass. The abundance of lava beds and stunning Cascade views, however, make this hike all Central Oregon.

After the trail leads through dense hemlock and lodgepole pine a short distance, you'll come out of the trees and see the Hand Lake Shelter. Walk directly up to the shelter, reaching it at 0.5 mile. This old three-sided cabin overlooks a pristine meadow with a humble display of wildflowers, including lupine and

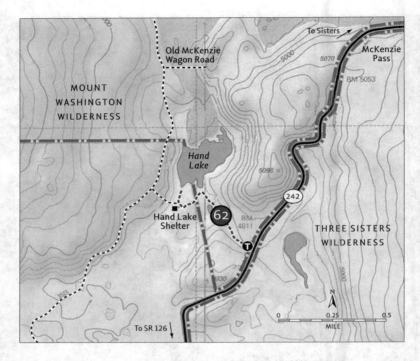

aster. A short side trail leads to the lake and a stunning view of Mount Washington.

A picnic at the beach makes this quick outing feel more like a day trip. When you're ready, retrace your steps back to your car. You'll still have plenty of time to explore the rest of McKenzie Pass.

EXTENDING YOUR TRIP

If historical sites are your thing, continue on the trail past the shelter to visit the Old McKenzie Wagon Road. At the junction, turn right toward Robinson Lake and continue another 0.6 mile to the faint wagon road crossing the lava on the right.

Opposite: Three Fingered Jack behind the 1923 cupola lookout

mount jefferson
and santiam pass

It seems like every region in Central Oregon has had to deal with fires recently, and the big ones have a long-lasting impact. When the B&B Fire swept through the Mount Jefferson Wilderness in 2003, it destroyed much of the area's forests. But today the once barren landscape is coming back in a beautiful way. Charred trees certainly remain, but bright green new growth is beginning to eclipse the old burn.

The hikes in this area are characterized by their stunning views of Three Fingered Jack and Mount Washington, gorgeous wildflowers, and the mesmerizing Metolius River. There are plenty of gorgeous lakes to see, and many have far less foot traffic than the ones just east of here in the Three Sisters Wilderness. Stop for a quick hike on your way over Santiam Pass, or make a dedicated visit another time—you won't regret it.

63 Black Butte

RATING/ DIFFICULTY	ROUNDTRIP	ELEV GAIN/ HIGH POINT	SEASON
****/4	4 miles	1550 feet/ 6436 feet	June–Nov

Map: Green Trails No. 590 Sisters; **Contact:** Deschutes National Forest, Sisters Ranger District; **Notes:** NW Forest Pass or $5 day-use fee. Privy at trailhead; **GPS:** N 44 23.71, W 121 38.89

Snow-covered peaks get all the love, but this dark Central Oregon summit should be on your list. While 6436-foot Black Butte is dwarfed by big Bachelor and the Three Sisters just across the way, the summit has 360-degree views, making it a premier vantage point for appreciating the entire Central Oregon landscape. And here's a fun fact: Black Butte is actually older than the higher-up jagged Cascades, although you'd never guess it. The brooding butte maintains its youthful symmetrical shape because it wasn't carved and eroded by glaciers like the other peaks were. Hike the Black Butte Trail for a great workout, stunning views, and an all-around wonderful day in Central Oregon.

GETTING THERE
From Sisters, take US Highway 20 west for 5.4 miles. Turn right for "Indian Ford Camp" on Forest Road 11. Go 3.7 miles and turn left onto FR 1110. Take the bumpy, gravelly, switchbacked road for 5 miles to the trailhead parking lot.

ON THE TRAIL
Begin by taking the upper trail on the left side of the parking lot. The trail immediately rises through a surprisingly lush area with mossy ponderosas and a fern-covered hillside. Patchy shade will keep the sun off your back for now. Enjoy it while you can, because it doesn't last for long. This steep hike is completely exposed for the second half, so it's wise to time your trip accordingly.

The soft path climbs steadily and pops out of the trees into the wide open within the first mile. Notice the change in flora as the shade disappears. Instead of moss and ferns, the now sunny slope is speckled with a wide variety of wildflowers, including red paintbrush, purple larkspur, and yellow balsamroot among weathered whitebark pine and thick snowbrush.

Pass through a small burn area at 1.6 miles, where the trail begins a brutal stretch. There's no refuge from the hot summer sun, and the incline doesn't let up. Take time to catch your breath. There are plenty of stopping

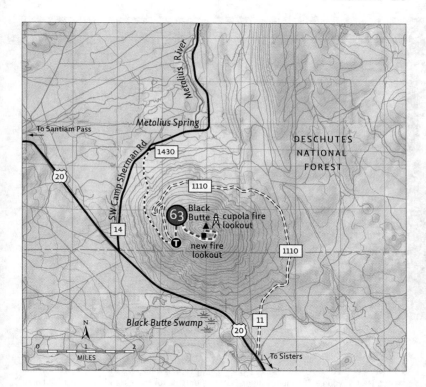

points to admire the views around you, so take advantage of them! If you look up, you'll also see the fire lookout towering high on the summit above you. The fire tower is actually one of several structures at the summit. You'll also find the original cupola-style lookout, an updated cabin, and debris from an old collapsed tower.

As you make your final push to the top of the now extinct volcano, you'll see that the last 0.25 mile of the trail was recently rerouted. The new trail provides better access to the antique cupola building, while also increasing privacy for the fire-lookout operations and living quarters near the tower. Please stay on this new trail out of respect for the fire-detection operations that go on up here. Wildfires are a serious issue in the high desert, and these folks help keep our forests safe.

This new trail takes you directly up to the historical cupola lookout, which was built in the early 1920s. Sit on one of the nearby benches and admire outstanding Cascade views stretching all the way to Washington's Mount Adams. It's nearly impossible to capture the entire spectacle with your camera, as it's too vast to fit in a single frame. Your

Hikers enjoy the view of Three Fingered Jack near the antique cupola–style lookout on Black Butte's summit.

best bet is to stand on a rock and take a panoramic shot. If you can't snap a winner, just put the camera away. You hike to get *away* from technology and everyday life, right? Find your favorite view, take a seat, and enjoy the beauty around you.

EXTENDING YOUR TRIP

Consider starting from the lower trailhead at the base of Black Butte and hiking all the way to the top. This historical path used to be a ranger and mule trail, but many skip it in favor of the easier midmountain trailhead. This lower trailhead was restored in 2013 and allows you to hike 10.5 miles roundtrip to the summit. To find this lower trailhead,

turn right onto FR 14 from US Highway 20. Continue for 3 miles, and then turn right onto FR 1430. The trailhead is on the right at the base of Black Butte.

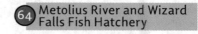

64 Metolius River and Wizard Falls Fish Hatchery

RATING/ DIFFICULTY	LOOP	ELEV GAIN/ HIGH POINT	SEASON
**/3	6.5 miles	150 feet/ 2770 feet	Year-round

Map: Green Trails No. 590 Sisters; **Contact:** Deschutes National Forest, Sisters Ranger District; **GPS:** N 44 31.35, W 121 37.96

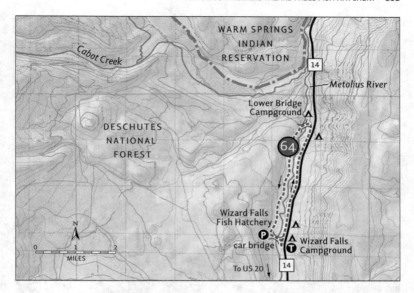

Over the course of a few miles, the Metolius River changes from calm and serene, to fast and violent, and then back to peaceful. Considering its humble beginnings at the calm headwaters south of here, the sections of white water around these parts seem out of place. The water's erratic nature, however, only makes this easy riverside stroll more beautiful. Start at the Wizard Falls Fish Hatchery before heading downstream. You'll pass a few campgrounds before crossing the river and returning on the opposite side.

GETTING THERE

From Sisters, take US Highway 20 west for 10 miles. Turn right onto SW Camp Sherman Road/Forest Road 14, keeping right at the fork at the 2.7-mile mark. Stay on FR 14 for another 7.7 miles. Then turn left onto gravel FR 1400 and go 0.25 mile, crossing the one-lane bridge and parking at the Wizard Falls Fish Hatchery.

ON THE TRAIL

From the fish hatchery, walk the main road and cross the bridge that you drove over on the way in. Back on the other side, turn left onto the trail to take an easy stroll downstream along the river's east bank. There aren't many major sights or exciting landmarks, but this gentle amble is sure to put your mind at ease. The flat trail is great for families.

The trail stays close to the riverbank, winding through mixed conifer forest as it passes two campgrounds. Did you notice how gorgeous the water is? As crystal clear as it is in calm spots, the brilliant blue within the rapids is even more striking.

The river habitat hosts all sorts of wildlife, namely nonthreatening critters like birds

This peaceful trail follows the Metolius River and passes several campgrounds.

and beavers. Look for dams in the river and osprey nests up high in the trees. Bald eagles also frequent this area, attracted by the hatchery and the many fish species that now run the river. You may also see American dippers and western tanagers. If you visit in May or June, you're likely to score views of fuzzy little Canada goose goslings.

At 3.25 miles, you'll approach Lower Bridge Campground. Turn left to take the bridge across the river. Then, on the other side, turn left to head upstream along the opposite bank. You'll enjoy the same gentle rambling all the way back to the fish hatchery.

When you're done with the hike, definitely check out the hatchery, where various organizations are working together to restore salmon and trout species to the river. Kids love the vending machines, where you can buy food to feed to the fish. The Metolius area is also a terrific location to explore in the wintertime when higher elevations are snowed-in.

65 Suttle Lake

RATING/ DIFFICULTY	LOOP	ELEV GAIN/ HIGH POINT	SEASON
***/3	3.7 miles	45 feet/ 3480 feet	Year-round

Map: Green Trails No. 590 Sisters; **Contact:** Deschutes National Forest, Sisters Ranger District, and Suttle Lake Resort; **Notes:** NW Forest Pass or $5 day-use fee. Dogs permitted on-leash. Water and restrooms at picnic area and campground; **GPS:** N 44 25.64, W 121 43.8

Remember when you sought fresh air, not because you had to get away from the stresses of daily life, but because that's where all the fun stuff was? Take yourself back to that feeling, and then re-create it with a trip to Suttle Lake. The lake is often bustling in the summertime—no shortage of activity here. It feels a little like summer camp, minus the food fights and wake-up calls. Break up the drive and walk this loop on your way over Santiam Pass. Pack the kids, the dog, and a picnic—let's make a day of it.

GETTING THERE

From Sisters, take US Highway 20 west for 13 miles. Turn left for Suttle Lake Resort and Marina, and follow signs for the day-use picnic area.

ON THE TRAIL

This loop takes Trail No. 4030 all the way around busy Suttle Lake. You'll pass cabins, campgrounds, and picnic areas that offer plenty of spots to jump in and embrace your inner child. You can hop on the trail at any of these access points, but to limit the amount of driving, just start at the day-use picnic area just past the lodge.

For such an easy-to-navigate trail, finding it from this parking lot isn't so obvious. After parking your car, backtrack about 30 yards by walking on the main road you drove in on until you see the trail on the right side of the road. This trail soon passes over the one-lane bridge via a guardrail lane. If you haven't connected with the trail yet, do so here.

This is the farthest you'll be from the lake for the entire hike. Soon enough, the trail rolls back toward the water, passing sandy beaches that slope to the shoreline. The trail is easygoing the entire way, mostly flat with a few ups and downs. It can be a bit windy when breezes roll across the water, but this helps keep the bugs at bay. Direction-wise, things are simple—just keep the lake on your right.

As you continue around the lake, you'll find that it's a perfectly comfortable hike for families and dogs. Solitude is sparse, but the kids can be as loud as they want and there are plenty of places for picnics and swimming.

A footbridge on the Suttle Lake loop

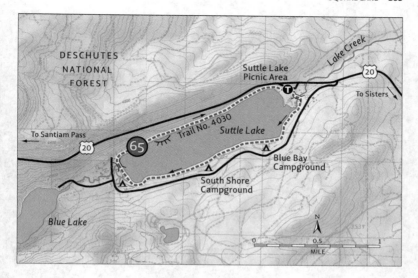

You'll also find plenty of bathrooms and water spots along the trail as you pass through campgrounds. This trip may lack the "Wow! I'm the only one around for miles!" feeling, but the celebratory atmosphere of vacationers enjoying the outdoors more than makes up for that.

Pass through a campground as you near the far end of the lake, and then cross a small footbridge at 2.2 miles to link up with the boat ramp. The route takes to the road here as it makes its way across the pavement, but just continue straight and you'll catch up with trail again on the other side.

Round the lake and enter the homeward straightaway. These last 1.5 miles parallel the highway, but surprisingly, they're the most scenic. Here you'll add Black Butte and Three Fingered Jack to the panorama. Set up your picnic at one of the small retaining walls along the shoreline and claim your own mini beach for the day. These walls are part

of the restoration efforts that have saved the trail from eroding too much of the shoreline. Continue on toward the parking area when you're ready.

66 Square Lake

RATING/ DIFFICULTY	ROUNDTRIP	ELEV GAIN/ HIGH POINT	SEASON
***/3	4 miles	450 feet/ 4780 feet	May–Nov

Maps: Green Trails No. 589 Three Fingered Jack, No. 590 Sisters; **Contact:** Deschutes National Forest, Sisters Ranger District; **Notes:** Free self-issue wilderness permit Memorial Day–Oct 31; **GPS:** N 44 26.49, W 121 47.46

It must have been a Monday when people assigned names to these lakes. Round Lake? Square Lake? Surely there

Colorful fall foliage stands out against the burned trees.

was a humble trail volunteer they could have honored instead! Oh well. Starting from Round Lake just outside the Mount Jefferson Wilderness, you'll soon cross over the boundary on your way to Square Lake. Though its name lacks creativity, there's nothing bland about the lake itself. The trail is comfortable, just as pretty in the sun as it is in cloudy weather. Even the old burn is scenic in its own way. In the fall, autumn color fills the empty space between the dead trees with bright bursts of orange, red, and yellow.

GETTING THERE

From Sisters, head west on US Highway 20 for 12 miles. Near milepost 89, turn right on Forest Road 12 toward Mount Jefferson Wilderness trailheads and drive 1 mile. Then turn left on FR 1210 toward Round Lake and go 5.5 miles. Turn right on FR Spur 1210/600; look for the sign pointing toward the Wilderness Retreat Camp. Drive another 0.6 mile. The trailhead is on the left before the road reaches Round Lake and dead-ends at the camp building.

ON THE TRAIL

Start on Round Lake Trail No. 4012. It ascends immediately from the trailhead, but not much. You'll only gain 400 feet over the course of the next 2 miles, all pretty gradual. As you hit the first turn in the trail, take advantage of a great view of Round Lake below. The lake isn't a perfect circle, but it's more round than the upcoming Square Lake is square.

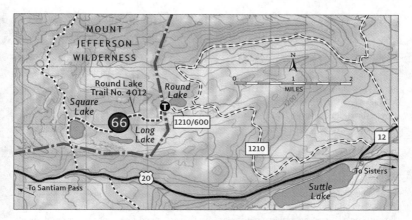

You'll proceed through an old wildfire burn, a scene dominated by standing logs and undersized new growth. Manzanita and snowbrush fill in large patches, quite gorgeous when flowering. Since most of the growth is still short, you'll be able to see all the way through the old forest to the surrounding ridgelines.

This is the kind of easygoing hike where you almost lose track of how long you've been on the trail. After 1.4 uneventful but enjoyable miles, look down to your left to find a pool of water shimmering at the bottom of the hill. That's Long Lake. As you peer down toward the lake, you'll also spot colorful mountain aspens as they make the switch to autumn shades. Their fall color is brilliant against the colorless burn.

In another 0.2 mile, the stubby forest starts to thicken. Continue into the trees, where you'll find Square Lake sitting peacefully at 2 miles. Three Fingered Jack's pointy spires loom on the horizon. While you may have had the trail to yourself, don't expect the lake to be empty. Head back the same way when you're ready.

67 Canyon Creek Meadows

RATING/ DIFFICULTY	LOOP	ELEV GAIN/ HIGH POINT	SEASON
****/3	5 miles	800 feet/ 5680 feet	July–Oct

Maps: Green Trails No. 589 Three Fingered Jack, No. 557 Mount Jefferson; **Contact:** Deschutes National Forest, Sisters Ranger District; **Notes:** NW Forest Pass or $5 day-use fee. Free self-issue wilderness permit Memorial Day–Oct 31. Privy at trailhead; **GPS:** N 44 29.54, W 121 47.66

Canyon Creek Meadows is just as beautiful as it sounds. In late July, throngs of wildflowers poke out of the ground and grace the meadows with color—all while the still snow-capped Three Fingered Jack hovers just beyond. As with most easily accessed attractions, this trail can get quite crowded, especially on summer weekends. Consider hiking early in the day for a little more solitude and perhaps to catch the sunrise bathing Three Fingered Jack in morning light.

GETTING THERE

From Sisters, head west on US Highway 20 for 12 miles. Near milepost 89, turn right on Forest Road 12 toward Mount Jefferson Wilderness trailheads and drive about 4 miles. Turn left on FR 1230 and follow it for 1.6 miles, staying left after crossing the creek. Turn left again onto FR 1234 and drive 5 washboard miles to the trailhead.

ON THE TRAIL

Head straight, following signs toward Canyon Creek Meadows. Like most hikes in this area, recovery is still taking place from a fire in the early 2000s. Begin by walking through this old burn, now much greener with new growth. Within 100 feet or so, you'll pass by Jack Lake on your left—blue waters with a grassy shoreline. Stay straight for the main trail.

Just shy of 0.4 mile, you'll enter the Mount Jefferson Wilderness and reach a junction

signaling the start of the loop. Turn left for Canyon Creek Meadows onto Trail No. 4010. Along the trail, you'll start to see sneak peeks of the wildflower show you'll get in the meadow. The way begins with a moderate ascent, climbing out of the burn and flattening out at the top of a ridge. Here, you'll start to make your way back down into older-growth forest. Pass over several creek beds (most of which are dry by the end of summer) and follow the narrow path into lower Canyon Creek Meadows at 1.8 miles.

With craggy Three Fingered Jack dominating the background and colorful wildflowers peppering the foreground, you'd be hard-pressed to find a more picturesque place. Look for tons of purple lupine, yellow bitterroot, and red Indian paintbrush, as well as magenta diamond clarkia and white arrowleaf buckwheat. Even in the fall, when

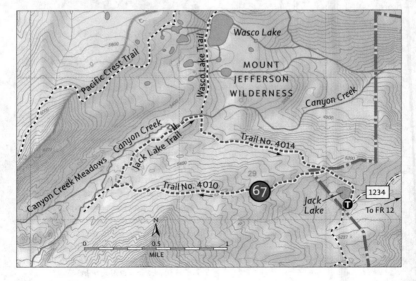

Clusters of white wildflowers near Canyon Creek Meadows

the curtain has closed on the big show, you'll still see heather, daisy-like fleabane, and several other varieties.

While the trail continues a bit more, it quickly peters out without much better views. Instead, turn right here onto the Jack Lake Trail to continue the loop. Hike along the creek for a bit, and within 1 mile you'll pass small Canyon Creek Falls before reaching a junction with the Wasco Lake Trail at 3.1 miles. Keep right onto Trail No. 4014 to finish up the loop back to your car.

EXTENDING YOUR TRIP

An easy side trip to Wasco Lake adds less than 1.5 miles roundtrip to your outing but is a great option if you feel like hunkering down for a picnic and quick swim. Exit the loop by turning left on the Wasco Lake Trail just past the waterfall. Reenter the loop when you're done.

68 Cabot and Carl Lakes

RATING/ DIFFICULTY	ROUNDTRIP	ELEV GAIN/ HIGH POINT	SEASON
****/4	9.6 miles	1100 feet/ 5495 feet	July–Oct

Maps: Green Trails No. 589 Three Fingered Jack, No. 557 Mount Jefferson; **Contact:** Deschutes National Forest, Sisters Ranger District; **Notes:** Free self-issue wilderness permit Memorial Day–Oct 31; **GPS:** N 44 34.43, W 121 43.55

This trailhead is a little hard to find, but it's well worth the bumpy back-roads trip for the splendor and solitude that await you. Burned almost to the ground during the 2003 B&B Fire, this area is finally looking normal again, with established new growth and fresh wildflowers. With Sugar

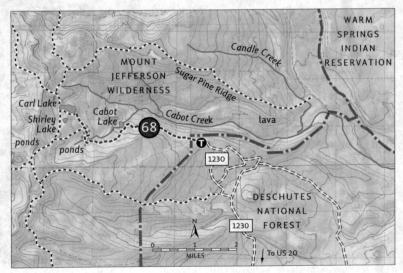

Sugar Pine Ridge as seen through the charred forest

Pine Ridge on your right, you'll make your way through vast expanses of creaky trees and then past a small lake and several ponds before rising up into Carl Lake's large alpine basin. This hike showcases what the Mount Jefferson Wilderness is all about.

GETTING THERE

From Sisters, take US Highway 20 west for about 12 miles. Near milepost 89, turn right on Forest Road 12 toward Mount Jefferson Wilderness trailheads and drive about 4 miles. Turn left on FR 1230. The road turns to gravel in 1.6 miles. Continue on FR 1230 for another 6.6 miles, first toward Sheep Springs and then to the Cabot Lake trailhead.

ON THE TRAIL

Shortly after leaving the trailhead, the path is completely flanked by thick snowbrush. In some areas, the shrubs are so thick that you would get completely lost if you were plopped down in the middle of them. You'd never find the trail if you weren't already on it. Each turn looks the same, like an *Alice in Wonderland* labyrinth. This is a hike you don't want to do too early in the season; wait until trail crews recarve a path through the growth and blowdowns. It's not a very crowded trailhead, so the chances of your running into someone if you get lost are pretty slim!

Continue on, looking past the charred

trees to beautiful views of Mount Jefferson and Sugar Pine Ridge. At 1.6 miles, you'll abruptly enter where the burn stopped. The snowbrush is replaced by ferns and burned stumps swapped for tall fir trees. As you make your way through the forest, you'll start up a few switchbacks before reaching Cabot Lake at 1.9 miles. A short and unmarked 0.1-mile side trail takes you down to the lake. Climb over downed trees on your way, and then reach calm water surrounded by trees.

Connecting back to the main trail where you left off, continue up the switchbacks toward Carl Lake. The hike is calm and peaceful the rest of the way, including the mild crossing of sometimes dry Cabot Creek. At around 3.75 miles, you'll approach the first of several ponds. You'll pass at least three more shallow pools, give or take, depending on the season and the amount of snowfall that year. One of the last ponds, at around 4.4 miles, has some pretty mountain views.

Continue through the forest, and then ascend another quick series of switchbacks before reaching Carl Lake's deep bluish-green waters at 4.8 miles. Admire the ridge-like rim that cradles this scenic glacier-carved basin. If you're lucky, you might even find some rare and tasty wild huckleberry bushes along the rocky shoreline. Relax before heading back the way you came.

EXTENDING YOUR TRIP

To add another little lake to your trip, continue around the left side of Carl Lake, turning left and heading less than 0.5 mile to Shirley Lake. Should you venture farther, make sure you're very experienced with backcountry navigation. Many area trails have been in no-maintenance mode since the 2003 fire and are impassable.

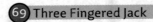

69 Three Fingered Jack

RATING/ DIFFICULTY	ROUNDTRIP	ELEV GAIN/ HIGH POINT	SEASON
****/4	10.5 miles	1500 feet/ 6280 feet	Aug–Oct

Maps: Green Trails No. 589 Three Fingered Jack, No. 557 Mount Jefferson; **Contact:** Deschutes National Forest, Sisters Ranger District; **Notes:** NW Forest Pass or $5 day-use fee. Free self-issue wilderness permit Memorial Day–Oct 31. Privy at trailhead; **GPS:** N 44 25.51, W 121 51.01

Three Fingered Jack is as gnarly as his name sounds—jagged, rough around the edges, and frankly a little unstable. Due to its eroding structure, summiting Three Fingered Jack is a tricky technical climb, requiring significant mountaineering expertise and equipment. So for hiking purposes, this precarious Cascade peak is best viewed from a bit of a distance. You can still get pretty close. This route takes you to an incredible viewpoint where you can appreciate Three Fingered Jack's impressive form without putting yourself in a compromising situation.

GETTING THERE

From Sisters, take US Highway 20 west for 20 miles. At Santiam Pass, across from Hoodoo Ski Resort, turn right for the signed Pacific Crest Trail. Drive 0.2 mile to the parking area.

ON THE TRAIL

Find the wilderness permit kiosk on the east side of the parking area. After you've filled out your pass, start down the beaten path and turn left on the Pacific Crest Trail (PCT) in a few hundred feet. As you head north, you'll notice the burned snags left from an old forest fire and the excessive shrubbery that has filled in around them.

After traveling on the PCT for just 0.2 mile, you'll intersect with Trail No. 4014, which travels to Square Lake. Keep left to continue on the dusty and well-worn PCT. As popular as this section of trail is, hikers have done a pretty good job of sticking to the beaten-down path, which has allowed wildflowers to flourish nearby. Look for paintbrush and lupine in season, among other varieties.

After another mile, near the 1.3-mile mark, keep right at the base of the rocky hill to stay on the PCT. This is a good spot to take a quick break, because the going gets tougher from here. Your breathing will be heavy as the trail begins to climb in earnest. The ridgeline also has several exposed sections that can be miserable in the summer sun. Drink plenty of water over the next few miles.

When you crest the ridge at 3.6 miles, you'll be rewarded with gorgeous Cascade views in every direction. As far as Three

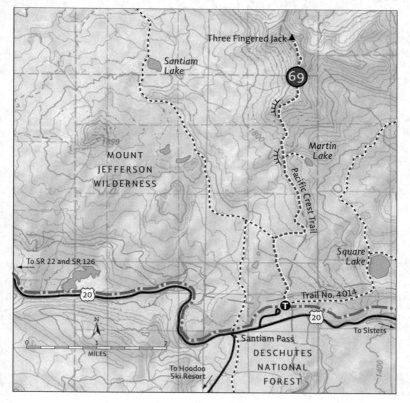

Yellow arrowleaf balsamroot

Fingered Jack goes, all you can see from here is the tip top of the summit. Luckily, better views await just a little farther ahead. As you traverse the ridge, look down to see Martin Lake far below. Ignore trails heading toward the lake and instead keep left, climbing briefly as you enter the comfort of a shaded forest.

At 5 miles, you'll finally be face to face with Three Fingered Jack's western flank and open scree slopes. Continue on for a little less than 0.25 mile for another impressive view of the eroding volcano's jagged spine and colorful layers. Scraggly cairns mark climbers' routes that head up the scree fields, but only continue on if you're an experienced climber, with a buddy, and equipped with the right gear. Otherwise, follow the PCT back down the way you came when you're ready.

Opposite: Smith Rock is one of the most beautiful places in the entire state.

crooked river
and smith rock

In all my years visiting Bend, I rarely explored north of the city. Don't repeat my mistake or you'll miss out on a stunning section of Central Oregon. The most widely known areas up here are the Cove Palisades and Smith Rock state parks, but don't stop there. Central Oregon's canyon country offers endless opportunities for exploring.

The Crooked River National Grassland encompasses more than 155,000 protected acres of land between Terrebonne and Madras. Falcons, golden eagles, and other birds of prey are prevalent. Wide plateaus parallel the horizon while stunning basalt cliffs stretch down hundreds of feet. These walls form stunning canyons that channel the area's rivers—the Deschutes, Metolius, and Crooked.

Crooked River in particular runs through these parts in a grand fashion, stretching from the east and flowing into the Deschutes River on its long journey to the Columbia River. The 500-foot cliffs of the Crooked River Gorge are made of columnar basalt from the Newberry eruption over a million years ago. The canyon was formed slowly as the Crooked River eroded the walls over time.

Every time I visit this area, I'm reminded of how varied Central Oregon is. The terrain here is nothing like the high-alpine areas, and that's what makes it so beautiful.

70 Maston Area Trails

RATING/ DIFFICULTY	LOOP	ELEV GAIN/ HIGH POINT	SEASON
***/3	5 miles	350 feet/ 3185 feet	Year-round

Map: BLM Maston Area Trails; **Contact:** BLM Prineville District; **GPS:** N 44 14.67, W 121 16.93

Look for deer prints near Cline Butte. Elk frequent the area as well.

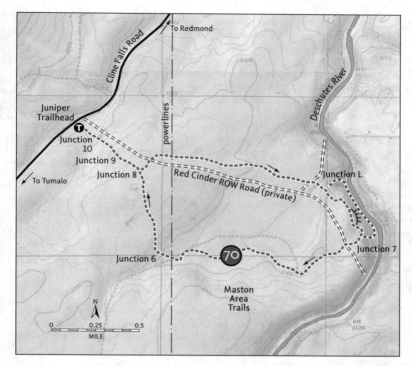

The Maston Area Trails are located between Cline Falls Highway and the western banks of the Deschutes River. This area used to be abused by vehicles, dumping, and target shooting, but it's received a significant upgrade. As part of the Cline Buttes Recreation Area, this spacious trail system features multiuse paths for hikers, bikers, and equestrians. There are plenty of routes to explore, but this easy loop to the canyon viewpoint is a good start. This hike starts from the northernmost access point, the Juniper Trailhead, which is conveniently located just 1.5 miles from Eagle Crest Resort.

GETTING THERE

From Redmond, drive State Route 126 west for 4 miles, and then take the Cline Falls Highway exit toward NW 74th Street. In 0.1 mile, turn right on Cline Falls Road and proceed for 2.6 miles to the Juniper Trailhead on your left.

ON THE TRAIL

From the Juniper Trailhead, take off on the trail. The Maston Area Trails system assigns a number for each junction, which you can view at a map posted at the trailhead. Very few junctions are actually signed with enough information to point you back to the trailhead if you get lost, so this is a good hike to do with a GPS unit. You'll reach the first such intersection at Junction 10, just 0.1 mile into the hike. Turn left, crossing straight through a few junctions for small side trails. At 0.3 mile, you'll reach Junction 9. Turn left and then left again at Junction 8 at 0.5 mile.

During early summer, a colorful smattering of desert flora dots the landscape. The old-growth juniper and sagebrush provide a teensy bit of shade, but not quite enough to keep you cool in the dead of summer. If you choose to visit during the hottest months, hit the trails in the morning. You'll see deer almost year-round, but winter also draws elk herds that traverse the mostly barren tundra. Even if there isn't much to look at trailside, you'll have plenty of views of the surrounding Cascades and Cline Buttes.

Cross over Red Cinder ROW Road at 0.7 mile and then under powerlines at 0.75 mile. Keep straight for the next mile. At this point, you'll reach an often-unsigned junction. Continue straight, crossing the cinder road again at 1.9 miles. The trail winds toward a scenic overlook of the canyon, which you'll reach at 2.2 miles.

This spot features an outstanding view of the rugged canyon walls and birds soaring above the Deschutes River far below you. Admire the striped layers on the walls, and notice how the hues vary depending on whether or not the sun is illuminating them.

Keep right at Junction 7 at 2.4 miles to begin your loop back to the trailhead. You'll head straight through several unofficial intersections before reaching Junction 6 at 3.75 miles. Turn right, following one of the only signs pointing you back toward Juniper Trailhead. In 0.7 mile, you'll be back at Junction 8, where you'll stay left. Retrace your steps the final 0.5 mile back to the trailhead.

EXTENDING YOUR TRIP

Add a side-trail extension to loop down to the riverbank at the base of the canyon. At an unsigned junction at 1.75 miles, turn left on the trail to Junction L. Turn right onto the pedestrian-only trail, which steeply descends into the canyon. Turn right and walk through the canyon for 0.4 mile before turning back uphill away from the river and catching up with the main trail at Junction 7.

71 Smith Rock: Misery Ridge and Monkey Face

RATING/ DIFFICULTY	LOOP	ELEV GAIN/ HIGH POINT	SEASON
*****/4	3.9 miles	800 feet/ 3320 feet	Year-round

Map: Oregon State Parks—Smith Rock, available at visitors center; **Contact:** Smith Rock State Park; **Notes:** $5 day-use fee. Dogs permitted on-leash. Water and restrooms available; **GPS:** N 44 21.57, W 121 8.15

Smith Rock is simply incredible. Some state parks are just glorified rest stops, but not Smith Rock. It impresses straight from the parking area, and it gets more and more outstanding as you hike deep into its splendor. For starters, the colorful cliffs feel like something right out of the Jurassic. Whenever I'm here, I picture pterodactyls soaring down from their high nests and through the canyon. The refreshing Crooked River cuts through the otherwise dry landscape, winding around the giant rock walls. There are several trails in the area, but this loop is the highlight reel.

A hiker and her dogs descending Misery Ridge on a hot day

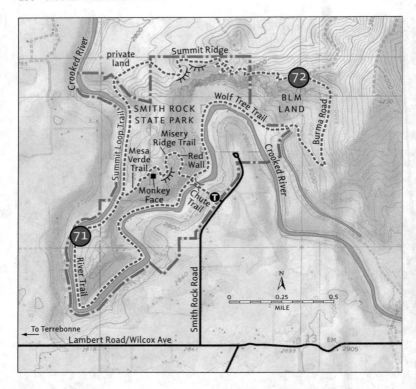

GETTING THERE

From Bend, drive north on US Highway 97 for 21 miles to Terrebonne. Turn right on NW Smith Rock Way/B Avenue and drive 0.5 mile. Then turn left on Lambert Road/Wilcox Avenue. Continue another 2 miles and turn left on Smith Rock Road into the park. Follow the paths near the visitors center to the trailhead.

ON THE TRAIL

From the main Smith Rock trailhead, take the Chute Trail down to the river and cross the footbridge. Keep straight and follow the Misery Ridge Trail straight up the switchbacks and oversized stairs. You'll soon pass the base of Red Wall, one of several climbing locations you'll see on this hike. In fact, if you choose to explore some of the side trails, you'll find that many of them simply lead to emergency sets of gurneys and crutches. It's a little unsettling how many of them there are.

Next, the trail turns upward from the canyon floor on the loose and rocky switchbacks for approximately 0.75 mile. This trail is called Misery Ridge for a reason. It's steep, dry, and completely exposed, so make sure to wear sunscreen and bring plenty of water. Go early in the day if you can. Climb steadily, feeling the burn as you bear down and reach the top of the ridge at 0.85 mile. Catch your breath and ogle at the sweeping western views of Cascade volcanoes, including Mount Bachelor, all Three Sisters, Mount Washington, Mount Jefferson, and even Mount Hood.

Continue across the flat top of the ridge until you're rewarded with head-on views of Smith Rock's most prominent landmark—Monkey Face. This 350-foot volcanic pillar attracts top climbing talent almost every day of the year. It's fun to watch the climbers dangle from the column—and then feel quite thankful that your feet are on solid ground.

From here, take the steep, descending switchbacks down the west side of the ridge, leading all the way to the base of Monkey Face. Turn left at the junction with the Mesa Verde Trail at around 1.1 miles. The trail descends to the river for about 0.4 mile before reaching a junction with the River Trail near 1.5 miles. Pay attention, because it's easy to get turned around. Keep straight on the left-hand trail.

The path continues south along the floor of the Crooked River Gorge, rounding the bend in the river and then continuing on the flat homeward stretch back to the bridge. If you decide to take a dip in the cool river, keep an eye out for rattlers. They like to lurk in shady areas under the rocks near the water. Cross the river on the footbridge and follow the park trails up the Chute Trail back to your starting spot, at just under 4 miles total.

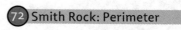

72 Smith Rock: Perimeter

RATING/ DIFFICULTY	LOOP	ELEV GAIN/ HIGH POINT	SEASON
****/4	7.2 miles	1400 feet/ 3590 feet	Year-round

Map: Oregon State Parks—Smith Rock, available at visitors center; **Contact:** Smith Rock State Park; **Notes:** $5 day-use fee. Dogs permitted on-leash. Water and restrooms available; **GPS:** N 44 21.57, W 121 8.15

This all-encompassing Smith Rock hike takes you around the park's perimeter. You'll start and end along the Crooked River, while the chunk in between takes you way beyond the rock walls and up the Summit Loop Trail for views of the entire park. There's a brief stint along a service road, but other than that and the crowds of people on nice days, this trail is all nature. This hike is also excellent for spotting wildlife, including deer and peregrine falcons.

GETTING THERE
From Bend, drive north on US Highway 97 for 21 miles to Terrebonne. Turn right on NW Smith Rock Way/B Avenue and drive 0.5 mile. Then turn left on Lambert Road/Wilcox Avenue. Continue another 2 miles and turn left on Smith Rock Road into the park. Follow the paths near the visitors center to the trailhead.

ON THE TRAIL
Start off down the steep Chute Trail to descend to the river. Cross the footbridge and turn left on the River Trail at 0.25 mile. As you make your way downriver, check out all the climbing routes along the steep canyon

A hiker enjoys the view from one of the highest vantage points in the park.

walls. Then turn toward the river and take a minute to look for playful river otters near the rocks or proud herons posing in the water. At 2 miles, continue following signs for the River Trail.

After another 0.5-mile stroll along the river, continue straight on the signed Summit Loop Trail. You'll quickly leave the soft dirt and make a rocky exposed traverse across the hillside. At 2.75 miles, you'll be back on dirt again. Turn around and check out the stunning rock walls you're leaving behind. Within 100 feet or so, the trail begins a 0.25-mile stretch through private property before entering the state park again at 3 miles.

The trail really starts to climb here, but within the next 0.3 mile, you'll see views of Mount Washington, Black Butte, and Mount Jefferson to your left. This stretch is also a great place to look for deer. In another 0.1 mile, turn right at the junction for a quick side trip to a viewpoint and an excellent reminder that you're still, in fact, in Smith Rock State Park. Then turn around and head straight at the junction to continue on the Summit Loop Trail.

You'll hit another inviting vantage point at 3.75 miles, this time trailside, as you finish the ascent to Summit Ridge. With gorgeous rock pinnacles all around, this is a perfect place to recover while you take in the incredible view. With the panorama of Smith Rock State Park in front of you, the work to get up here is all worth it. Spin around to take in views of Sherwood Canyon and Gray Butte (Hike 73) nearby.

After enjoying the views from the top of the lofty basalt walls, continue up to the summit's plateau. The Gray Butte Trail enters from the left, but you'll turn right to reach Burma Road just before the 5-mile mark. You're crossing into BLM land here. This service road is slippery, a bit boring compared to where you've been and annoying at times, but it's the most efficient way to get back down to the river. At 5.8 miles you'll cross over the canal and reenter the park. Immediately turn right on the Wolf Tree Trail.

This is a *steep* and slippery descent with very little traction. Take it slow. At 6 miles, turn right to stay on the Wolf Tree Trail, and then cross over a scree field before moving into the trees. You can hear the river close-by, and soon enough you'll see it. At 6.9 miles,

turn left to go over the footbridge and then back up the Chute Trail to where you began.

73 Gray Butte

RATING/ DIFFICULTY	ROUNDTRIP	ELEV GAIN/ HIGH POINT	SEASON
***/3	3.8 miles	800 feet/ 4250 feet	Year- round

Map: USFS Crooked River Grasslands; **Contact:** Ochoco National Forest and Crooked River National Grassland; **GPS:** N 44 25.73, W 121 5.43

If Smith Rock is a bit too crowded, take a step back and head to Gray Butte instead. Just down the road from the gorgeous but busy state park,

Gray Butte's brushy hillsides on a sunny day

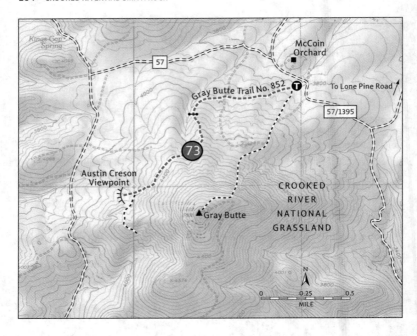

this little butte is the high point on this side of Terrebonne. An out-and-back takes you part-way up Gray Butte to an unobstructed view of the Cascades and the Crooked River National Grassland. For something so close to a busy area, the Gray Butte trailhead isn't easy to find. Horse trails, ATV tracks, and a complete lack of signage make things confusing back here. Watch your car's odometer and be prepared for unmaintained roads and missing signage.

GETTING THERE

From Bend, drive north on US Highway 97 for 21 miles to Terrebonne. Turn right onto NW Smith Rock Way/B Avenue and drive 5 miles. Then turn left on Lone Pine Road. Proceed 7.1 miles, passing Skull Hollow Campground and a Gray Butte sign. Then turn left onto the unsigned and bumpy Forest Road 57/1395 and drive 2.7 miles. Stay right, and then find the primitive trailhead on the left in another 0.6 mile.

ON THE TRAIL

Before starting out, look across the road at the McCoin Orchard. It was built in 1887, and the government purchased the land from the McCoin family in the 1930s. The orchard is easy to miss because the trees are no longer in pristine rows, but many still bear fruit. Once on the trail, you'll trade fruit trees for juniper and sagebrush. Because this trail doesn't get much use, a large variety of wildflowers happily flourish up here. Take Gray Butte Trail No. 852 west.

Follow the single-track trail around the ridge and through a metal gate at 0.9 mile. Unless signed otherwise, leave open gates open, but reclose closed gates after you pass through. The trail only climbs slightly, but the ground can be tricky depending on conditions. Some spots have loose scree, while others are littered with cow and horse manure. Hikers heading out after a good downpour will encounter notorious Gray Butte "gumbo"—thick clay mud that sticks to just about everything. It's miserable to drive in, but even worse to walk in. Aim to hike this one when it's dry, but before it gets too hot.

At 1.9 miles, turn right to take the very short side trail to the rocky ledge of the Austin Creson Viewpoint on the western side of Gray Butte. Named for a trail planner who was influential in establishing this trail, this vantage point affords amazing views of the surrounding area. After you've enjoyed the view for a bit, head back to the main trail. While the trail does continue down Sherwood Canyon, the loop hikes in this area get pretty confusing, so it's better to simply turn back down the way you came. Look for grazing cows among the colorful wildflowers that dot the hillside in the spring and early summer.

EXTENDING YOUR TRIP

If reaching the tip-top, 5108-foot summit of Gray Butte is important to you, skip the main trail and opt for this direct route. Turn south off the main trail about 0.1 mile from the trailhead and head straight up. Use the communication towers at the top as your focal point. This off-trail scramble is a steep 1.5 miles and 1300 feet of vertical gain to the summit. On clear days, you can see all the way south to Mount Shasta in California.

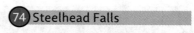

74 Steelhead Falls

RATING/ DIFFICULTY	ROUNDTRIP	ELEV GAIN/ HIGH POINT	SEASON
***/1	1 mile	130 feet/ 2455 feet	Year-round

Map: USGS Steelhead Falls; **Contact:** BLM Prineville District; **Notes:** Privy at trailhead; **GPS:** N 44 24.68, W 121 17.56

The high desert can be awfully hot, dry, and dusty in the summer. What better way to cool off than a peaceful swimming hole at the bottom of a pretty waterfall? If that sounds like the perfect day, and if you don't mind sharing the space with cliff-jumping daredevils, look no further than Steelhead Falls. Not a fan of getting wet? The riverside hike along the Deschutes is completely gorgeous all on its own.

GETTING THERE

From Bend, drive north on US Highway 97 for 21 miles to Terrebonne. In 0.5 mile, turn left on Lower Bridge Road. Drive 2 miles and turn right on McCain Road/43rd Street. Drive 1.8 miles, following signs for Crooked River Ranch. Turn left on Chinook Road and go 1 mile, then left on Badger Road for 1.8 miles, and then right on Quail Road for 1.2 miles. Then take the second left onto gravel River Road and drive 0.8 mile to the trailhead.

ON THE TRAIL

This hike is part of the Steelhead Falls Wilderness Study Area. This special designation has helped preserve the area, but local conservation groups are seeking permanent federal protection. Nice! This is a busy, in-and-out kind of trailhead, so play it safe and leave your valuables at home. This

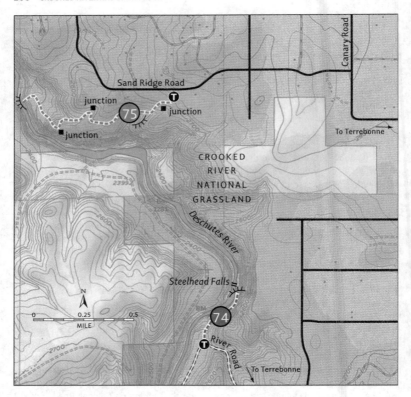

hike is only 1 mile, so you shouldn't need to bring much.

Directionally, this is a simple hike. From the parking lot, the trail travels downriver and reaches the falls in 0.5 mile. The route is fairly easy, although steep in parts. Along the way, look for lizards sunning themselves on the warm rocks. Watch out for rattlesnakes too, especially if you're running around barefoot near the rocks by the water. It may be a good idea to keep your pooch on a leash, although it isn't required.

As you approach the falls, you can see the water tumble over the edge into the swirling pool below. The falls themselves are about 20 feet high, but 30-foot rocky cliffs make a semicircle around them. You'll see plenty of youngsters jumping off the high rocks, but there are calmer wading and swimming areas slightly downriver.

Beyond the pool on both sides of the river, high canyon walls stretch to the sky, striped with colorful evidence of volcanic ash and river sediment from the past seven million years. Steelhead Falls is named for the salmon that used to jump up the river here,

Cliffs lining the quick hike to Steelhead Falls

before dams were constructed downstream. To the left of the falls, you can still see the brickwork remains from an old fish ladder.

If you're planning on swimming, the water is all snowmelt, which means it's pretty dang cold until at least mid-June. This withdrawn little spot is well known, so it's unlikely that you'll have it to yourself in the summer. If you'd rather skip the crowds, winter is a great time to visit (if you don't plan to swim).

75 Sand Ridge

RATING/ DIFFICULTY	ROUNDTRIP	ELEV GAIN/ HIGH POINT	SEASON
***/3	2 miles	450 feet/ 2715 feet	Year-round

Map: USGS Steelhead Falls; **Contact:** BLM Prineville District; **GPS:** N 44 25.79, W 121 17.89

The trails here are primitive, mostly used by anglers and in-the-know folks who live near Crooked River Ranch. There are many loop options, but the area is confusing enough as it is, so stick to an out-and-back your first time here. This hike lures you in with short mileage, stunning sights, and a downhill start. But what goes down must come back up. You'll be sweating at the end—especially in the summer, when the canyon is sweltering hot.

GETTING THERE

From Bend, drive north on US Highway 97 for 21 miles to Terrebonne. In 0.5 mile, turn left on Lower Bridge Road. Drive 2 miles and turn right on McCain Road/43rd Street. Drive 1.8 miles, following signs for Crooked River Ranch. Turn left on Chinook Road and drive 2.4 miles. Turn left on Mustang Road and go 1.1 miles. Turn right on Shad

You don't always have to see wildlife to know it's nearby!

Road and continue for 2.4 miles. Then take a left on Canary Road. In 0.3 mile, turn right on Sand Ridge Road. You'll see the small dirt lot on the left side of the road in 0.5 mile.

ON THE TRAIL

Take the faint Sand Ridge Trail from the parking area toward the canyon. At this point, the trail is lined with a small rock boundary defining the way, making it quite easy to follow. Within the first 200 feet, you'll reach a small junction. Stay right as you traverse a mesa high above the Deschutes. Sagebrush and clusters of desert wildflowers decorate the ground around you.

This is a weird area. It's safe, but sometimes it feels a little eerie. Maybe that has something to do with the completely licked-clean animal bones that lie scattered just off-trail—hints that wildlife frequent this area. It's a strange feeling knowing that you probably aren't alone, even though the trail is so seemingly lonely.

At 0.25 mile, you'll have a quick view of the river below. Stay straight and ignore the little paths that beg you to explore off-trail. The "main" trail is marked with irregularly placed cairns—roughly every 30 feet or so. At 0.5 mile, go left.

The distinctive stripes on the canyon walls are stunning, especially with the tops of the Cascades poking up just over the canyon rim. At 0.75 mile, turn right, and reach a viewpoint just 0.2 mile later. From here, a short switchback descent takes you past a rockslide to the canyon floor. At 1 mile, the trail peters out, but there's a lovely shady spot to sit and enjoy the tranquility of the canyon. Rest up. While the sandy trail was slippery on the way down, it's a workout on the way back up.

 **76 Alder Springs Trail**

RATING/ DIFFICULTY	ROUNDTRIP	ELEV GAIN/ HIGH POINT	SEASON
****/3	6 miles	950 feet/ 2600 feet	Apr–Nov

Map: USGS Alder Springs; **Contact:** Ochoco National Forest and Crooked River National Grassland; **Notes:** Closed Dec 1–Mar 31. Creek crossing required—difficulty depends on flow, highest in spring; **GPS:** N 44 26.02, W 121 21.22

This trail used to be fairly empty, but the secret of this incredible area is out. From Cascade views at the top of the canyon to the convergence of two major waterways at the bottom, this hike is sure to please all. Look for colorful high-desert blooms, such as monkey flower, columbine, green-banded mariposa lilies, and abundant arrowleaf balsamroot. Wildlife-wise, the trail is closed four months of the year to protect local deer populations. Also make sure to watch out for sneaky rattlesnakes that often hang out under hot rocks and near the river.

GETTING THERE

From Bend, drive north on US Highway 97 for 21 miles to Terrebonne. In 0.5 mile, turn left on Lower Bridge Road. Drive 12 miles, turn left on Holmes Road, and go 2 miles. Turn right on Forest Road 6360 at milepost 7. After 4.2 bumpy miles, turn right on FR Spur 040 at the "Alder Springs" sign and proceed another 0.8 mile to the trailhead.

ON THE TRAIL

Start atop the juniper- and sage-covered mesa high above Whychus Creek, complete

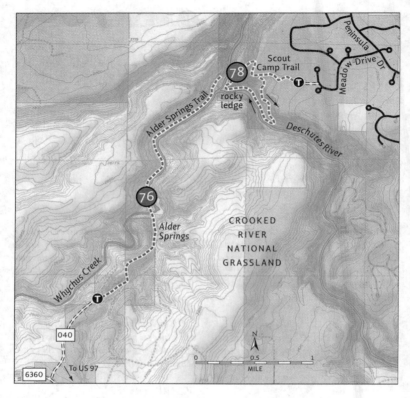

with views of the Cascades and a scattering of wildflowers lining the trail. Follow the trail downhill, staying right at a junction at 0.2 mile to bypass a side trip down to an old bridge crossing. After the junction, continue across the plateau for another 0.8 mile, where you'll cross an often-dry drainage ditch before beginning a steep descent into the canyon.

At 1.3 miles, you'll need to ford a 15-foot-wide section of Whychus Creek to continue on. The creek's depth and swiftness depend on water flow. While it's highest in the

spring, you can count on getting your shoes wet year-round. As you climb out of the water, you'll be on the edge of Alder Springs' scenic meadows.

The river turns the otherwise arid ground into a lush oasis. With high canyon walls looming above, this is an awesome lunch spot if you're happy with the distance so far. If not, proceed through the meadow on a softly undulating trail.

Once you're back down in the canyon, a user trail continues along the water for another 1.5 miles to the confluence of

Fiery reddish-orange desert paintbrush

Whychus Creek and the Deschutes River at 3 miles. Enjoy the incredible scene from the rocky crag by the river before turning back.

EXTENDING YOUR TRIP

Wish you could explore the territory on the other side of the river? The water is definitely impassable here at the confluence, but Hike 78 accesses the opposite terrain via the Scout Camp Trail.

77 Lone Pine Trail

RATING/ DIFFICULTY	ROUNDTRIP	ELEV GAIN/ HIGH POINT	SEASON
***/3	1.8 miles	300 feet/ 2400 feet	Year-round

Map: BLM Otter Bench Trail System; **Contact:** BLM Prineville District, and Crooked River Ranch; **Notes:** Privy at trailhead; **GPS:** N 44 27.77, W 121 16.98

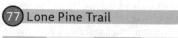 *Welcome to canyon country. Describing the views along this stretch of the Crooked River Gorge feels like writing a new verse for "Home on the Range." No need to don cowboy boots, but the 300-foot rock walls, sweet-smelling sagebrush, and endlessly blue sky are straight out of an old western. Start along the west rim of the dramatic canyon, and then descend steeply to the river below.*

GETTING THERE

From Bend, drive north on US Highway 97 for 21 miles to Terrebonne. In 0.5 mile, turn left on Lower Bridge Road. Drive 2 miles and turn right on McCain Road/43rd Street. Drive 1.8 miles, following signs for Crooked River Ranch. Turn left on Chinook Road and drive 5.9 miles. The road names change several times (from Chinook to Clubhouse to Ranch House Road), but just stay on this main road. At an odd three-way intersection,

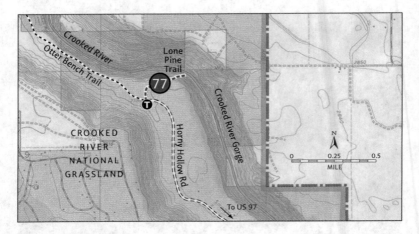

continue straight onto Back Hill Road/Horny Hollow Road, and continue 0.7 mile through a residential area until the road ends at the trailhead.

ON THE TRAIL

Ignore the easy-to-spot signage for the Otter Bench Trail at the back of the parking lot. Instead, park on the right-hand side and find the less trod Lone Pine Trail to the northeast. The grass bordering the parking lot is sometimes overgrown, which makes spotting the trail tricky. Look for the path heading toward the gorge and then upriver.

This trail is relatively new and occupies land managed by the Bureau of Land Management, Crooked River National Grassland, and Oregon Department of Fish and Wildlife. Until recently, this area was abused by dumping and off-road vehicles. Trail development has helped control erosion and preserve this gorgeous landscape. Note that private property surrounds much of this trail system, so please stay on defined trails.

For the first 0.25 mile, go north and take the trail upstream. This section is mostly flat, but there are plenty of opportunities to get tripped up by the rocky trail. In the spring, look for colorful wildflowers among the sagebrush, notably, yellow displays of arrowleaf balsamroot. Soon enough, you'll see the high canyon walls and the Crooked River below.

This section of river above Lake Billy Chinook is federally designated as Wild and Scenic. As such, it's a prime location for seeing wildlife. You'd be hard-pressed to find roaming buffalo, but you might see deer, bobcats, or rattlesnakes. Raptors also nest just downriver, so there's a good chance you'll see them soaring through the canyon on the way back to their lofty nests.

As the trail reaches the edge of the gorge, proceed down steep switchbacks until you reach the canyon floor at 0.9 mile. From the river, you'll have breathtaking views of rimrock cliffs and columnar basalt. Pick any of the outstanding spots along the water to

Descending into Crooked River Canyon

fish or just sit and enjoy the majesty of the canyon. The Crooked River Gorge is truly one of the beauties of Central Oregon. Retrace your steps on the way back.

EXTENDING YOUR TRIP

Explore the Crooked River a little farther by venturing out on the Otter Bench Trail. The scenery along the trail is much like the Lone Pine Trail, but you finish at a gorgeous overlook. The Otter Bench Trail begins by traveling west before turning north. In 2.5 miles, continue on the Opal Canyon Loop, which adds another 3 miles. Total, the roundtrip to the viewpoint is approximately 8 miles.

78 Scout Camp Trail

RATING/ DIFFICULTY	LOOP	ELEV GAIN/ HIGH POINT	SEASON
****/43	2.3 miles	700 feet/ 2750 feet	Year-round

Map: BLM Scout Camp Loop Trail; **Contact:** BLM Prineville District; **GPS:** N 44 27.66, W 121 19.29; **See map at Hike 76.**

This new trailhead was constructed in 2010 along with a few others to increase access to the gorgeous Bureau of Land Management area along the Deschutes River Canyon. Maybe visitors don't know it

A little hole in an old juniper is a perfect home for critters.

exists, or maybe they overlook it in favor of the Alder Springs trailhead across the river. Either way, they're missing out. This hidden gem boasts a view-packed loop into the canyon to the convergence of the Deschutes River and Whychus Creek. Don't miss this one.

GETTING THERE

From Bend, drive north on US Highway 97 for 21 miles to Terrebonne. In 0.5 mile, turn left on Lower Bridge Road. Drive 2 miles and turn right on McCain Road/43rd Street. Drive 1.8 miles, following signs for Crooked River Ranch. Turn left on Chinook Road and drive 2.4 miles. Turn left on Mustang Road and go 1.1 miles. Turn right on Shad Road and drive 1.4 miles. Turn right on Peninsula Drive and go 3.1 miles before turning left on Meadow Drive. Go 0.5 mile and turn right on Scout Camp Trail (yes, the road is called a trail). You'll find the trailhead 0.2 mile down the gravel road.

ON THE TRAIL

Head west from the parking lot on a flat trail that passes sagebrush and ancient junipers. In the springtime, this desert plateau also hosts dry-climate blooms. After a flat 0.25 mile, you'll begin a 700-foot descent toward the river. Luckily, tight switchbacks lessen the blow.

At 0.4 mile, you'll come to a three-way junction—the beginning of the loop. Turn left, taking time to admire the white-water rapids underneath the striped canyon walls. This area gets quite warm in the summer, and even though the river is much too wild here for swimming, you'll probably be itching to get close to the water. Cruelly, the trail makes a hard right just shy of the canyon floor at around 0.75 mile.

After a mostly flat stretch just above the river, the trail turns uphill at 1.25 miles. You'll find this stretch either super fun or quite obnoxious, depending on how you feel about obstacle courses. The trail will seemingly dead-end at an 8-foot ledge. No worries! Remember when you were a kid? Channel those memories and scramble over the rock

to where the trail continues on the other side. Fun, right?

You'll soon reach the confluence of the Deschutes River and Whychus Creek, perhaps climbing over a few small boulders along the way. The Alder Springs Trail (Hike 76) ends on the other side of the canyon, so you may see people over there. Absolutely don't try to cross the river. Instead, admire the amazing rock formations all around you, including the stripy rainbow-colored rock called the Fin.

As you climb out of the canyon, allow yourself a few breaks to inhale the scent of ponderosa pine and juniper and enjoy the views. The steep, gravelly climb reaches the loop junction at 1.75 miles. Turn left, following the trail back across the plateau to your car.

79 Rimrock Springs

RATING/ DIFFICULTY	ROUNDTRIP	ELEV GAIN/ HIGH POINT	SEASON
**/1	1 mile	20 feet/ 3100 feet	Year-round

Map: USFS Crooked River National Grassland; **Contact:** Ochoco National Forest Service and Crooked River Grassland; **Notes:** Dogs permitted on-leash; **GPS:** N 44 29.77, W 121 3.35

The Rimrock Springs Wildlife Management Area is a marshy refuge in the middle of a juniper and sagebrush desert that attracts a variety of animals. The main trail is ADA accessible and quite short, making it a great outing for all skill levels. While the wildlife management area is in good hands, its overseeing agencies have taken an unconventional

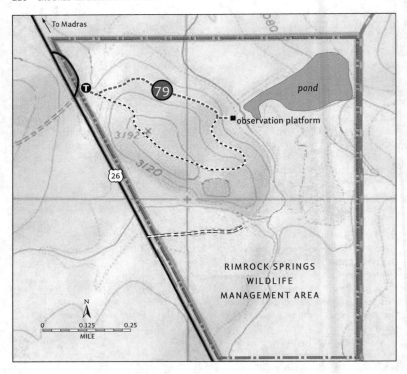

approach to maintenance. *To discourage the vandalism, dumping, and other sketchy activities that had been taking place in the parking lot, officials simply removed roadside signage and restrooms. The trail itself is safe and in good condition, and removing some of the human-made aspects has probably made the area even more attractive for wildlife.*

GETTING THERE

From Madras, take US Highway 97 south for 1.2 miles and turn left onto US 26. Continue for 9.4 miles, and turn left into the likely unmarked Rimrock Springs trailhead parking area.

ON THE TRAIL

Leave the parking lot and begin walking on the trail, staying left within the first 100 feet or so to keep on the paved, barrier-free path. The flat trail winds through an arid juniper and sagebrush landscape for 0.5 mile before reaching the wetland pond, which was created by damming some of the spring-fed waters.

Installing the observation platform was a proactive measure to prevent erosion, providing hikers with an awesome spot to sit and enjoy the views without wading into the soggy wetland and disrupting wildlife. Birds are almost always present, especially during

Deer in the Rimrock Springs Wildlife Management Area

nesting season. Several types of waterfowl, songbirds, and birds of prey are common. Bring a pair of binoculars if you want to get a closer view.

Other frequent visitors include pronghorn, beavers, bats, snakes, lizards, and rabbits. Wildlife sightings are common but not guaranteed. Up your odds by giving yourself plenty of time and visiting at dawn or dusk. Even if you miss the wildlife, the panoramic views of the grasslands and surrounding Cascades are well worth the quick stroll. Turn back when you're ready.

EXTENDING YOUR TRIP

At the viewing platform, leave the paved trail and continue on a gravel path, which visits a second viewing platform before looping back around to the main trail. Turn left to hike the last 100 feet or so back to the trailhead. This full loop measures 1.3 miles.

80 Tam-a-lau Trail

RATING/ DIFFICULTY	LOOP	ELEV GAIN/ HIGH POINT	SEASON
*****/3	6.5 miles	650 feet/ 2620 feet	Year-round

Map: Oregon State Parks—Cove Palisades State Park; **Contact:** Cove Palisades State Park; **Notes:** $5 day-use fee. Must register at trailhead. Park open 7:00 A.M.–10:00 P.M. Dogs permitted on-leash. Water and restrooms available at day-use area; **GPS:** N 44 32.08, W 121 17.28

There's nothing quite like Lake Billy Chinook. The human-made reservoir was built in the mid-1960s by damming flows from the Deschutes, Crooked, and Metolius rivers. The two prominent landmarks here are the

217

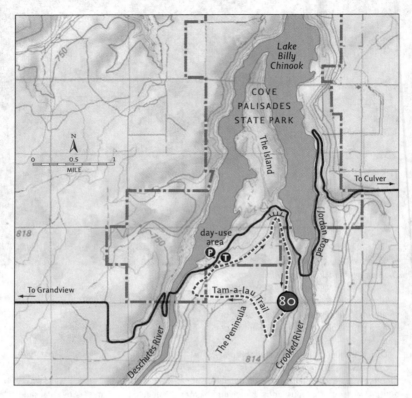

Peninsula and the Island. After an increase in visitation started to disrupt the ecological integrity of the Island, it was designated as a research natural area and closed to hikers. Several agencies came together in 1997 to create the Tam-a-lau Trail, giving visitors a way to keep exploring this gorgeous terrain while still preventing erosion. The trail features incredible views of the basalt walls and surrounding landscape. The trail is open year-round, although it can be excruciatingly hot and busy in the summer.

GETTING THERE

From Bend, head north on US Highway 97 for 21 miles to Terrebonne. Near milepost 106, turn left on Culver Highway/State Route 361 and continue for 2.5 miles. Turn left on C Street and keep following signs for Cove Palisades State Park. In 0.9 mile, turn right on SW Feather Drive. In 0.8 mile, turn left on Fisch Lane. In 0.5 mile, keep right onto Frazier Drive. Then in 0.5 mile, turn left on Jordan Road. From here, keep straight on the main road into the canyon. Pass over a bridge at 4 miles. In another 1.1 miles, turn right for

Stunning views of Lake Billy Chinook from atop the Peninsula

the Upper Deschutes Day Use Area. Pay for your parking pass on the way in, and then keep right to the parking lot.

ON THE TRAIL

The easiest way to get to the trail is to retrace your steps back up the Upper Deschutes Day Use Road to the main park road. Turn left and immediately locate the trail sign on the other side of the street. At 0.25 mile, you'll reach the main trailhead and an informational kiosk. You'll need to sign in at the trail register here.

Turn right to proceed on the official Tam-a-lau Trail. It starts out slightly wooded, with clusters of juniper and pine and plenty of sagebrush. After the first flat stretch, you'll begin your ascent on a series of switchbacks and a few sets of railroad-tie steps. Your heart rate will start climbing with the elevation, but incredible views give you plenty of excuses to stop and catch your breath. At 1.25 miles from the trailhead kiosk and 1.5 overall, you'll crest the plateau and reach the loop junction.

Keep left at the junction to begin the absolutely stunning loop portion of the hike. Signs remind you to stay on the trail, but the path parallels the breathtaking edge of the rimrock, so there's no reason to deviate. Views abound in every direction, so take it all in! You'll start up high above the Deschutes River Arm, with views of the Cascades in the background. At 2.75 miles from your car, you'll reach a viewpoint at the tip of the Peninsula, looking across to the Island on the other side of the road. The loop and views continue along the east side of the plateau, above the Crooked River Arm.

In about 1 mile from the viewpoint, the trail turns inland and descends slightly another 1.25 miles back to the junction to close the loop at 5 miles from where you started. Take a left and admire the dramatic canyon walls one more time as you head back to the trailhead. After signing out at the register, retrace your steps to your car at the Upper Deschutes Day Use Area.

81 Willow Creek Canyon

RATING/ DIFFICULTY	ROUNDTRIP	ELEV GAIN/ HIGH POINT	SEASON
***/3	6 miles	700 feet/ 2470 feet	Year-round

Map: USGS Madras West; **Contact:** City of Madras Public Works; **Notes:** Dogs permitted on-leash; **GPS:** N 44 37.65, W 121 8.31

Madras gets overlooked on the grand Central Oregon landscape. North of Redmond, it's often seen as nothing more than a last stop between Bend and Portland. But Madras is worth a trip all by itself. Start out on the new, steep paved path heading up the M Hill, so named for the big white M marking the city of Madras. Descend the other side and hop onto the Willow Creek Canyon Trail. This trail stretches 7 miles all the way to Lake Simtustus, but even a few miles will yield outstanding canyon views.

GETTING THERE
From downtown Madras, turn west on D Street, which quickly turns into Culver Highway/State Route 361. In 0.5 mile, you'll see the trail crossing the road. Turn left onto SW H Street, and then turn right into the parking lot at the Madras Bike and Skate Park. Follow the trail across the road.

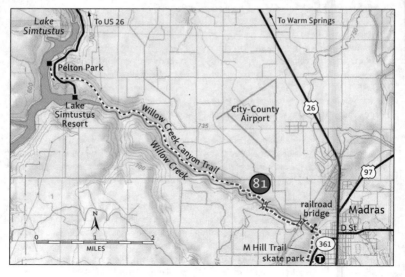

The trail winds between two rock walls in the Willow Creek Canyon.

ON THE TRAIL

The city of Madras has done quite a few upgrades to its trails over the past few years. Start on the newly paved M Hill Trail, which ascends to a nice view of the city before descending the opposite side. At 1 mile, you'll follow the trail across the road and then turn left at the fork. In less than 0.25 mile, you'll cross the road again and pass through a gate onto the gravelly Willow Creek Canyon Trail.

You'll follow an old railroad spur for a little while, crossing under a big bridge and continuing on to enter the canyon. High volcanic cliffs grace both sides of the trail and look more and more wild the farther you descend into the canyon. Willow Creek meanders nearby, although it often dries up in summer. The lack of water and the canyon's tendency to trap heat make this hike a poor choice for dogs, at least in hot weather.

At 1.6 miles, stay straight over an often-dry creek crossing. You'll cross a footbridge at 2 miles. It's hard to find a good turnaround spot on this hike, as it always feels like a big open viewpoint is "just around the corner." It's oh so tempting to keep going. The canyon is stunning, but it's a lot of the same until you get to the lake, and the trudge back can feel monotonous if you've gone farther than your body can handle. It's better to call it a day before you're too tired, so that you can actually enjoy the beauty around you. The 3-mile mark has some pretty views and makes a good turnaround point. Retrace your steps out of the canyon. As you head back up the steep M Hill on the way to your car, you'll be happy you turned around when you did.

EXTENDING YOUR TRIP

If you really want views of the lake, it's better to hike the Willow Creek Canyon Trail one-way. Park a second car at Pelton Park so you can walk all the way to the shores of Lake Simtustus—a 7.5-mile excursion, including the M Hill at the beginning. From Lake Simtustus Resort, drive north up the hill for 0.5 mile and find the trail on the north side before the road starts downhill. If this parking area is full, park down at the resort.

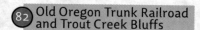

82 Old Oregon Trunk Railroad and Trout Creek Bluffs

RATING/ DIFFICULTY	ROUNDTRIP	ELEV GAIN/ HIGH POINT	SEASON
****/3	2.5 miles	900 feet/ 2100 feet	Year-round

Map: USGS Gateway; **Contact:** BLM Prineville District; **Notes:** Bluffs subject to seasonal wildlife closure Jan 15–Aug 31. Privy at campground; **GPS:** N 44 48.77, W 121 5.76

This intriguing rail-to-trail conversion travels through the Lower Deschutes River Canyon. Designated as both an Oregon Scenic Waterway and a federal Wild and Scenic River, the Deschutes flows through a colorful rimrock canyon here, a favorite recreational spot for hikers, mountain bikers, anglers, and rafters. This route takes the steep climbers' trail to the base of Trout Creek Bluffs. The trail up to the bluffs is subject to seasonal closure to protect nesting golden eagles. The closure doesn't affect the lower trail, though, so you'll have options for exploring year-round.

GETTING THERE

From Madras, take US Highway 97 north for 3.5 miles and turn left on Cora Drive. Drive 8.2 miles, keeping left at 3.9 miles when the road changes to Clark Drive. Pass through the little town of Gateway. Just after crossing the railroad tracks, turn right at Clemens Drive and proceed another 5 gravelly miles. Turn left into the Trout Creek Recreation Area. Stay left to find the trailhead at the day-use area at the far end of the campground.

ON THE TRAIL

Start off on the wide and flat trail on the south side of the river, crossing over a cattle guard almost immediately as you head upstream. The entire stretch of the canyon is gorgeous, but this hike is particularly scenic. The old railroad grade that you're walking on is a leftover from the early 1900s Deschutes Railroad War. Back then, the Deschutes Railroad and the Oregon Trunk Railway were in a dead heat trying to be the first to complete a line from the mouth of the Deschutes to Bend.

At 0.7 mile, take the unmarked climbers trail to the left. This narrow, steep, and slippery path couldn't be more different from the one you just left. Press on for a tedious 0.5 mile up to the base of the most significant landmark on the trail—the Trout Creek Bluffs. These incredible basalt columns look

View of the Deschutes River from the base of the Trout Creek Bluffs

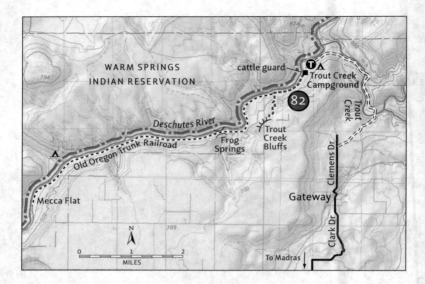

like seamlessly sandwiched pillars, forming a nearly perfect flat mesa. While green hued at times, the whole face turns golden when the sun illuminates it.

Most people on the lower trail are anglers, so very few ascend the stunning bluffs. If you share the space with anyone, it will likely be a few climbers who jab their fingers in the tight cracks to ascend the columns. Scramble the final stretch over some giant boulders, and then pick a good spot to catch your breath while you enjoy the stunning views of the vibrant Deschutes River twisting through the canyon. Look for raptors and golden eagles making shadows as they soar overhead.

After a nice relaxing break, retrace your steps down the hill and through the canyon. You're more likely to fall on the way down the steep hill, so take it slow and watch your footing.

EXTENDING YOUR TRIP

For a longer and calmer hike, or if the seasonal wildlife closure is in effect, stay on the railroad grade for another 1.25 miles to the Frog Springs footbridge. Still can't get enough? The trail continues another 5 miles to Mecca Flat. Both trail stretches are as wide, flat, and free flowing as the river that runs alongside it.

Opposite: Summer storm clouds above Chimney Rock

prineville and ochoco mountains

The Ochoco National Forest is tucked away outside Prineville, off Central Oregon's most beaten paths. Because this area is hardly a thriving metropolis, it's easy to assume that it's a pain to get to. Not true! Major thoroughfares provide easy access to the Ochoco Mountains. From Bend, getting to Prineville takes about as long as driving to Newberry Caldera or the lower-elevation hikes off Cascade Lakes Highway.

Home to the Mill Creek Wilderness, this region is full of beautiful old-growth forests, rambling slopes, and colorful wildflowers. It also hosts a wide variety of historical sites, especially old ruins from the mining heyday.

The Ochocos are currently threatened by proposals to establish off-highway-vehicle (OHV) trails cutting through the forest. These secluded wildlands host many animal species, including Rocky Mountain elk, the rare redband trout, and mule deer.

Because the Ochocos act as a corridor for wildlife traveling between the Cascades and the Blue Mountains, it's important to limit disruptions to the area. Several conservation agencies are working to do just that.

The Ochocos are generally wilder and less maintained than Central Oregon's other national forests, so stick to the well-defined trails or make sure you have the navigational skills to stay on track.

83 Chimney Rock

RATING/ DIFFICULTY	ROUNDTRIP	ELEV GAIN/ HIGH POINT	SEASON
****/3	2.75 miles	550 feet/ 3615 feet	Year-round

Map: BLM Prineville Reservoir Recreation Area; **Contact:** BLM Prineville District; **Notes:** Privy at trailhead; **GPS:** N 44 8.11, W 120 48.79

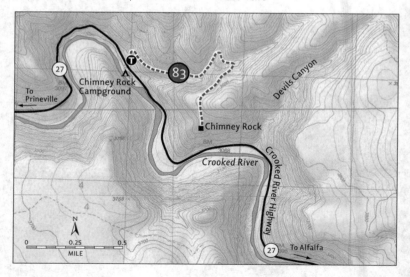

Crooked River as seen from the base of Chimney Rock

No, this isn't the iconic rock from the Oregon Trail. Surprisingly, that famous landmark is in Nebraska. This is Oregon's Chimney Rock, and it's located in the gnarled wonder of the Crooked River Gorge. Just downstream of the Prineville Reservoir, you'll find a lush, grassy oasis underneath high basalt canyon walls. Anglers love this stretch of river, and on any given day you'll see them wading into the shallow river among blue herons, both trying to get closer to their catch. The scenic, winding drive through Crooked River Gorge is worth the trip all on its own. The view from Chimney Rock is just a sweet bonus!

GETTING THERE

From Prineville, take Crooked River Highway/State Route 27 south for 15.7 miles. The trailhead is on the left, directly across from the Chimney Rock Campground.

ON THE TRAIL

The single-track path ascends immediately from the parking lot with moderate switchbacks. After traversing up the hillside, the trail cuts through a small canyon filled with juniper and sage. The trail then meets up with a dry riverbed and skirts a fence before turning toward the right up the ridge.

Follow a few more switchbacks and notice the scattered wildflowers that decorate the exposed slope. Watch your footing, because there are plenty of loose rocks and roots to trip you up. Be especially careful as you near the top. The narrow path hugs the hillside on your left, but don't test your luck with the steep basalt drop-offs on the right.

The trail snakes up to the top of a plateau and crosses over a 50-foot dry waterfall. If you need a quick breather, there's a bench at a fantastic lookout spot at 1 mile. Sit down and look out over the canyon, admiring the dramatic lichen-lined basalt walls stretching all the way down to the river below. These same cliffs provide habitat for nesting eagles, falcons, and ravens.

After a short descent, you'll reach Chimney Rock and more expansive views of the canyon and the Cascades off in the distance.

Walk right up to the bench that sits in front of the pillar, but don't venture much farther. It's a long drop down, and the basalt isn't stable enough for exploring. Hang out here and enjoy the views before heading back the way you came. Watch your step on the way down.

84 Steins Pillar

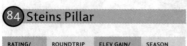

RATING/ DIFFICULTY	ROUNDTRIP	ELEV GAIN/ HIGH POINT	SEASON
***/3	4.1 miles	700 feet/ 5570 feet	Late Mar– Nov

Maps: USFS Ochoco National Forest, USGS Steins Pillar; **Contact:** Ochoco National Forest, Lookout Mountain Ranger District; **GPS:** N 44 23.68, W 120 37.44

While this hike technically lies just outside the Ochoco National Forest's boundaries, it leads to views of one of the area's most significant landmarks. Steins Pillar is an impressive monolith—kind of a poor man's Smith Rock. It's named after late-1800s explorer Major Enoch Steen, his last name misspelled so frequently that it just stuck. The trip is one of the more accessible Ochoco hikes, which makes it a good first-time venture into this area. Note that the altitude peaks smack-dab in the middle, so you'll have to climb going both ways.

GETTING THERE
From Prineville, take US Highway 26 east out of town for 8 miles. Just past milepost 28, turn left on Mill Creek Road. Drive 5 miles

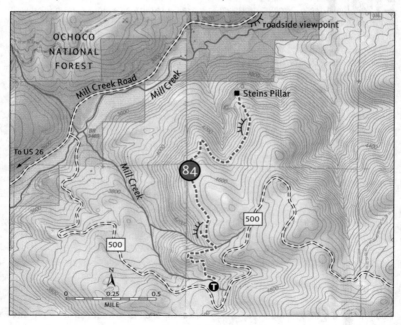

Steins Pillar stands tall just outside the Ochoco National Forest.

and continue straight on the gravel road for just under 2 miles. Turn right on Forest Road 500 for 2 bumpy miles to the trailhead.

ON THE TRAIL

The first part of this trail is pretty well maintained, although the trail is often carpeted with pine needles, and you'll probably have to hop over blowdown after strong storms. Almost immediately, cross a sometimes-dry tributary of Mill Creek. Large boulders look like they were hurled into the forest, a stark contrast to the petite wildflowers that adorn the slopes in spring and early summer. You'll start off on flat ground in a deep forest, but the treescape gets thinner as you gradually begin climbing.

Cross another creek bed at 0.5 mile, and at 0.8 mile reach a small clearing with views of the very far away tip-tops of the Three Sisters. Climb just a bit more, reaching the trail's high point at 1 mile. In another 0.2 mile, you'll reach a fork. Take the left fork for a viewpoint less than 0.1 mile away. Go back to the main trail and take the other fork to continue to Steins Pillar.

Keep descending, and come to another viewpoint of the pillar at 1.8 miles. You'll also pass two rocky formations on the left, but they're just posing as the big one. Stay the course on the trail. You'll begin descending quite steeply on switchbacking wooden stairs for 0.25 mile to the base of the pillar.

From here you can really appreciate the enormity of this monolith. Steins Pillar is over 350 feet high and 120 feet wide. The rock itself is composed of forty-four-million-year-old rhyolite ash, gradually chiseled away by the elements to create the large tower you see today. Look for the cavern at the base of the pillar. Overall, this is a

fantastic place to have a picnic and take in the views of the Mill Creek valley before heading back.

If you want to see the pillar but don't have time to do the hike, there's a pretty good roadside viewpoint. It's actually a better place for photographs than the pillar's base. Instead of turning on FR 500, continue straight on Mill Creek Road another 1.25 miles to a good pullout with a bit of information about how the pillar was formed.

85 Twin Pillars

RATING/ DIFFICULTY	ROUNDTRIP	ELEV GAIN/ HIGH POINT	SEASON
***/4	6 miles	600 feet/ 5850 feet	Apr–Nov

Map: USFS Ochoco National Forest; **Contact:** Ochoco National Forest, Lookout Mountain Ranger District; **Notes:** Free wilderness permit at trailhead; **GPS:** N 44 30.86, W 120 31.74

The Twin Pillars are located in the Mill Creek Wilderness within the Ochoco National Forest. It's far less crowded here than at nearby Steins Pillar (Hike 84), but this is still one of the more popular and accessible attractions in the area. For more solitude and a higher likelihood for wildlife viewing, start from the more remote northern trailhead as described here. The elevation gain is very comfortable, with the exception of the last climb and occasional scrambling up to the base of the pillars. Because of past forest fires and intermittent maintenance, trails here are sometimes difficult to follow. Come prepared with navigational skills and the self-awareness to know when it's time to turn back.

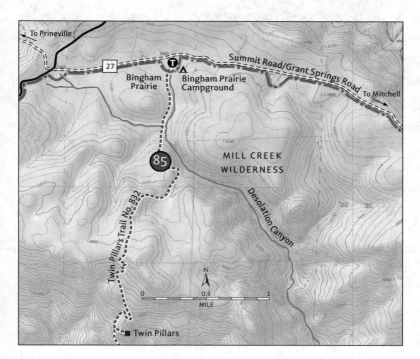

GETTING THERE

From Prineville, take Main Street north out of town for 11 miles to the Ochoco National Forest boundary, at which point the road becomes Forest Road 27/McKay Creek Road. Continue for another 12 miles, and keep right at the "Twin Pillars Trail No. 832" sign to turn onto gravel FR 27/Summit Road/ Grant Springs Road. Drive another 0.5 mile to the Twin Pillars north trailhead at Bingham Prairie Campground.

ON THE TRAIL

Before you head out, check out the meadow at the adjacent Bingham Prairie Campground. This open pasture features a spring and a small pond, which make it a great place for wildlife viewing. Look for birds, elk, and mule deer. Rarer sightings include mountain lions, black bears, and bobcats. On the other side of the coin, you'll almost certainly see sheep and cows, as grazing is permitted in this area. No matter what kind of wildlife you encounter, let them be and don't approach any of the animals.

Head south on Twin Pillars Trail No. 832, which is mostly flat as it winds through ponderosa and lodgepole pines. Because the trail isn't regularly maintained, expect to climb over downed trees. If the brush is thick, make sure to check for ticks at the end of the day. At 0.5 mile, you'll cross the creek

Grazing cows are a common sight in the Ochocos.

and reach the rim of Desolation Canyon. This jagged valley is as deserted as its name implies, but the rocky cliffs are beautiful. Follow the ridge as the trail begins to climb, reaching the highest point on the trail near the 1-mile mark.

The trail descends gradually as you approach the pillars. At 2.8 miles, turn left for a 0.2-mile scramble up the loose rocky hillside to the base of the pillars. Admire the 2000-foot lichen-covered Twin Pillars and the impressive Mill Creek Wilderness views that surround you before returning the way you came.

86 Cougar Creek

RATING/ DIFFICULTY	ROUNDTRIP	ELEV GAIN/ HIGH POINT	SEASON
***/4	7 miles	1200 feet/ 4200 feet	Mar–Nov

Maps: USFS Ochoco National Forest, USGS Lookout Mountain; **Contact:** Ochoco National Forest, Lookout Mountain Ranger District; **GPS:** N 44 32.83, W 120 26.85

🏠 ⭐ *This trail is buried deep in the Ochoco National Forest, so not many visitors make it far enough along US Highway 26 to hike this historical route. The Cougar Creek Trail follows the path travelers used when they trekked between Prineville and the John Day River. Those early settlers picked a pretty route with panoramic views of the surrounding forests, hills, and meadows. This area was hit by a fire in 2014, so for the next few years you can expect significant debris and blockage from fallen trees that may make navigation difficult. This trail is also fairly hilly, so beginners may want to skip this one.*

GETTING THERE

From Prineville, take US Highway 26 east for 28 miles. Turn left onto Forest Road 27 and proceed for 5 miles. Keep right at the fork to continue onto FR 250. After 4 miles,

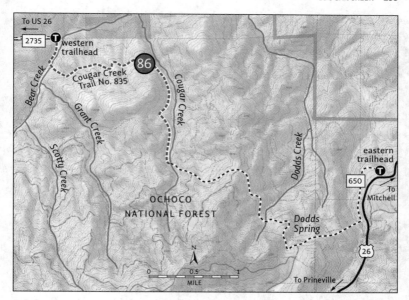

turn right on FR 2735 and drive another 4 miles. Look for the Cougar West trailhead on your right.

ON THE TRAIL

The trail parallels Bear Creek for the first 0.25 mile or so before turning left to cross it and continue on Cougar Creek Trail No. 835. This historical pack trail was used between 1915 and 1922, but it's just as wild today, if not more so. Forest fires have changed the landscape and marred parts of the trail. Do your best to stay on the trail to prevent further erosion and trail damage. Hikers, mountain bikers, and equestrians all use this route. Alliances of all three user groups have worked hard over the years to maintain this trail. Look for yellow diamond markers among the trees if you feel like you've lost the official path.

Near the 2-mile mark, you'll begin hiking alongside Cougar Creek. Depending on the season, it may be dry. At 2.5 miles, the trail starts to gradually gain elevation. Be careful as the trail traverses over rocky sections. The cliffs are steep in spots, and rattlesnakes have also been known to hide among the rocks. These rocky spots are generally nice viewpoints, so take time to appreciate the surrounding views of the northern Ochoco National Forest.

At 3.5 miles, you'll bump into Cougar Creek. This is a good turnaround spot. Simply retrace the old pack trail to the trailhead.

EXTENDING YOUR TRIP

A one-way 8.2-mile hike is possible with a car shuttle. Leave a car at the Cougar East trailhead by staying on US 26 another 5 miles before turning left on FR 650. On the

A Steller's jay perched on a boulder

hike, you'll begin a steep climb to the high point on the trail just after crossing Cougar Creek. The elevation on this old road hovers right around 4750 feet before descending and flattening out. Cross Dodds Creek, then Dodds Spring, and turn left on FR 650 at 7.5 miles. This final stretch travels through a recent timber sale along the logging road until it reaches the eastern trailhead.

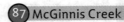

87 McGinnis Creek

RATING/ DIFFICULTY	LOOP	ELEV GAIN/ HIGH POINT	SEASON
**/3	5.2 miles	450 feet/ 5000 feet	Late Mar– Nov

Maps: USFS Ochoco National Forest, Bandit Springs Trail Map; **Contact:** Ochoco National Forest, Lookout Mountain Ranger District; **Notes:** Privy at trailhead; **GPS:** N 44 29.21, W 120 23.83

While the Bandit Springs Trail System is primarily visited by wintertime cross-country skiers and snowshoers, the area is ideal for families looking for easygoing day hikes. Various routes abound, but this loop visits all the highlights. Wind through old ponderosa pine forests before making a steep side trip to a scenic three-sided shelter. As you continue around the perimeter of the winter recreation area, you'll cross a pretty creek and wander across calm meadows. This friendly trail system is also an excellent place to spot wildlife. Be on the lookout for elk, deer, cougar, and all kinds of high-desert critters.

GETTING THERE
From Prineville, take US Highway 26 east for approximately 29 miles. After milepost 48, turn into the Bandit Springs area on your left.

ON THE TRAIL
The junctions in this trail system are marked with letters M through Z and blue diamonds posted high up on trees (to ensure the markers are still visible above the winter snowline). From the parking area, turn right

to start on the Ponderosa Trail. This trail provides access to all other paths, and it's fairly flat. In 0.8 mile, at Junction P, continue straight onto the McGinnis Creek Trail.

The McGinnis Creek Trail parallels FR 27 here, twisting a bit as it gains about 200 feet. The loop is mostly flat, with a few up-and-down sections to keep things interesting. At junction O, turn right to keep climbing to Junction N. The McGinnis Creek Trail heads left at this four-way intersection, but before continuing on the loop, turn right onto Ridge Trail No. 802A. Look for the blue diamonds along a tight curve. This trail climbs the ridge for 0.5 mile to Junction M and then turns right for another 0.1 mile. Look for a faint

trail heading to your right down the slope. This path leads about 200 feet to a three-sided shelter facing south, looking out from the ridge. It's a nice spot to have a snack if you're hungry.

Turn back the way you came, and head back to Junction N. To continue the loop, turn right to pick up the McGinnis Creek Trail again. Stay right at Junction S and proceed through a moderate burn area from the 2000 Mill Creek Fire. Cross McGinnis Creek and continue another 0.5 mile to Junction Y, where you'll stay right. Stay right again at Junction Z. As the path proceeds across a meadow for 100 yards or so, it may grow faint. Just continue through the meadow

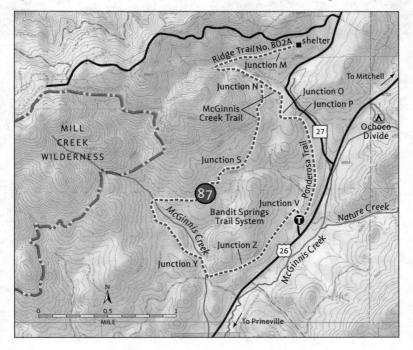

Sometimes cows and hikers share the same trails out here.

until you reach Junction V at the road. Turn right to walk the finishing leg of the Ponderosa Loop back to the trailhead.

88 Lookout Mountain

RATING/ DIFFICULTY	LOOP	ELEV GAIN/ HIGH POINT	SEASON
***/4	6 miles	1200 feet/ 6930 feet	May–Oct

Maps: USFS Ochoco National Forest, USGS Lookout Mountain; **Contact:** Ochoco National Forest, Lookout Mountain Ranger District; **GPS:** N 44 20.39, W 120 21.54

The Lookout Mountain trail traverses large hillsides in the Mill Creek Wilderness, passing an old cabin and plenty of roaming cows on the way to a captivating viewpoint. Pretty as it is, this trail has a way of making even the directionally capable feel somewhat disoriented. It's hard to keep your bearings along this looping, swerving, winding route. Signage is inconsistent, and because the trail numbers have changed over the past few years, your old map might lead you astray. Bring a compass and GPS unit, and take a photo of the map at the trailhead to help you find your way.

GETTING THERE

From Prineville, take US Highway 26 east for 13 miles and turn right onto Forest Road 23 near milepost 34. Just past the ranger station at 8 miles, turn right onto FR 42. Stay on FR 42 for 6.5 miles, and then turn right on gravel FR 4205 to follow signs for Independent Mine. Continue 1 mile to the trailhead at the end of the road.

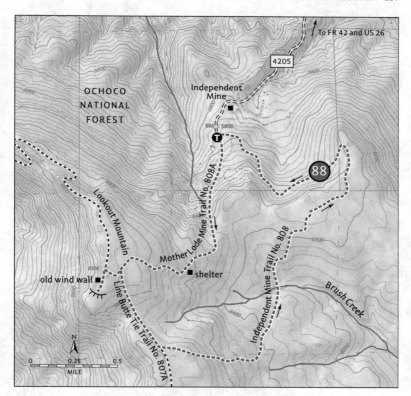

ON THE TRAIL

Three trails leave from this trailhead. Start climbing Mother Lode Mine Trail No. 808A, a beaten-down path that leads up to the Lookout Mountain summit. Trees provide shade here, but as you get to the top, the trail becomes more exposed. By summer, the wildflowers and skunk cabbage are all dried up from the intense sun and arid climate of Central Oregon, but in the fall, a few colorful snags brighten up small patches of green forest.

At 1.5 miles, you'll pass a fun snow shelter that looks like it was made with life-size Lincoln Logs. Decorated with American flags and outdoor gear, the three-sided shelter even has a wood-burning stove—quite popular with snowshoers and cross-country skiers in the winter. Step back onto the trail and continue another 0.25 mile to a junction near the summit. Turn right toward the unofficial summit viewpoint.

Walk into the sagebrush and toward the pile of rocks—remnants of a wind wall that

An ax on the side of the snow shelter on Lookout Mountain

used to protect an old lookout up here. Amid all the familiar Cascade views, you'll see the thoroughly forested rolling Ochoco hills, small peaks, and an assortment of lakes sitting in the foreground of the big expanse of blue sky.

When you're ready to loop back, return to your last junction and turn right on Line Butte Tie Trail No. 807A. At 2.4 miles, turn left on Independent Mine Trail No. 808. This will lead you on a winding route over the plateau before making a slow descent through open fields. Be on the lookout for cows, wild horses, and deer. At 3.6 miles, you'll pass over Brush Creek. You'll gain 200 feet or so over the next mile before starting a gradual descent to your car. You'll pop out just to the side of the trail you started on.

EXTENDING YOUR TRIP

For a visit to the old Independent Mine, see Appendix I.

89 Walton Lake

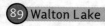

RATING/ DIFFICULTY	LOOP	ELEV GAIN/ HIGH POINT	SEASON
***/2	2 miles	200 feet/ 4350 feet	Year-round

Maps: USFS Ochoco National Forest, USGS Ochoco Butte; **Contact:** Ochoco National Forest, Lookout Mountain Ranger District; **Notes:** Dogs permitted on-leash. Privy at campground; **GPS:** N 44 25.91, W 120 19.65

Walton Lake is a sparkling and scenic camping, fishing, swimming, paddling, and all-around summer fun spot in the middle of the Ochoco wilderness. This route adds a bit of extra pizzazz to the lake loop by starting on a hillside 0.5 mile above the water, across from the Round Mountain Trail. The easy descent adds a bit of mileage to this otherwise short hike and lets you see the lake from above before walking alongside it.

GETTING THERE

From Prineville, take US Highway 26 east for 13 miles and turn right onto Forest Road 23 near milepost 34. Just past the ranger station at 8 miles, turn left onto FR 22. Pass the Walton Lake Campground entrance at 7 miles, and in another 0.4 mile find the roadside pullout on your left across from the Round Mountain Trail.

ON THE TRAIL

From the pullout, find the trail sign and follow the path down Walton Lake Trail No. 809. Another trail travels uphill in this area, so if the sign says "Round Mountain Trail," you're on the wrong side of the road.

As you head downhill, make your way through old-growth ponderosa and Douglas-fir. Scattered western larches turn canary

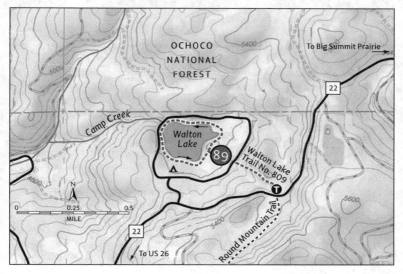

A nice flat path curves around Walton Lake's shoreline.

yellow in the fall. You'll likely hear campers nearby, but the trail is otherwise quite calm. As the lake comes into view, the narrow trail weaves through a mountain meadow. Stay on the trail where you can watch your footing, as sometimes there are bee nests hidden in the grass.

At 0.5 mile, you'll reach the intersection with the 1-mile lakeside loop. Turn right and follow the cattail-lined path along the lake. Because it's stocked with rainbow trout and catfish each summer, Walton Lake is a fun fishing spot. It's also a great place for bird-watching. Look for belted kingfishers, white-headed woodpeckers, spotted sandpipers, cinnamon teals, and a variety of blackbirds.

The trail itself has undergone renovations over the past few years to increase usability and accessibility. It's a flat, comfortable path, perfect for families looking for more of a walk than a hike. As you make your way around the lake, there's a pleasant day-use area for picnicking near the campground. If you'd prefer to opt out of the first part of the hike and only do the lakeside loop, you have the option of starting at the campground instead. If you park here, you'll need to display your Northwest Forest Pass or pay a $5 day-use fee.

Follow the trail the rest of the way around the lake. At 1.5 miles into the hike, connect back to the spur trail to your car, following the "To Round Mountain Trail No. 805A" sign.

90 Eagle Rock Agate Beds

RATING/ DIFFICULTY	ROUNDTRIP	ELEV GAIN/ HIGH POINT	SEASON
**/3	3.6 miles	700 feet/ 4290 feet	Mid-Apr– Nov

Maps: USFS Ochoco National Forest, BLM Central Oregon Rockhounding Map; **Contact:** Ochoco National Forest, Lookout Mountain Ranger District, and BLM Prineville District; **GPS:** N 44 11.72, W 120 38.99

Just beyond the Prineville Reservoir stands a rocky monolith called Eagle Rock. Geologically speaking, this landmark is an eroding welded tuff. In layperson's terms, it's a big and beautiful old landmark that happens to be a popular rockhounding location. Agate is the name of the game here, with plume, moss, dendritic, and botryoidal all available. Kids love an excuse to hit rocks with a hammer, so bring them along. Hike up bumpy forest roads to a nice view of the surrounding landscape, including an aerial view of Eagle Rock.

GETTING THERE
From Prineville, take Combs Flat Road/Post–Paulina Road/State Route 380 east for 14 miles. Just past Eagle Rock, turn right on the unmarked gravel road and park on the side.

ON THE TRAIL
Cross the cattle guard and turn left. This road is subject to a seasonal closure between

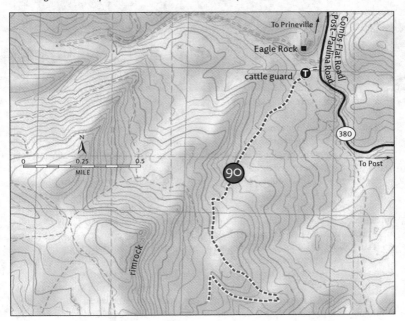

Eagle Rock and the surrounding agate beds

December 1 and April 15 to protect wintering deer, but this only applies to motor vehicles. Since you're headed up on nothing but your own two feet, you're in the clear. Start climbing the bumpy road, which quickly begins to wind up and away from Eagle Rock.

This prominent landmark is the leftover remains of a welded tuff. Slow erosion of these volcanic ash deposits created its interesting form, which looks like gradated columns. If you turn around at any point during the hike, you'll have a nice view of Eagle Rock.

At 0.9 mile, you'll reach a junction. Turn right, and then proceed another 0.4 mile.

The rimrock walls above you make an outstanding backdrop to a rockhounding adventure, so it's worth continuing on to the collection site.

Walk another 0.2 mile down the gravel road. From here, follow the faint trails that steeply ascend the hill for about 0.25 mile. Stay left for another 150 yards or so and start looking for good agate chunks on the ground. Even if you don't bring tools, there are plenty of smaller pieces scattered around the hillside to pick through.

The Bureau of Land Management has set apart certain locations for legal collection of rocks, minerals, and gemstones. Basic wilderness principles, however, still apply. Don't ransack the place; it's only legal to take a few mementos. Also, make sure to leave the terrain as you found it, being careful to dig no deeper than four feet and fill in all holes before you leave. Check with the local BLM office on current collection rules before you dig.

If you're interested in the thick bands of black chalcedony hidden in the cliffs, you'll need a healthy dose of determination and caution. The material is both difficult and dangerous to remove from the unstable basalt. Instead, admire the rocky face from farther back. Sticking to the agate-rich sections that slope from the base of the rimrock down to the flats below is a better bet. These sections are known as "agate floats"—over time, the rock is carried ("floating") over the slope and settles in a particular spot. If you find some agates, you can generally follow a "float" to find the other main sources. Head back down the hill when you're done prospecting. If you feel like it, it's worth the short but steep walk to Eagle Rock's base for a close-up view.

Appendix I
10 Quick Hikes to Get You Out on the Trail

Paulina Falls

RATING/ DIFFICULTY	ROUNDTRIP	ELEV GAIN/ HIGH POINT	SEASON
***/2	0.6 mile	300 feet/ 6280 feet	June–Oct

Map: USFS Deschutes National Forest; **Contact:** Deschutes National Forest, Crescent Ranger District, and Lava Lands Visitor Center; **Notes:** NW Forest Pass or $5 day-use fee. Access road closed in winter. Dogs permitted on-leash. Privy at trailhead; **GPS:** N 43 42.67, W 121 16.99

There are several long day hikes in the Newberry National Volcanic Monument, but this one is less than a mile with great views of a double waterfall along Paulina Creek.

Getting there: From Bend, take US Highway 97 south for 20 miles toward La Pine. Turn left for Newberry Caldera/Paulina and East Lakes near milepost 161, onto Paulina/East Lake Road 21. Drive 12.5 miles and turn left into the Paulina Creek Falls Picnic Area. From the picnic area, begin on the paved trail to a viewpoint accessible directly from the parking lot.

Wake Butte

RATING/ DIFFICULTY	ROUNDTRIP	ELEV GAIN/ HIGH POINT	SEASON
**/2	0.6 mile	250 feet/ 4700 feet	Year-round

Map: USFS Deschutes National Forest; **Contact:** Deschutes National Forest, Bend–Fort Rock Ranger District; **GPS:** N 43 49.7, W 121 36.49

Lonely, out-of-the-way Wake Butte offers solitude and a gorgeous panoramic view of a vast carpet of evergreen forest. Short and steep, the trail climbs 250 feet over just 0.3 mile, making it ideal for calming down active kiddos and restless legs.

Getting there: From Bend, drive US Highway 97 south for 11 miles to exit 153. Keep right at the fork, drive 2 miles to a roundabout, and go straight through it. The road name changes from South Century Drive to Upper Deschutes Road and finally to Forest Road 40. In 4 miles from the roundabout, turn left toward Crane Prairie to stay on FR 40. Drive 5 miles and turn right at the signed Wake Butte trailhead near milepost 11.5. Find the narrow, unsigned but obvious trail on the left side of the parking loop.

Tumalo Falls

RATING/ DIFFICULTY	ROUNDTRIP	ELEV GAIN/ HIGH POINT	SEASON
****/1	0.5 mile	115 feet/ 5125 feet	May– early Nov

Maps: USGS Tumalo Falls, Bend Adventure Map; **Contact:** Deschutes National Forest, Bend–Fort Rock Ranger District; **Notes:** NW Forest Pass or $5 day-use fee. Access road closed in winter. Dogs permitted on-leash. Privy at trailhead; **GPS:** N 44 1.91, W 121 33.98

Impressive 97-foot Tumalo Falls crashes into a lush pool at the base of a basalt canyon, and it's located just steps from the parking lot, offering visitors instant gratification but almost always crowds as well.

Getting there: From US Highway 97 in Bend, take exit 139 and follow Reed Market Road west toward the Old Mill District. Stay straight for 3 miles, during which the road changes to Mount Washington Drive. At the Skyliners Road roundabout, take the third exit to turn left and turn onto gravel Tumalo Falls Road/Forest Road 4603 for another 2.5 miles to the trailhead. If you're not lucky enough to snag a spot in the upper lot, park along the gravel road with the rest of the visitors. Once you've reached the main trailhead at the upper lot, the trail is an obvious path by the trailhead board.

Dee Wright Observatory

RATING/ DIFFICULTY	LOOP	ELEV GAIN/ HIGH POINT	SEASON
***/1	0.75 mile	100 feet/ 5375 feet	July–Oct

Map: Green Trails No. 590 Sisters; **Contact:** Willamette National Forest, McKenzie Ranger District; **Notes:** Access road closed in winter. Dogs permitted on-leash. Privy at trailhead; **GPS:** N 44 15.61, W 121 48.08

At the crest of McKenzie Pass, explore a short but fascinating Oregon Trail interpretive path and the Dee Wright Observatory fortress. This short excursion makes a great add-on to one of the other scenic trails along this highway.

Getting there: From Sisters, go west on State Route 242 for just under 15 miles. At the summit of McKenzie Pass, turn left into the Dee Wright parking area. From the parking area, cross the highway and walk toward the small castle-like observatory, then turn

right for the interpretive trail that winds through the old Belknap Flow.

Head of the Metolius

RATING/ DIFFICULTY	ROUNDTRIP	ELEV GAIN/ HIGH POINT	SEASON
**/1	0.5 mile	25 feet/ 3125 feet	Year-round

Map: Green Trails No. 590 Sisters; **Contact:** Deschutes National Forest, Sisters Ranger District; **Notes:** Dogs permitted on-leash. Privy at trailhead; **GPS:** N 44 26.04, W 121 38.05

This short and simple trail to Metolius Springs offers a beautiful example of how volcanic activity dramatically altered the landscape of Central Oregon. Here at the spring, you can see the river bubbling right out of the ground—with a gorgeous backdrop to boot.

Getting there: From Sisters, take US Highway 20 west for 10 miles. Turn right onto SW Camp Sherman Road/Forest Road 14. Drive 4.4 miles, keeping right at the fork and following signs to the Metolius Springs parking lot entrance. Head toward the big, log-encased Head of the Metolius sign to start your hike.

Head of Jack Creek

RATING/ DIFFICULTY	ROUNDTRIP	ELEV GAIN/ HIGH POINT	SEASON
**/1	0.8 mile	30 feet/ 3215 feet	Year-round

Maps: Green Trails No. 589 Three Fingered Jack, No. 557 Mount Jefferson; **Contact:** Deschutes National Forest, Sisters Ranger District; **Notes:** NW Forest Pass or $5 day-use fee. Privy at campground; **GPS:** N 44 28.80, W 121 43.26

Completely flat and soft, this tranquil trail gets young kids out for a quick creekside romp.

Getting there: From Sisters, head west on US Highway 20 for 12 miles. Near milepost 89, turn right on Forest Road 12 toward Mount Jefferson Wilderness trailheads and drive about 4 miles. Turn left on FR 1230 and follow it 0.6 mile. Cross the creek and turn left on cinder FR 1232. Proceed for 1.5 miles, keeping left onto FR 470 and passing the campground to reach the trailhead. Walk the trail, staying right when you reach the creek to keep toward the headwaters.

Redmond Caves

RATING/ DIFFICULTY	ROUNDTRIP	ELEV GAIN/ HIGH POINT	SEASON
**/2	0.75 mile	100 feet/ 3000 feet	Year-round

Map: BLM Redmond Cave Map; **Contact:** BLM Prineville District and City of Redmond Parks and Recreation; **Notes:** Bring a headlamp; **GPS:** N 44 14.85, W 121 10.66

Explore five separate caves formed from a collapsed lava tube—one of the only cave sites in Central Oregon without a seasonal bat closure, so you can visit year-round.

Getting there: From Bend, take US Highway 97 north for 17 miles toward Redmond. Take exit 124 for the Redmond Airport. At the end of the off-ramp, turn right and follow SE Airport Way for 1 mile to the parking area on the left.

Balancing Rocks

RATING/ DIFFICULTY	ROUNDTRIP	ELEV GAIN/ HIGH POINT	SEASON
**/1	0.5 mile	50 feet/ 2250 feet	Year-round

Map: USGS Fly Creek; **Contact:** Deschutes National Forest, Sisters Ranger District; **GPS:** N 44 34.51, W 121 25.41

Walk to odd hoodoo formations that are the result of three different layers of volcanic tuffs that erode at different speeds. The fragile capstones that remain appear to be just on the verge of toppling off the columns and down the hillside. Look at but please don't touch these precarious sculptures.

Getting there: From Bend, head north on US Highway 97 for 21 miles to Terrebonne. Near milepost 106, turn left on Culver Highway/State Route 361 and continue for 2.5 miles. Turn left on C Street and keep following signs for Cove Palisades State Park. In 0.9 mile, turn right on SW Feather Drive. In 0.8 mile, turn left on Fisch Lane. In 0.5 mile, keep right onto Frazier Drive. Then in 0.5 mile, turn left on Jordan Road. From here, keep straight on the main road into the canyon. Pass over a bridge at 4 miles and then a single-lane bridge 3 miles later. Keep on for the next 12 miles, following the paved road as it changes from Jordan Road to Graham Road and finally to Montgomery Road. When the road turns to gravel, drive another 0.2 mile and find the unmarked lot on the right. Locate the hidden path entry point at the back of the parking area.

Independent Mine Ruins

RATING/ DIFFICULTY	ROUNDTRIP	ELEV GAIN/ HIGH POINT	SEASON
***/1	0.75 mile	60 feet/ 5800 feet	Apr–Oct

Maps: USFS Ochoco National Forest, USGS Lookout Mountain; **Contact:** Ochoco National Forest, Lookout Mountain Ranger District; **GPS:** N 44 20.51, W 120 21.39

Remnants of the Central Oregon mining boom, this old excavation complex has the feel of a cowboy ghost town. There's just enough historical charm and eeriness to make the trip quite entertaining for kids.

Getting there: From Prineville, take US Highway 26 east for 13 miles and turn right onto Forest Road 23 near milepost 34. Just past the ranger station at 8 miles, turn right onto FR 42. Stay on FR 42 for 6.5 miles, and then turn right on gravel FR 4205 to follow signs for the Independent Mine. In 0.7 mile, park in the lot on the right side of the road, for the Baneberry trailhead on the left. From the parking lot, cross the road and follow signs for Baneberry Nature Loop Trail No. 812. Cross a few dry creek beds, and at 0.15 mile take a side trail left and walk into the tree grove and down to the old buildings.

Black Mountain Lookout Tree

RATING/ DIFFICULTY	ROUNDTRIP	ELEV GAIN/ HIGH POINT	SEASON
**/2	0.4 mile	175 feet/ 5300 feet	Late Mar– Nov

Maps: USFS Ochoco National Forest, USGS Keys Creek; **Contact:** Ochoco National Forest, Lookout Mountain Ranger District; **GPS:** N 44 22.67, W 120 5.65

Hike across slippery pine needles and clamber over downed branches to reach an old fire lookout built right into a 100-foot ponderosa pine. It should go without saying, but please don't climb the tree.

Getting there: From Prineville, take US Highway 26 east for 13 miles and turn right onto Forest Road 23 near milepost 34. Just past the ranger station at 8 miles, turn right onto FR 42. Stay on FR 42 for 9.5 miles toward Big Summit Prairie before turning left at the gravelly FR 30 toward Mitchell. Drive 1.8 miles, stay right at the junction, and drive another 2.7 miles. Park along the right side of the road. This spot is unsigned, so watch your odometer. Cross the road and look up the hill through the trees. You should be able to see the lookout at a clearing at the top of the hill. Scout out your own path, as there is no official trail.

Appendix II
Contact Information

Bureau of Land Management (BLM) Prineville District
www.blm.gov/or/districts/prineville
(541) 416-6700

City of Bend Parks and Recreation
www.bendparksandrec.org
(541) 388-5435

City of Madras Public Works
www.ci.madras.or.us
(541) 325-0313

City of Redmond Parks and Recreation
www.raprd.org/parks-trails
(541) 548-7275

Crooked River Ranch
www.crookedriverranch.com
(541) 548-8939

Deschutes National Forest
www.fs.usda.gov/centraloregon

Bend–Fort Rock Ranger District
(541) 383-4000

Cascade Lakes Welcome Station
(541) 383-4000

Crescent Ranger District
(541) 433-3200

Sisters Ranger District
(541) 549-7700

Lava Lands Visitor Center
www.fs.usda.gov/centraloregon
(541) 593-2421

Mount Bachelor Resort
www.mtbachelor.com
(800) 829-2442

Ochoco National Forest and Crooked River National Grassland
www.fs.usda.gov/ochoco

Crooked River National Grassland
(541) 416-6640

Lookout Mountain Ranger District
(541) 416-6500

Oregon Department of Transportation
www.oregon.gov/odot/hwy/region4
(503) 588-2941 or 511

Oregon State Parks
www.oregonstateparks.org

Cove Palisades State Park
(541) 546-3412

La Pine State Park
(541) 536-2428

Pilot Butte State Park
(541) 388-6055

Smith Rock State Park
(541) 548-7501

Pine Mountain Observatory
http://pmo.uoregon.edu
(541) 382-8331

Sisters Trail Alliance
www.sisterstrails.com
(541) 719-8822

Suttle Lake Resort
www.thelodgeatsuttlelake.com
(541) 595-2628

Willamette National Forest
www.fs.usda.gov/willamette

McKenzie Ranger District
(541) 822-3381

Appendix III
Conservation and Trail Organizations

Central Oregon Trail Alliance
PO Box 555
Bend, OR 97709
www.cotamtb.com

Crooked River Watershed Council
498 SE Lynn Blvd
Prineville, OR 97754
www.crookedriver.deschutesriver.org
(541) 447-8567

Deschutes Land Trust
210 NW Irving Avenue, Suite 102
Bend, OR 97701
www.deschuteslandtrust.org
info@deschuteslandtrust.org
(541) 330-0017

Deschutes River Conservancy
700 NW Hill Street
Bend, OR 97701
www.deschutesriver.org
(541) 382-4077

Friends and Neighbors of the Deschutes Canyon
www.fansofdeschutes.org
fansofdeschutes@gmail.com
(541) 771-3267

Friends of the Metolius
PO Box 101
Camp Sherman, OR 97730
www.metoliusfriends.org
clearwater@metoliusfriends.org

Oregon Natural Desert Association
50 SW Bond Street, Suite 4
Bend, OR 97702
www.onda.org
onda@onda.org
(541) 330-2638

Oregon Wild, Central Oregon Office
2445 NE Division Street, Suite 303
Bend, OR 97701
www.oregonwild.org
info@oregonwild.org
(541) 382-2616

Sierra Club, Juniper Chapter
16 NW Kansas Avenue
Bend, OR 97701
www.oregon2.sierraclub.org
/juniper-group
junipergrp@yahoo.com

Sisters Trail Alliance
PO Box 1871
Sisters, OR 97759
www.sisterstrail.com
trails@sisterstrails.com
(541) 719-8822

Upper Deschutes Watershed Council
700 NW Hill Street
Bend, OR 97701
www.upperdeschuteswatershed
council.org
(541) 382-6103

Index

About the Author

Brittany Manwill has lived in the Pacific Northwest her entire life, hopping around different cities in both Oregon and Washington before finally settling in Central Oregon. She fell in love with the outdoors at an early age and has hiked all over the Pacific Northwest. She's also an avid runner, skier, and cyclist. She's usually up for trying any outdoor activity at least once. She loves half marathons and bike races but will never do another triathlon.

She loves the feeling of accomplishment that comes from summiting Cascade peaks but equally enjoys clearing her mind with a walk along the Deschutes River. When Brittany's not enjoying Central Oregon's stunning scenery, she loves to travel and explore new places. Hiking through the Alps, backcountry skiing Canada's Selkirk Mountains, and extensively backpacking through Yosemite top her list of favorite travel adventures so far.

Brittany worked in marketing before making a change to better align her work with her passions. She is the founder of Mazama Bar—a company that makes all-natural energy bars for outdoor adventure. That leap into the outdoor industry ultimately led her to start writing.

Day Hiking Bend and Central Oregon is Brittany's first guidebook. She's also a gear tester and regular contributor for *Washington Trails Magazine*. Brittany graduated from the University of Oregon with a major in business and a minor in journalism. She lives in Bend with her favorite hiking companions: her husband, Derek; their son, Rowan; and their happily hyper rescue dog, Tonka. For more information on her work, please visit www.brittanymanwill.com.

1% for Trails
Outdoor Nonprofits in Partnership

Where would we be without trails? Not very far into the wilderness.

That's why Mountaineers Books designates 1 percent of the sales of select guidebooks in our Day Hiking series toward volunteer trail maintenance. Since launching this program, we've contributed more than $14,000 toward improving trails.

For this book, our 1 percent of sales is going to the Oregon State Parks Foundation. The foundation develops funding for programs and projects in Oregon State Parks, including the purchase and protection of land at Fort Rock Cave and Smith Rock State Park. Through its "Sustainable Parks" campaign, the foundation promotes water conservation, recycling and solar upgrades in several Central Oregon state parks. It also provides interpretive signage, expanded accessibility, bicycle shelters, and other improvements for trails throughout the state park system.

Mountaineers Books donates many books to nonprofit recreation and conservation organizations. Our 1% for Trails campaign is one more way we can help fellow nonprofit organizations as we work together to get more people outside, to both enjoy and protect our wild public lands.

If you'd like to support Mountaineers Books and our nonprofit partnership programs, please visit our website to learn more or email mbooks@mountaineersbooks.org.

MOUNTAINEERS BOOKS

recreation · lifestyle · conservation

MOUNTAINEERS BOOKS is a leading publisher of mountaineering literature and guides—including our flagship title, *Mountaineering: The Freedom of the Hills*—as well as adventure narratives, natural history, and general outdoor recreation. Through our two imprints, Skipstone and Braided River, we also publish titles on sustainability and conservation. We are committed to supporting the environmental and educational goals of our organization by providing expert information on human-powered adventure, sustainable practices at home and on the trail, and preservation of wilderness.

The Mountaineers, founded in 1906, is a 501(c)(3) nonprofit outdoor activity and conservation organization whose mission is "to explore, study, preserve, and enjoy the natural beauty of the outdoors." One of the largest such organizations in the United States, it sponsors classes and year-round outdoor activities throughout the Pacific Northwest, including climbing, hiking, backcountry skiing, snowshoeing, bicycling, camping, paddling, and more. The Mountaineers also supports its mission through its publishing division, Mountaineers Books, and promotes environmental education and citizen engagement. For more information, visit The Mountaineers Program Center, 7700 Sand Point Way NE, Seattle, WA 98115-3996; phone 206-521-6001; www.mountaineers.org; or email info@mountaineers.org.

Our publications are made possible through the generosity of donors and through sales of more than 600 titles on outdoor recreation, sustainable lifestyle, and conservation. To donate, purchase books, or learn more, visit us online:

MOUNTAINEERS BOOKS
1001 SW Klickitat Way, Suite 201 • Seattle, WA 98134
800-553-4453 • mbooks@mountaineersbooks.org • www.mountaineersbooks.org

Mountaineers Books is proud to be a corporate sponsor of The Leave No Trace Center for Outdoor Ethics, whose mission is to promote and inspire responsible outdoor recreation through education, research, and partnerships • The Leave No Trace program is focused specifically on human-powered (nonmotorized) recreation • Leave No Trace strives to educate visitors about the nature of their recreational impacts and offers techniques to prevent and minimize such impacts • Leave No Trace is best understood as an educational and ethical program, not as a set of rules and regulations • For more information, visit www.lnt.org, or call 800-332-4100.